BUTLER'S LIVES OF THE SAINTS

CONCISE, MODERNIZED EDITION

EDITED BY BERNARD BANGLEY

PARACLETE PRESS

BREWSTER, MASSACHUSETTS

Butler's Lives of the Saints

2007 Second Printing
2005 First Printing

ISBN 978-1-55725-422-1

Library of Congress Cataloging-in-Publication Data

Bangley, Bernard, 1935–
Butler's lives of the saints : concise, modernized edition / by Bernard Bangley.
    p. cm.
  Includes index.
  ISBN 1-55725-422-2
1. Christian saints—Biography. I. Title.
BX4655.3.B35 2005
282'.092'2—dc22   2005015564

10 9 8 7 6 5 4 3 2

Published by Paraclete Press
Brewster, Massachusetts
www.paracletepress.com

Printed in the United States of America.

❦ Contents

Fr. Alban Butler
1710–1773

❦ Introduction

Beneath the various councils and actions that are buoys and channel markers in the river of church history, there are some very real people. They aspire and pray, think and plan, guide and direct, hurt and bleed. Some of their names are familiar to many of the people of the world. Others worked and died in obscurity.

The best way to discover the qualities of life in Christ is to mingle with genuine Christians. The friends we keep have a way of shaping our interests, preferences, and moral judgments. Every new generation rediscovers the difference between the values of our culture and the virtues of Christianity. This version of *Lives of the Saints* presents examples and inspiration for devout living in modern society.

But for any reader this book can provide still more. The saints remind us of a reality and a power beyond the merely earthly. Because they are clearly as human as we are, it is reasonable to expect that the same dimensions they explore are available to us. We also can live with an awareness of the presence of God.

Like many characters in the Bible, some of our saints have rough edges and crooked seams. As King David and Simon Peter demonstrate serious or annoying flaws, so do the individuals who followed them through centuries of Christian experience. These saints are very much like the rest of us.

Hagios is the New Testament Greek word that translates into English as saint. It appears sixty-two times. Paul addresses letters to "all the saints" in a particular location. Linguistically it means "separate from common condition and use; dedicated, hallowed," but Paul uses the word as an equivalent for "church members"—all of us who are a part of the Body of Christ.

The popular idea that a saint is a person who never does anything wrong, is good and pure to the core, and lives the perfect life of holiness, is not supported by reality. Saints are entirely human. We put them in stained glass windows, carve statues of them, and erect churches in their names. We have sought every way possible to isolate them from ourselves and to make them something other than we are. We say to ourselves, "They did not know the pressures we know or experience the stresses of everyday life. They are simply too distant from our concerns to have any kinship with us." We push the saints as far from us as we can place them. That way, we do not have to aspire to be what they are. We push their example away, protesting, "I'm no saint," but yet we are traveling the same path.

The purpose of this book is to give not only Catholic readers a reader-friendly collection, but also to invite those of other religious traditions to share knowledge of, and respect for, these exemplary Christians. Many are only vaguely familiar with the saints of the Roman Catholic Church other than a few with celebrity status and those whose "feast days" are now associated with secular holidays. The sketches in this book will answer questions and fill in gaps of knowledge.

The Roman Martyrology is the official list of Catholic saints. It has grown and changed from ancient to modern times, with a recent edition appearing in 2001. *Acta sanctorum* is a huge and growing sixty-four volume work started in 1643. Written in Latin, the valuable information it contains is not widely accessible.

The first collection of lives of the saints intended for general readers was *The Golden Legend* by Jacobus de Voragine. Published in the thirteenth century, it recounts the lives of one hundred and fifty-nine saints in a devout but exaggerated style. Jacobus had little interest in gathering credible historic facts, preferring to emphasize the mysterious side of religious life.

Five centuries later, Alban Butler, an English priest, devoted thirty years of sustained research for a work he called *Lives of the Primitive Fathers, Martyrs, and Other Principal Saints*. Published in four volumes from 1756 to 1759, it contains sixteen hundred biographies with commentary and came to be known as *Butler's Lives of the Saints*. Butler opened the way to popular interest in the Church's saints, and many still consider it the standard guide for English readers. There have been many revisions, each version less like the original, because Butler was more effective as a researcher than as a writer; his verbose and flowery English presents challenging reading today.

Butler's distinctive contribution to stories about saints was to turn attention away from the superhuman, miraculous themes that are prevalent in earlier works. He gives us saints who are examples of Christian living and provide inspiration for the living of our own lives, in every time and circumstance. "They were once what we are now, travelers on earth. They had the same weaknesses we have. We have difficulties; so had the saints."

The sources drawn upon by compilers are called *acta* and *hagiography*. Local congregations often put into writing the circumstances of the deaths of their members during the years of Roman persecution. These eyewitness *acta* circulated among churches as a means of encouragement and guidance. The original "acts" of some martyrs still survive. A generous portion of Polycarp's *acta* is included in the February 23 selection—the earliest example of its kind in existence today.

When Roman persecution ended in the fourth century, *acta* evolved into fanciful documents. Writers plugged gaps in knowledge with spurious inventions of the pious imagination. Sometimes the introduced material is merely fictional decoration, bordering on the absurd. A set of common themes developed as stock material for saintly biography, or *hagiography*. Resistance of attraction to the opposite sex (often under very colorful circumstances—Bernard of Clairvaux is said to have jumped into a pond of cold water), miraculous escapes, and spiritual gymnastics of all kinds may be repeated under many different names. The quality of existing hagiography varies from outstanding to the cheapest pulp fiction. The *Acta of Bibiana* lies at the opposite pole from that of Polycarp. Her accounts are recognized as medieval romantic fiction.

I have avoided an impressive list of ecclesiastical terms in this edition of *Lives of the Saints*. "Oblate," "holy see," "prebend," "lector," "tonsure," and other ecclesiastical jargon are not always immediately meaningful to modern readers. Such terms as "bishop," "archbishop," "nun," "sister," "monk," and "friar" are more widely recognized and are used as required.

Canonization is the Church's way of making something official. The sixty-six books approved for inclusion in the Bible are the *canon* of Scripture. The word means "standard" or "rule." There are many other sacred writings of Judeo-Christian origin that did not make the cut. Scholars call them *non-canonical*.

Early saints did not travel through anything similar to today's process of canonization. The local congregation declared someone a saint. With the passage of time, the Vatican worked out a carefully organized procedural plan, and the journey to sainthood must travel through the proper paths of bureaucracy. It now takes more than local enthusiasm. Careful documentation, long hours of deliberation, and financial resources are required. This, of course, is a needed and welcomed screening of candidates, but it results in a list of saints that is crowded with people from religious orders. These groups are equipped to see the job through to completion. If you would like to see the process at work today, visit the following internet website: http://www.motherteresacause.info/

Here, in simple outline, are the four steps that lead to the canonization of an individual as a saint today.

A local congregation nominates an individual for sainthood. They present this request to a group called the Magisterium at Rome.

The Magisterium declares such a nominee to be "Venerable" if there is evidence that such a person either was martyred because of hostility toward Christianity, or exemplified Christian virtues to a heroic degree.

One becomes "Blessed" at the next stage of the journey to sainthood. An excruciatingly detailed examination of the proposed individual's life, writings, comments, and activity—together with openness to objections—makes this a slow procedure. If the candidate is not a martyr, a verifiable miracle is required.

"Saint" is a term applied to those who can survive repeated examination and be associated with a second miracle. Miraculous healings are most commonly recognized today and may occur before or after the death of the person nominated.

This edition of *Lives of the Saints* follows the general calendar, ascribing a particular saint to a specific month and day. From earliest times, a saint's "feast day" is associated with that individual's death, or "birthday into heaven." There has been great flexibility in this schedule over the years, with movement from one day to another to avoid certain calendar conflicts. The Second Vatican Council of 1963–1965 expressed concern that the feasts of the saints might "take precedence over the feasts which commemorate the very mysteries of salvation." Vatican II took the position that "many of them should be left to be celebrated by a particular Church or nation or religious community; only those should be extended to the universal Church which commemorate saints who are truly of universal significance." The most recent revision of the official calendar accomplished this in 1969.

Various sources list a wide choice of possible feast days for individual saints. More than one saint is assigned on many days, and individual saints are assigned different days. In order to include some when there was serious competition for a day, two or three are off by one day when compared with the official list.

Several factors directed the selection of saints included in this edition. To keep it faithful to Alban Butler's original concept, only those who are officially recognized by the Roman Catholic Church are included. To avoid cluttering the pages with "St." and "Bd." I ordinarily make no distinction between fully canonized saints and those who are presently labeled "blessed." To make the collection under these covers as broad as possible, preference is often given to women, laity, recent candidates for sainthood, country of origin, and above all, spiritual relevance for today. Rather than overly repeating familiar themes, I have given special attention to the distinctive aspects of interesting individuals.

Many saints are not included. The Church has never assumed that even its extensive official list is complete. Moreover, only God knows many saints. "All Saints" receive recognition on November 1 in order to include those remaining.

There are inconsistencies and minor mistakes in most of the published material on this vast subject. There is no way an individual compiler of saint's lives can be an expert on each one. Specialists will certainly find errors even though the competent staff at Paraclete Press and I have worked together to make this book as accurate as possible.

Preparing this volume at points left me a little limp. Physical and mental violence among Christians is distressing to witness, and there is a steady pattern of it through history. The "church fight" is nothing new. Few of the saints, if any, lived an idyllic life of prayer and meditation, untroubled by the behavior of others. For that matter, the internal spiritual struggles of individual saints are even more distracting. At the same time, it is stunning to see faith in God at work for good and positive advances in both individuals and communities. Alban Butler declared, "The saints are a 'cloud of witnesses over our head,' showing us that a life of Christian perfection is not impossible." The perfection they show us is far from being spotless or insulated from real life. When we realize this, we will see the possibilities for ourselves.

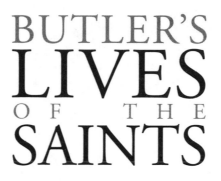

BUTLER'S
LIVES
OF THE
SAINTS

Peter of Atroa (773–837)

Ministry under duress

Ephesus is a popular archaeological site on the western coast of today's Turkey. The apostle Paul established a Christian congregation there on his first missionary journey, remaining there three years, ministering to first-generation Christians. About seven hundred years later, Peter of Atroa was born to Christian parents in the neighborhood of Ephesus.

Peter had natural spiritual interests, and at eighteen, he became a monk, and a few years later, an ordained priest. As he began a pilgrimage to Jerusalem, a mystical vision turned him and his companion aside with the inspiration to build a monastery. A strong work resulted and Peter became the monastery's leader at the age of thirty-two. People sought him because of his reputation as a healer and because of his sensitive spirit.

The early ninth century was a difficult time for Christians in that part of the world. Persecution increased with each passing year, and Peter worked fervently to protect his monks from harm. He died on the first day of January, 837, in the chapel choir, while his brother monks sang around him.

Basil the Great (329–79)

Clear thinking

Popular heresy has always been a threat to basic Christian doctrine. It was rampant in the early centuries, and one attractively expressed teaching was Arianism. The controversy began in Alexandria, in about 320, as a dispute between Arius and his bishop. Arius thought that Christ was neither fully God nor fully human, but something in between. This idea was not acceptable to orthodox Christian doctrine, but the notion gained a considerable following. The Church prepared the Nicene Creed in an effort to correct such heresies.

Basil the Great lived during the height of the Arian controversy (239–379), and he had an important part in the process of resisting it. It is worth noting that Basil's father, mother, grandmother, one of his sisters, and two of his brothers are also officially recognized saints, pointing to a remarkable family life.

Basil worked against steady opposition and received little support from other leaders in the Church even as he was championing the Church's teaching. Libraries preserve many of his books and letters today. The members of his flock loved him because he was an outstanding pastor who often visited among them. He preached to large gatherings twice a day, took care of the poor, and had a hospital built. One of the greatest personalities in church history, Basil did a superlative and enduring work in one of the most difficult times the Church has ever faced.

JANUARY 3

Genevieve (ca. 422– ca. 500)

✍ *Wholesome faith*

Genevieve was a little shepherd in fields near Paris when Germanus (May 28) saw her and envisioned her saintly future. He noticed her listening intently to his sermon preached in Nanterre, a small village about eight miles from Paris. He asked to meet the child and had a quiet conversation with her. When she expressed an interest in service to God, Germanus spoke to her parents, predicting that Genevieve would lead a holy life and bring many others to God. He met with her a second time the next morning, giving her a medal engraved with a cross as a reminder of her dedication to Christ.

Genevieve remained at home, growing up in a wholesome, prayerful environment. When her parents died, she moved into the city of Paris and lived with her godmother. She began to live a life dedicated to religious interests, and continued to do so for thirty years. Neighbors accused Genevieve of acting a part and being a hypocrite, considering her mystical experiences to be pretense and deceit. Their hostility grew to the point that they considered drowning her, but Germanus intervened and persuaded them to overcome their animosity.

In 451, when Attila the Hun overran Gaul, the residents of Paris panicked and made plans to flee for their lives. Genevieve urged them to trust God, telling them that Paris would be spared if they had faith. In fact, Attila turned away from Paris and attacked Orléans. Genevieve died in 512 at the age of eighty-nine. Many residents of modern Paris still have a high regard for her, and some are doing charitable works in her name.

JANUARY 4

Elizabeth Ann Seton (1774–1821)

❧ *Oneness in Christ*

Elizabeth Ann Seton was the first person born in the United States to be recognized as a saint. She began life as an Episcopalian, growing up in New York's high society. She married the wealthy merchant William Magee Seton, when she was nineteen, and she mothered five children. After a decade of stable and happy marriage, William's business went into bankruptcy, and soon afterward, he died of tuberculosis.

Attracted to Catholicism for years, Elizabeth Ann converted in 1805. Most of her friends were not able to understand this change, and some of them even began to shun her. To support her children, she opened a school in Boston. Her school was independent of the Church, but she organized it in a manner similar to a religious community. Based on this experience, the archbishop asked Elizabeth Ann to open a Catholic girl's school in Baltimore, Maryland—the beginning of the parochial school system in America. She founded the Sisters of Charity in 1809 to oversee the work.

Elizabeth Ann died at Emmitsburg, Maryland, on January 4, 1821. In September, 1975, Pope Paul VI formally canonized her.

Near her death, Elizabeth Ann wrote a statement of faith that reads like poetry:

Link by link, the blessed chain
One Body in Christ—He the head we the members
One Spirit diffused thru' the Holy Ghost in us all
One Hope—Him in heaven and Eternity
One Faith—by his Word and his Church
One Baptism and participation of his sacraments
One God our dear Lord
One Father We his children—he above all through all and in all.
Who can resist, all self must be killed and destroyed by this artillery of love—one, one, one. Who could escape this bond of unity, peace, and love? O my soul, be fastened link by link, strong as death, iron, and Hell as says the sacred Word.

JANUARY 5

Genoveva Torres Morales (1870–1956)

❦*Happiness is harmony with God*

Both of Genoveva's Spanish parents and four of her brothers and sisters had died by the time she was eight. Genoveva alone survived to care for their home and had the difficult task of rearing José, her younger brother. At ten, she began reading books on religious subjects, and concluded that happiness was to be found in doing God's will. She determined to practice this with her life.

When Genoveva was thirteen an infected leg became gangrenous and required amputation. Doctors removed her left leg in her home without the benefit of sufficient anesthesia. For the remainder of her life, Genoveva walked on crutches and coped with persistent pain.

At fifteen, she began nine years with the Sisters and other children at the Mercy Home run by the Carmelites of Charity. During this time she became a proficient seamstress and deepened her devotional life. Commenting on her discovery of spiritual liberty during her years at the Mercy Home, Genoveva wrote, "I loved freedom of heart very much, and worked and am working to achieve it fully. It does the soul so much good that every effort is nothing compared with this free condition of the heart."

In 1911, when Genoveva was 41, she accepted the assignment to begin a new kind of religious community—one intended for poor women who could not support themselves. She organized the first such community in Valencia. In time, she established other communities in scattered Spanish locations. Necessary administrative detail crowded in upon her personal prayer life and added spiritual distress to the physical pain that was her constant companion.

She had a reputation for kindness and openness to others. Her good humor was legendary, and she would even joke about her physical condition. "Even if I must suffer greatly, thanks be to God's mercy," she said, "I will not lack courage."

Genoveva died on January 5, 1956.

JANUARY 6

John de Ribera (1532–1611)

✍ *The influence of circumstance*

John grew up in Seville, Spain, in a gracious environment of family and church. His father, Peter de Ribera, a devout Christian, was an important political figure. Educated at the University of Salamanca, John became an ordained priest at the age of twenty-five and remained at the university to teach theology.

Because his leadership abilities were extraordinary, he was appointed bishop, against his wishes, in 1562. After fulfilling that responsibility with distinction for six years, he became archbishop of Valencia. This difficult and fatiguing position he held for forty-two years. Unfortunately, John de Ribera shared a popular notion of his people that the Moors who lived in the excellent agricultural region of Valencia were "sponges who suck up Christian wealth."

He agreed with the 1609 edict expelling them from Valencia. This action resulted in horribly brutal behavior and damaged the local economy. He died two years later in 1611. The Church made an unusual statement honoring the personal virtues of God's servant, but did not accept his political views.

Raymund of Peñafort (ca. 1175–1275)

Organizing and codifying

Raymund, a Spanish Dominican who held a doctorate in law, made a significant contribution to codifying church law. Born in Catalonia, he studied and taught in Barcelona. At the age of forty-seven he exchanged his academic career for life with the Dominicans, and soon after, Rome asked him to come and organize the decrees issued by the popes and church councils of the previous century. The five-volume result, *Decretals*, became the standard reference for church regulations until recent times.

At sixty, Raymund became archbishop of Aragon. He never enjoyed this position, and after two years, an illness led to his resignation. The next year the Dominicans chose Raymund to head their Order. He took his work seriously, faithfully visiting by walking to each Dominican community.

With Raymund's background in law, he decided to revise the Dominican Order's constitution, writing in a provision that the head of the Order could resign. When the Dominicans approved his new constitution, he immediately resigned from office at the modern retirement age of sixty-five.

But his life was not nearly complete. He lived approximately another thirty-five years. He used this time to teach, even guiding Thomas Aquinas (see January 28). Raymund of Peñafort devoted great effort in these remaining years to fighting heresy and trying to convert the Moors in Spain to Christianity. In 1256, he wrote his master-general that ten thousand Muslims had been converted and baptized under his leadership.

JANUARY 8
Thorfinn (d. 1285)
✇ *Faithful in obscurity*

The Norwegian Thorfinn died at a Cistercian monastery in Belgium. During his life he did not attract much attention, and after he was buried, most people all but forgot him.

About fifty years later construction workers accidentally broke open his tomb. Instead of a disagreeable odor, there was a strong, pleasing scent. The abbot asked his monks about the man interred on the site and found one of them, the aged Walter de Muda, who remembered Thorfinn. Walter recalled that Thorfinn had impressed the community with his gentle, yet strong personality. De Muda had actually written a little poem praising Thorfinn that was entombed with him. Searchers found this poem on parchment, undeteriorated after five decades. The abbot took this as a sign that it was important to perpetuate the memory of Thorfinn, and asked Walter to write everything he could remember about him. All that we know about this saint today may be read in Walter's sketchy recollections and the tribute he paid him with his poem. He remembered Thorfinn as a kind, patient, generous man, whose gentle nature was combined with a strong moral character.

JANUARY 9
Julian and Basilissa (fourth century)
✇ *Acts of charity*

Husband and wife, Julian and Basilissa turned their home into something of a hospital for the poor. In this facility, they provided a refuge for the helpless and the homeless, and as many as a thousand people came under their care.

Julian and Basilissa lived in fourth-century Egypt where their expression of personal Christian dedication resulted in many acts of charity and penance. We do not know many details of their lives, though it is certain Julian outlived his wife by many years. Both of them died as martyrs for their faith.

JANUARY 10
Leonie Aviat (1844–1914)
❦Saintly influence

Leonie was born in Sézanne, France, in 1844. She developed spiritually at the Monastery of the Visitation in Troyes. The influence of Francis de Sales (January 24) permeated her experience there. With this preparation, she founded a congregation committed to Salesian spirituality and to the evangelization and education of young textile workers.

From France, Leonie's work spread to Italy, Mexico, and many other places worldwide. Inspired by Francis de Sales, she worked for the happiness of others and was faithful to her resolution "to forget myself entirely." She died in Perugia, Italy, on January 10, 1914.

JANUARY 11
Thomas of Cori (1653–1729)
❦A life of prayer

Thomas, who became an orphan at fourteen, was left alone to take care of his sisters. He supported his family by herding sheep, and this gave him time to reflect on spiritual matters. When his sisters were married, Thomas became a Franciscan and was ordained a priest in 1683.

A commentator writes that Thomas of Cori was not so much a man who prayed as a man who became prayer. At the same time, Thomas admitted that even with his intense dedication to prayer he experienced spiritual dryness for about forty years.

Thomas devoted himself to visiting with others in various regions of Italy. He preached with lucidity, in a straightforward and persuasive style. While he attempted to live a thoroughly Franciscan life, he patiently and kindly encouraged others who were not as spiritually mature as himself. Personal humility characterized his demeanor.

JANUARY 12

Bernard of Corleone (1605–67)

❧ *Change of life*

His parents, who tended a small vineyard in Sicily, named him Philip. While he received no formal education, he did learn to be a cobbler. After his father died, Philip made and repaired shoes to support himself and his mother.

During the seventeenth century, Spanish mercenaries occupied Sicily. Proficient in the use of swords, they taught young Philip the art of swordsmanship. He gained a reputation for being the best "blade" in Sicily. He used his sword to protect women and peasant neighbors from abuse by the soldiers. One incident provoked a duel in which Philip seriously wounded his opponent. Seeking sanctuary, he ran to a local church and hid there. In the quiet of that place, the young man reviewed his life and decided it was meaningless.

In December of 1631, at the age of twenty-seven, Philip joined the Franciscans in Caltanisetta, and received the religious name of Bernard. Not only did he change his name, but he radically changed his manner of living. Instead of reaching for his sword when provoked, he now responded with silence.

Bernard of Corleone turned his former violence toward others into merciless violence toward himself. Self-discipline became a central task for him as he advanced rapidly in a life of devotion to God.

In the manner of Francis of Assisi (October 4), he had a loving and healing relationship with animals. People brought their sick pets and farm animals to him with remarkable results. He practiced a ritual of praying the Lord's Prayer over an animal and then leading it three times around a cross in front of his church. His life was in harmony with all of God's creation.

Bernard of Corleone died in 1667 at the age of sixty-two, an uneducated cobbler and sword fighter who won his greatest duel—with himself.

JANUARY 13
Hilary of Poitiers (ca. 315–67)
Quiet studies

After receiving a good education in rhetoric and philosophy, Hilary married and had a daughter. In 350, following lengthy and serious study, he became a Christian convert.

Leadership qualities quickly brought Hilary to positions of responsibility in the Church. By 353 he was a bishop, and for the remainder of his life he championed the cause of orthodox Christian doctrine that was challenged by the growing popularity of heresies. Augustine and Jerome expressed great respect for his clear thinking and persuasive abilities. He demonstrated a compassionate love for heretics while yet combating their heresy. Described as gentle and courteous, he was a friendly person whose writing on Christian doctrine remains engaging in our day.

Hilary died at the age of fifty-two.

JANUARY 14
Sava of Serbia (1174–1237)
Guiding others

Sava called himself an "unworthy, lazy monk." An easy-going man, he never became heavy-handed with those under his oversight. His gentle guidance proved effective in the training of young monks. He invariably came down on the side of kindness and leniency.

Born in Bulgaria, the third son of Prince Stephen Nemanya (who won independence for the Serbs), Sava became a monk in 1191. Five years later, his princely father abdicated and joined him in his religious vocation. These two monks, father and son, founded a monastery at Mount Athos which became the center of Serbian culture.

Sava translated Scripture and other books into the Serbian language. The Mount Athos monastery, named Khilandari, still possesses some of his hand-written work.

JANUARY 15
Arnold Janssen (1837–1909)
❧ *An idealistic dream*

Arnold Janssen grew up on his family farm in Germany. After studying mathematics, science, and philosophy, he attended seminary in Muenster. In 1861 he became an ordained priest and began to work as a schoolteacher.

Appointed director of the Apostleship of Prayer, Arnold began to mingle with Christians of other denominations. He traveled to many places, often walking. A growing interest in mission work led him to give up his teaching responsibilities and devote his full energy to promoting missions in Germany and beyond. He began a popular magazine, *The Little Messenger of the Sacred Heart.*

The civil government in Germany during the late nineteenth century began to restrict the Church. Anti-Catholic laws resulted in the imprisonment of bishops and the exile of priests. Arnold looked for ways to make the best of a bad situation. He proposed that some of the expelled priests could become missionaries, or at least they could help train them. His ideas received little support. People argued that he was too idealistic, and that Germany was not ready to begin such a grand project. Janssen responded, "The Lord challenges our faith to do something new, precisely when so many things are collapsing in the Church."

Promoting his project in the *Little Messenger,* he began fundraising. German politics complicated his search for a house to use for the training of priests. He shopped for real estate across the Netherlands border, and bought property in Steyl. There the Church founded the Divine Word Missionaries in 1875. Four years later, the first two missionaries departed for China.

A steady flow of eager students came into Steyl. Improvements to the house required the labor of many volunteers who engaged in what they considered mission work. Janssen had not anticipated this enthusiastic blossoming of his idea. Women also arrived to work in the kitchen and later formed the Holy Spirit Missionary Sisters. The first Sisters went to Argentina in 1895.

Arnold Janssen died at the house in Steyl at the age of seventy-one, on January 15, 1909. Today, more than six thousand Divine Word Missionaries work in sixty-five countries, and almost four thousand Holy Spirit Missionary Sisters serve in thirty-five countries. A farm boy's idealistic dream continues to bear a rich spiritual harvest.

JANUARY 16
Honoratus of Arles (ca. 350–429)
❦ *Searching*

Honoratus was born in the fourth century to a Roman family working for their government in Gaul. As a young person, he abandoned pagan worship of idols and became a Christian. He moved with his brother Venàntius, to Greece and attempted life as a religious hermit. Their circumstances were difficult, exposing them to physical hardships. Venantius became ill and died. Honoratus, also quite sick, returned home and established a monastery on one of the Mediterranean islands that bears his name today.

He became archbishop of Arles, assuming responsibilities that consumed the final three years of his life.

JANUARY 17
Anthony of Egypt (ca. 251–356)
❦ *Surrendering everything*

Credit for the concept of monasticism goes to Anthony. He is considered the father of all monks. Growing up in a Christian home in Egypt, Anthony lost his parents early, inheriting a small fortune. When he reached the age of twenty Christ's words about selling what you have and giving it to the poor touched him profoundly. He determined to practice Christ's teaching literally. Once he had arranged for the care of his younger sister, he sought solitude in the desert for prayer and meditation. His experiences during the next twenty years of his life parallel those of the temptation of Christ.

Many came to Anthony for spiritual direction and advice. The emperor Constantine wrote, requesting his prayers. Anthony set up a scattered group of cells that were the world's first suggestion of a monastery. He expected to become a martyr during the Roman persecution of Christians in 311, but did not, even though he went to Alexandria while openly wearing his identifying white tunic of sheepskin in order to encourage other Christians.

Living beyond one hundred years, Anthony actively opposed the Arian heresy (see the January 2 entry). The story of his life was influential in the conversion of Augustine (August 28).

JANUARY 18

Christina Ciccarelli (sixteenth century)
Caring for the poor

Christina was an Italian who became an Augustinian nun. While she stayed far from any public spotlight, her profound spirituality became well-known. She had great concern for the needs of the poor, working with other nuns to provide them with essentials. On January 18, 1543, the day of her death, the children of Aquila, where her convent was located, paraded in the streets mourning her death.

JANUARY 19

Canute IV, King of Denmark (1043–86)
Meeting a challenge

Canute became king of Denmark in 1081. Much of the Danish nation was at least nominally Christian because of the labor of English missionaries. Canute worked to strengthen the Church in his country by law and financial subsidies.

A series of political misjudgments, including an attempt to claim the crown of England, led to his downfall. The Danish people did not support his taxing them for religious purposes and rebelled against him. An angry mob gathered outside the church where Canute was praying. As he knelt, receiving the holy Eucharist, someone threw a spear through a church window, striking and killing this king of Denmark.

JANUARY 20

Sebastian of Rome (third century)

ᵂ*Suffering for Christ*

Impressive legends exist about Sebastian, but we know few details about the life of this famous Roman martyr. He lived in a time when it was dangerous to be a Christian. One legend contends that the Romans arrested him and threw him in prison, where two other Christian prisoners were ready to renounce their faith in order to save their lives. Sebastian's encouragement not only gave them strength, but reached the ears of others outside the prison bars, leading to additional conversions.

The legend of Sebastian's death is frightening. Romans, the story goes, tied him naked to a tree and used him as a target for archery practice. Many Renaissance paintings portray this incident. After he was left to die, a widow came to bury him, but she was astonished to discover that somehow breath was still in him. She took him home and tended to his wounds. After his recovery, she pleaded with him to escape the risks of living as a Christian in Rome. Instead, he went to Diocletian and demanded that he stop persecuting Christians. Shocked to discover that the young man had survived the target practice, Diocletian ordered the immediate execution of Sebastian. He was then clubbed to death.

Agnes (ca. 292– ca. 305)

꧁*Sexual equality*

The story of Agnes, who died at the executioner's hand as a thirteen–year-old adolescent, reveals a courageous effort of a young woman to define herself as a human being in Christ, in spite of the crushing attempt of her culture to identify her strictly in terms of sex. Her stand against the prevailing attitudes of the society around her is a brave declaration of independence.

An extraordinarily beautiful child, Agnes was born to a wealthy Roman family. As she approached puberty, many men began to express an interest in her. She did not respond positively to their advances. She told them, "Jesus is my only husband. I am already promised to the Lord." One disappointed suitor denounced her as a Christian and she was brought before the governor. When an offer of lavish gifts did not change her mind, the governor put her in chains. Agnes refused to back down, even after being tortured. When pain did not work, the Romans tried humiliation. The Roman governor sent her to a house of prostitution where any man might have his way with her. Because she radiated such an aura of purity (*Agnes* is the Greek word for *pure* and is but a step away from *agnus*, which means *lamb*) no man would touch her. According to the ancient written record of her life, one man who dared to gaze lustfully at her naked body lost his eyesight. Exasperated men condemned her to die by the sword, a punishment she accepted as cheerfully "as others go to their wedding."

Agnes has been an extraordinarily popular saint through the centuries. Perhaps she is a corrective to the idea that men should have a dominant place in human society. She saw herself as a child of God while her cultural environment attempted to identify her strictly in terms of sex. Agnes refused to play by the rulebook of her time and place.

JANUARY 22
Vincent Pallotti (1795–1850)
✒ *Inspired living*

The son of a Roman grocer, Vincent Pallotti was not the best student early in life. His teacher commented, "He is a little saint, but a bit thick-headed." His studies improved, and he was ordained to the priesthood in 1817 at the age of twenty-three. With a doctorate in theology and philosophy, he became a college professor, but eventually devoted himself to pastoral work full-time. His personal diary records his spiritual insight:

Not the intellect, but God.
Not the will, but God.
Not the soul, but God.
Not the goods of the world, but God.
Not riches, but God.
Not honors, but God.
Not distinction, but God.
Not dignities, but God.
Not advancement, but God.
God always and in everything.

Ahead of his times in both activity and thought, Pallotti became a target of some major dirty tricks handed out by other clergy who were apparently jealous of him. Ultimately, though, some who had mercilessly attacked him became ardent admirers and supporters.

Vincent Pallotti wrote, "Holiness is simply to do God's will, always and everywhere." He provided education and practical instruction for many kinds of laborers and craftsmen, attempting to give them pride in the quality of their work. He would literally give another the shirt off his back. Once, he dressed as a woman in order to approach the bedside of a man who said he would shoot any priest who came near him.

One comment about him beautifully summarizes his fifty-five years of life. "He did all that he could. As for what he couldn't do—well, he did that too." He died in Rome on January 22, 1850.

JANUARY 23
John the Almsgiver (d. ? 616)
ᗡ Generosity

John was the son of a governor of the island of Cyprus. When death claimed all the other members of his family, John moved to Alexandria, Egypt, about the year 608. He became a patriarch. The Church in Egypt was splitting into factions, but his personal integrity and his careful approach to almsgiving gained the respect of everyone.

John lived a simple life, calling the poor his masters. He would give all he could to help them, even to the point of giving away his own bedding. He worked strenuously on behalf of the poor, demanding accurate weights and measures, distributing money at his disposal to hospitals and monasteries. He built poorhouses and maternity hospitals. He spent an astonishing amount on disaster relief and in rescuing captives. He gave a ship loaded with corn to a merchant who was ruined by a couple of shipwrecks. The merchant sold the corn at a good profit in famine-struck Britain and was back in business.

Like anyone who works for charity with the general public, John developed an eye for freeloaders. Some came to him in disguise, hoping he would not recognize that he had already given them handouts. They need not have bothered. John continued to help them generously. He would sit all day on a bench in front of the church every Wednesday and Friday in order to provide everyone with free and easy access to his attention. Generosity begets generosity, and others began to follow his example.

JANUARY 24
Francis de Sales (1567–1622)
ᗡ Wholesome religion

"Live, Jesus!" That is the often repeated motto of Francis de Sales. If ever there was a genuine example of a thoroughly Christian life that is within the grasp of everyone, we can find it in this bishop

17

of Geneva. A few complained that he made sainthood too easily attainable.

Francis de Sales went to Geneva during troubled times. The Protestant reformation was sweeping across Switzerland at full speed. New Calvinists were making life difficult and dangerous for Catholics. Instead of pointing out the flaws in Protestant doctrine and attempting to suppress it, Francis de Sales understood the larger significance of the movement. A diplomat in the finest sense, he approached the Calvinists with love and gentleness. He established his home base a few miles away from Geneva in Annecy, France.

Francis had been born to wealthy parents in Savoy in 1567. They wanted him to be a lawyer and paid his way through college until he had earned a doctorate in law. There are many examples in history of parents who misguided remarkable children into the wrong profession. Francis de Sales said, "God does not want me to embrace the life for which my father destines me." He became a priest in 1593.

The life of Francis de Sales demonstrates the extraordinary value of a calm, gentle approach to difficult issues, combined with genuine spiritual depth. Sometimes, it may be necessary for Christians to be boldly combative, but the patient, loving pattern of Jesus himself results in remarkable success. Francis is a supreme example of applied Christianity. He truly "lived Jesus" as Christ lived in him.

Many sought Francis de Sales as their spiritual director. His correspondence with Madame de Chamoisy evolved into one of the most remarkable devotional books ever published on prayer and Christian living. *Introduction to the Devout Life* gives sane, understandable, and healthy spiritual advice that ordinary people who live and work in a secular world can effectively practice every day. His illustrations and metaphors are memorable. "When little bees are caught in a storm they take hold of small stones so they can keep their balance when they fly. Our firm resolution to stay with God is like stability to the soul amid the rolling waves of life."

One of the great spiritual relationships existed between Francis de Sales and Jane de Chantal (December 12). Their combined efforts resulted in the foundation of the Order of the Visitation in 1610.

Death came relatively early to Francis de Sales, but his fifty-six years have left a permanent mark on the Church. Through his writings and example, he continues to direct the formation of the human spirit.

JANUARY 25

The Conversion of Paul (ca. 4 B.C.– ca.64)

✍ *Confronting Christ*

Saul of Tarsus was a dedicated, enthusiastic Jew with a passionate interest in fulfilling the requirements of complex and detailed Jewish religious Law. The intelligent young man made the distressing discovery that the harder he tried to behave correctly, the farther the ideal life receded from his grasp. He had his heart set on being a righteous person, but his goal was not attainable. He began to feel disillusionment, and doubted that he would ever please God by strict observance of the Law. There can be no doubt that he was a well-behaved person. Anyone would have called him "good."

Many modern Christians do not realize they are as trapped in a system of attempting to win God's favor by good works as was Saul of Tarsus. "Righteousness by the law" motivated Saul to persecute Christians. This is a complex and multifaceted issue. One element is probably his own dissatisfaction with the religion he had inherited. For whatever package of reasons, Saul became a serious threat to the young Christian Church. He was present when Stephen, the first Christian martyr, was stoned, and Saul approved the action.

The ninth chapter of the book of Acts relates the story of Saul's conversion. He was on his way to Damascus with letters permitting him to arrest Christians and return them to Jerusalem for punishment. As he traveled, a bright light immobilized him as the risen Christ asked, "Saul, Saul, why do you persecute me?" Blinded by the experience, Paul had to be led by the hand into Damascus. A Christian named Ananias then visited him at the Lord's command, restored his sight, and baptized him. An astonishing change took place. Paul began to speak in public, giving the message that Jesus is the Son of God. The transformation of Paul is one of the most significant moments in human history. Paul's spiritual insight into the meaning of the life and the crucifixion of Jesus gave substance and character to his writing on basic Christian doctrine.

JANUARY 26

Paula (347–404)

⫷*Supporting role*

Paula began life in 347 as a member of the Roman aristocracy. She was a happily married mother until she became a widow at thirty-two. Another widow, Marcella, consoled Paula and led her into religious life. The famous Jerome (September 30) became Paula's friend and spiritual director. It was he who wrote her biography.

When Jerome traveled to the Holy Land in 385, Paula followed. She spent part of her fortune helping Jerome establish a monastery for men, a convent for women, and a guesthouse for pilgrims in Bethlehem. For the remainder of her life, Paula led the women's community and devoted time to assisting Jerome in his scholarly studies. Already proficient in Greek, she now began to learn Hebrew. Jerome's great Latin translation of the Bible from the original languages owes much credit to Paula's capable assistance.

Paula's death at the age of fifty-six on January 26, 404 prompted Jerome to write a touching letter to her daughter. "I cannot say enough to do justice to the virtues of the holy and venerable Paula. From a noble family, she was even nobler in holiness." Her grave is under the Church of the Nativity in Bethlehem.

JANUARY 27

Enrique De Osso Y Cervello (1840–96)
✎ *Teaching others*

The youngest of three Spanish children born to Jaime de Ossó and Michaela Cervelló in 1840, Enrique grew up in a devout Christian home. With natural aptitude for religious work, he became a priest in 1867. He said that his ideal was to love Jesus more each new day, and to make him known and loved by others. He decided that Christian education would be the tool that could transform society and as a result founded organizations dedicated to the task.

JANUARY 28

Thomas Aquinas (1225–74)
✎ *Faith and reason*

Benedictine monks in Italy's Monte Cassino reared the brilliant Thomas Aquinas from the age of five. His parents wanted to give him every opportunity to prepare for a significant religious life. Thomas was very compatible with the monks and remained with them until he was thirteen.

After studying at the University of Naples, Thomas informed his parents that he wanted to become a Dominican friar. This came as a shock to them. The Dominicans were a modern group of religious beggars, the technical term for which was *mendicants*. His parents wanted him to become a more respected Benedictine and perhaps bring them honor at Monte Cassino. They kidnapped him and locked him away for a year in their castle. Thomas used this time to study the *Sentences* of Peter Lombard, memorize much of the Bible, and to look for fallacies in Aristotle's writing. When he refused to change his mind about the Dominicans (or as his parents would have said, "refused to come to his senses") they allowed him to return to the Dominican Order of Preachers.

During his studies at Cologne, Thomas was a quiet, reserved student, preferring to listen rather than to speak. His competitive classmates gave the chubby new arrival the nickname, "Dumb Sicilian Ox." One of his teachers, noticing the intelligence of Thomas, said, "One day the lowing of this "Dumb Ox" will be heard around the world."

Eventually, Thomas Aquinas received a doctorate at the University of Paris, where he then began to teach. In this location, he began to write and publish commentaries on Scripture and books on philosophy. His fondness for the pagan Aristotle resulted in concern among Church leadership. He also stirred up controversy by insisting that theological discussion could attend equally to conflicting ideas before reaching a conclusion. This seemed to challenge the authority of the Church.

Preparation of his masterpiece, *Summa theologiae*, began in 1266. This was the first systematic approach to writing out Church doctrine. Thomas wanted to show the logic of Christian ideas. God's revelation does not disable human reason. As portions of this vast work began to circulate, some began to challenge and criticize Thomas. The Dominicans in Naples gave him a refuge from the heated controversies regarding his ideas. They wanted him to finish his *Summa*, but he never did. In December, 1273, he firmly put down his pen. After a significant religious experience he said, "I can't continue writing. Everything I have written seems to me like so much straw compared to what I have seen and what has been revealed to me."

When he died the next year, he was only forty-nine.

JANUARY 29

Gildas the Wise (ca. 500– ca. 570)

❧ *Prophetic voice*

As a young Briton, Gildas began practicing self-denial as a serious Christian commitment. He went to Wales as a refugee and became a monk. For a while he was something of a traveling hermit, but the details are extremely sketchy.

In 540 Gildas wrote his most famous book, *De Excidiis Britanniae*, in which he records vividly the failure of British leaders and clerics to live exemplary lives and make moral decisions. As did the Old Testament prophets, he told a suffering people that their own sins were responsible for their troubles. Their immorality was making the Anglo-Saxon invaders successful. Gildas attempted to awaken the conscience of the sixth-century British people with the strongest denunciatory verses he could find in the Bible. That Gildas had a working knowledge of Scripture, Virgil, and Ignatius is clearly evident in his book, and is a credit to this individual's effort to keep faith and the human mind alive in barbaric times.

JANUARY 30
Bathild (d. 680)
Transforming circumstances

Somewhere around 630, pirates abducted a young English girl named Bathild and transported her on a ship to France. The pirates sold her as a household slave to the comptroller in the king's palace at Neustria. Bathild did not struggle against her circumstances, but carefully learned to do the housekeeping chores required of her, while remaining polite and gentle.

King Clovis II found Bathild attractive and married her in 649. When the king died, she and her sons continued to rule that section of France. Because of her own experience, she took an active part in suppressing the slave trade and worked to release those already captured.

Queen Bathild's position allowed her to support religion in many ways. She opened a seminary for the training of clergy and a convent for nuns. Ultimately, she abandoned her royal privileges and entered the convent herself. The only thing that distinguished her from the other nuns was her extraordinary humility and strict obedience to her religious superiors. While at the convent, she devoted herself to caring for the sick and the poor.

After a painful, lingering illness, she died on January 30, 680.

JANUARY 31

John Bosco (1815–88)

✑*Loving the unlovely*

Born on an Italian farm in 1815 and ordained a priest in 1841, John Bosco began early in his ministry to work with young people in difficulty. He opened a boarding house for boys and asked his own mother to be the housekeeper. There he taught the boys ways to earn a living in various trades. This ministry quickly expanded. In 1854 Bosco founded a religious order focused on working with young people. He called the order Salesians, honoring Francis de Sales (January 24) whom he greatly admired. Cooperating with Mary Mazarello (May 14) he also helped to start the Daughters of Mary to work with girls.

Bosco's critics charged that his trust in God's providence was much greater than his actual financial resources. Others thought he was not strict enough with the boys under his care. The young men themselves, however, loved John Bosco. One eager boy crashed through a glass door wanting to meet with John as he was seen walking by on the street. John Bosco believed that Christian love provides the best guidance for young people. Punishment is not necessary when youths are engaged in interesting, creative activity. His approach was preventive instead of repressive. Bosco entertained the young people with acrobatics, juggling, and magic tricks. Getting and keeping assistants to work with the children according to his methods was a difficult and frustrating task. He continued to be personally involved in the care of his charges, and the struggle to raise funds, until the end of his life.

Bosco's doctors warned him that he was wearing himself out and needed to find time for total rest. He never took their advice. Two years later, before daylight on January 31, 1888, he died.

FEBRUARY 1

Brigid of Ireland (? 450– ? 525)

❧ *Love is a spendthrift*

Brigid is a saint with almost no existing historical record. Most of what we have about her is legendary and rooted in Irish pagan folklore. Her fifth-century birthplace may have been near Kildare, Ireland, and it is possible that St. Patrick (see March 17) baptized her.

Religion in Ireland was going through a radical transition from paganism to Christianity in the time of Brigid. The tales about her seem to reflect that tension. Her name is that of the Celtic sun goddess. Brigid exemplifies generosity and compassion with a feminine, nurturing slant. One story relates that when she was a slave girl she gave away her master's money with such enthusiasm that he freed her in order to save a little of his wealth. If Christ turned water into wine, legend states that Brigid followed his example, supplying eighteen churches with beer from one barrel, and turned water into milk that cured a woman with leprosy. The sick and the poor thronged around her.

Brigid became a nun and then the abbess of the monastery at Kildare. There is even a report that she became the first, and only, female bishop. Dublin's national museum claims to have her jewel-studded silver and brass shoe.

FEBRUARY 2

Simeon and the Presentation of the Lord (first century)

❧ *Expectations fulfilled*

Simeon lived to old age before Christ was born. He was waiting to see God's Messiah. A devout man, Simeon lived with an awareness of the presence of God. He embodied the hope of his nation that God would one day send his anointed Christ. Rome occupied Israel with a heavy hand, and corruption was commonplace among people of all nationalities. Simeon had divine assurance that he would not die until he had seen the long-anticipated Messiah.

At the temple in Jerusalem, Simeon saw a peasant couple from Galilee who had with them a baby boy less than two months old. Joseph and Mary had obeyed Jewish Law and had come for the ceremony of purification. This required a mother to offer a burnt offering of a lamb. If a lamb was too expensive, she could substitute a pigeon or a dove. The couple from Nazareth brought the offering of the poor. God revealed to Simeon that the child they held was the one he had been expecting.

The old man took the baby in his arms and uttered a beautiful prayer of thanksgiving and a prophecy, interpreting for all time the significance of the birth of this holy child. Simeon's horizons expanded, allowing him to grasp a larger concept of the work Jesus would accomplish, calling him "a light to the Gentiles" as well as the fulfillment of Jewish expectations. From the beginning when God made a covenant with Abraham, a universal blessing of the world through the Hebrew people was a part of the promise.

Returning the baby to his mother, Simeon told Mary of things to come: Both joy and sorrow waited for her because of this child.

FEBRUARY 3

Blaise of Sebaste (d. ? 316)

Healing ministry

Most of our information about Blaise of Sebaste is unreliable. He may have been bishop of Sebaste in Armenia (part of modern Turkey) early in the fourth century. One persistent legend claims that he saved the life of a boy who had a fish bone stuck in his throat. Blaise prayed for the child who then coughed up the bone. As his reputation spread, people flocked to him for physical and spiritual healing.

During a period of religious persecution, Blaise was arrested and imprisoned, but that did not stop his healing ministry. Even as he was on his way to jail, a desperate mother begged him to heal her child, and he did.

Blaise became a Christian martyr about 316.

FEBRUARY 4
John de Britto (1647–93)
🖋 *Missionary effort*

In an effort to reach Indian nobility, John de Britto, a Jesuit from Portugal, dressed and behaved according to the tradition of the Brahmin caste. Unfortunately, his ministry was not welcomed. John and his students were severely persecuted and physically harmed.

After a brief return home in Lisbon, John de Britto recovered enough to resume his duties in India. For three years he continued his difficult mission in hostile and threatening conditions. Eventually, the Rajah Raghunatha had him arrested for teaching what was considered to be subversive things regarding worship of the traditional gods of the nation. In a letter written the day before his execution, John wrote: "The only crime with which I am charged is that I teach the religion of the true God and do not worship idols. It is indeed glorious to suffer death for such a crime! That is what fills me with happiness and joy in our Lord. I await death, and I await it with impatience. It has always been the object of my prayers. It forms today the most precious reward of my labors and sufferings."

The next morning, February 4, 1693, a large crowd saw John de Britto decapitated. When news of his execution reached Lisbon there was a memorial service. John's mother attended, wearing a festal gown instead of mourning garments.

FEBRUARY 5
Philip of Jesus (1575–97)
🖋 *Missionary hardship*

Mexico City was the birthplace of Philip de las Casas. His pious parents had moved to Mexico from Spain. As a teenager Philip experimented with the religious life at the Franciscan Convent of Santa Barbara in Pueblo, Mexico. But then his father sent him to the

Philippines with funds to begin a shipping business. Still attracted to the religious life, he entered the Franciscan Convent in Manila during 1594. He became a friar and worked with the sick.

Yielding to his family's desire to see him again, Philip began a voyage home to Mexico, but a storm wrecked his ship on a reef off the coast of Japan as the boat attempted to enter a port. During this storm, Philip had a vision of a white cross over Japan, but the cross turned blood red. Japanese people seized the ship's cargo, while a local warlord accused those on board of being pirates and of spying for Spain in advance of an invasion. All aboard were condemned and murdered. Young Philip's death came by crucifixion on February 5, 1597, at Nagasaki, Japan. Philip embraced the cross on which he was to die, calling it a "happy ship" that would convey him to heaven.

FEBRUARY 6

Paul Miki and his Companions

(1562–97)

❦ *Faith survives*

A group of Jesuit missionaries led by Francis Xavier (December 3) introduced Christianity to Japan in 1549. The labor of two years resulted in a tiny group of committed converts. More missionaries followed, and the Japanese Church began to flourish. The record claims as many as three hundred thousand new Christians, most of them living in and around the port city of Nagasaki. The future of Christianity in Japan looked promising.

Human politics and power struggles prove a perennial hazard for secure and creative living, however. In the late sixteenth century, the rulers of Nagasaki grew suspicious of Spanish and Portuguese colonialism, and suspected missionaries as advance agents in that process. The work of Christian missions seemed a threat to their control. In 1587, one of the warlords (*shoguns*), Hideyoshi, gave an order to expel all missionaries. Most of them voluntarily complied, but a few remained and continued to work.

Ten years after handing down his decree, Hideyoshi condemned three Japanese Jesuits, six Franciscans, and seventeen of the Japanese laity to death. He had all twenty-six of them crucified in public in 1597. Paul Miki, a Japanese native, was one of the Jesuit victims. From his personal cross, Paul cried out, "As I come to this supreme moment of my life, I am sure none of you would think I want to deceive you. I tell you plainly: There is no way to be saved except the Christian way. My religion teaches me to pardon my enemies and all who have offended me. I do gladly pardon the Emperor and all who have sought my death. I beg them to seek baptism and be Christians themselves."

Following these executions, the authorities in Japan began a gruesome crackdown on Christianity. They demanded that people step on an image of Christ or Mary. The penalty of death awaited all who refused, along with their families. The result was a Japanese Christian community that was familiar with martyrdom and suffering. The Passion of Christ became central in Japanese spirituality, with the cross as a symbol of endurance and faith. Kept alive in secret, the Christian church in Japan became virtually invisible for two hundred years. Tens of thousands of Japanese passed Christianity from generation to generation, practicing baptism, memorizing Latin prayers, keeping feast days. When Japan began to open to the Western world in the mid-nineteenth century, Christian spiritual descendants of Paul Miki and his companion martyrs emerged to rebuild Christianity openly in Japan.

FEBRUARY 7

Edigio Maria of St. Joseph (1729–1812)

⁊ *Simple saintliness*

Edigio began his life in Taranto, Italy. His poor father died when Edigio was eighteen, and it became his responsibility to care for his family. When these duties were fulfilled at the age of twenty-five, he joined the Franciscans and serve as a cook and porter for his remaining fifty-three years at a hospice in Naples. His concern and care for the poor earned him the title "Consoler of Naples." He urged everyone he met to love God.

FEBRUARY 8

Josephine Bakhita (1869–1947)

❧ *Discovery of faith*

The people of Africa's Sudan know Josephine Bakhita as "*nostra Madre Moretta*" (our black mother). Her parents did not give her the name Bakhita. The captors who sold her into slavery applied it, called her "Bakhita," which means "fortunate." The nine-year-old girl's frightening abduction while working in the fields with her mother erased her memory of her actual family name. Arab slave traders sold her five times in the markets of El Obeid and Khartoum, and subjected her to all the moral and physical humiliation that accompanies human slavery. All her attempts to escape failed.

Callisto Legnani, an Italian consul, bought Bakhita in Khartoum. With Legnani, life became extraordinarily different. No one beat her. Her overseers treated her in a civilized and gentle manner. She actually began to enjoy working in the consul's house. When the consul returned to Italy, Bakhita asked to go with him.

In Genoa, the consul transferred Bakhita to the Michieli family, which took her to Zianigo where she became a babysitter for their daughter. Then the responsibilities of ownership and management of a hotel on the Red Sea took the Michieli family away, and Bakhita went to live with the Sisters of the Institute of the Catechumens in Venice. Now Bakhita discovered that God was behind the pleasant behavior of the Italian families she had known. She found clear answers to the searching questions she had been asking herself. Following a few months of formal instruction, the Sisters baptized Bakhita in 1890 and gave her a new name, Josephine. That was a happy and memorable day for her. For the rest of her life others could often see her kissing the baptismal font and saying, "Here, I became one of the daughters of God."

Mrs. Michieli returned from her Red Sea enterprise and sought Bakhita. With complete confidence, Bakhita asked to remain with the sisters, serving God. A new Italian law abolishing slavery provided the young African with the freedom to choose, and Mrs. Michieli reluctantly concurred. Bakhita remained, giving herself to the service of the Lord for another fifty years; sewing, cooking, doing embroidery, and keeping the door. While on door duty, she would gently touch the heads of children as they came to school. Her lovely voice blessed them and made them feel loved. "Be good. Love the Lord. Pray for those who do not know him. It is a great grace to know God." Her simplicity and smile were genuinely appealing. It took her twenty years to comply with a superior's order to write her autobiography, which was published in 1930. She began to travel, telling others her remarkable life story.

Bakhita's mature years were disturbed with a painful illness, which confined her to a wheelchair. When asked how she was, she would reply, smiling, "As the Master desires." The agony of her final illness caused her to relive her years as a slave. She asked those who attended her, "Please loosen the chains. They are heavy." Bakhita died February 8, 1947. One of her comments summarizes her spiritual life. "If I was to meet those slave raiders who abducted me and those who tortured me, I'd kneel down to them and kiss their hands, because, if it had not been for them, I would not have become a Christian or a religious person."

FEBRUARY 9

Miguel Cordero (1854–1910)
Teaching ministry

An Ecuadorian schoolteacher, Cordero had a distinguished academic career at the turn of the twentieth century. He specialized in languages and in writing textbooks for children. As the first indigenous de la Salle Brother, he was particularly adept at teaching religion to young people. He led an intense, personal prayer life and acquired a reputation for overflowing warmth and humor.

He was never in good health, so his intense labor in Europe was Cordero's undoing. He found the climate in Belgium and France uncomfortable and moved to Barcelona in 1909. Unfortunately, the political situation there resulted in anti-religious activity. The government safely evacuated Miguel Cordero and others, but his health steadily declined until pneumonia took his life. His remains were returned to Ecuador in 1936.

FEBRUARY 10

Scholastica (ca. 480– ? 543)

✍*Faithful kin*

Tradition states that Scholastica and Benedict of Nursia (July 11) were fraternal twins, and that Scholastica became the first Benedictine nun. Their parents had prayed for children for many years and when they came, they loved them dearly.

Scholastica met with her brother once a year for prayer and spiritual conversation in a house some distance from Benedict's monastery. Gregory the Great's (September 3) book *Dialogues* contains the only biography of Scholastica we have, and provides us with some delightful narratives of these visits. When they met for their last time together, Scholastica begged her brother to remain after supper for more conversation regarding the delights of heaven. Benedict's rule required him to return to his monastery for the night and he declined the invitation. Scholastica bowed her head and prayed that God would come to her assistance. Almost immediately, a violent storm began to rage outside. Benedict and his fellow monks were not able to leave. Benedict said, "God forgive you, sister. What have you done?" She replied, "I asked a favor of you and you refused. I asked it of God, and God has granted it." Good and sensible rules yielded to human need. They stayed up all night, discussing holy things.

It was the last time they met. Three days later, Scholastica died.

Benedict of Aniane (ca. 750–821)
Revitalizing

Benedict, a Visigoth who began life named Witiza, served royalty in Southern France before becoming a monk in Dijon at the age of twenty. He practiced asceticism, following the Benedictine Rule and taking the name of the saint. Returning home in 779, he built a little hermitage near a creek named Aniane. The hermitage grew into a great monastery with more than three hundred monks, and from that place. Benedict guided monastic reform throughout France. Earlier Viking attacks and secular ownership of monasteries had seriously wrecked both the physical structures and the quality of religious life. Benedict of Aniane dedicated his life to restoring the Rule of Benedict in France. The code he prepared radically and permanently altered Benedictine life. It became less severe, emphasizing art and education.

Benedict wore himself out with his labor and died at the age of seventy-one.

Meletius of Antioch (d. 381)
Earthly mediation

In 313, Constantine officially recognized Christianity as a legal religion. The gruesome years of Roman persecution were over, but Meletius of Antioch still faced a difficult spiritual challenge as he confronted a popular heresy, Arianism, which taught that Jesus was less than divine. When Meletius became bishop of Antioch in 361 he began twenty years of intense struggle, championing the cause of Christian orthodoxy. His sincerity and gentle manner were good diplomatic tools, but the task he faced was enormous.

In a remarkable incident, a group of church leaders were instructed to deliver a sermon on Proverbs 8:22, "The Lord created me at the beginning of his work." It turned out to be something of a theological sparring match. George of Laodicea interpreted the text in an Arian sense. Acacius of Caesarea came up with a wildly heretical document, and when it came Meletius's turn, he handled it as an explanation of the incarnation of Christ. The Arians were enraged with his response. They persuaded the emperor Valens to banish Meletius to Armenia. The split in the Church at Antioch was complete and lasted until Valens died in 378. With the emperor's death, the Arian persecution ceased and Meletius was allowed to return.

The ending of open hostility did not mean the end of controversy, because power struggles persisted. Meletius continuing to deal with them. In 381 the second ecumenical council met in Constantinople and Meletius presided. While this meeting was in progress, Meletius died. The painful schism in the church would continue for another generation.

FEBRUARY 13

Modomnoc O'Neil (sixth century)

✎ *Taste of honey*

An Irish monk, Modomnoc was a monastery beekeeper who carried the royal O'Neil family name. After a time in Wales, he moved into a hermitage at Tibraghny near Kilkenny, Ireland. It may be that he became a bishop, but that there is no way to confirm this.

There is a delightful legend about Modomnoc O'Neil. He was a passenger on a ship that was returning him to Ireland when some of his bees followed him, swarming on the boat's framework. They traveled with him to the Emerald Isle and became the origin of a fine strain of honeybees in that country.

FEBRUARY 14

Valentine (d. ? 269)

❧Love in action

Valentine would be astonished by the way so many generations have celebrated his day. He would look with wonder at the hearts school children cut from folded red construction paper. "Be my valentine" printed on candy hearts, the exchange of imaginative and colorful cards, and gifts of fancy chocolates have little to do with this saint. The association began centuries ago in England, apparently because an observant bird watcher noticed that British birds begin courting in preparation for nesting around the middle of February, or on St. Valentine's Day.

Valentine was a third-century Roman priest who devoted himself to helping Christians who were suffering persecution under Claudius II. Arrested, he appeared before the prefect of Rome, who attempted to persuade him to renounce his faith. Valentine stood firm in his faith and was beaten with clubs and then decapitated. His execution day was February 14.

FEBRUARY 15

Sigfrid (d. ? 1045)

❧Missionary to the North

When Norway's King Olaf Tryggvason (July 29) became a Christian, he asked Ethelred, king of England, to send missionaries to his country. Three quickly responded: Sigfrid, John, and Grimkel. The trio not only worked in Norway, but also in Sweden, where Sigfrid established his headquarters in Växjö. Sigfrid converted and baptized Sweden's king in a spring pond near Husaby that now carries the name "Sigfrid's Spring." Miraculous events have happened at that spot.

The Englishman Sigfrid conducted an energetic ministry at Växjö for many years. When he died around 1045, he was buried in the church there.

Onesimus (first century)
❧ Conversion

The New Testament contains a one-page letter from Paul to Philemon. Paul wrote the letter on behalf of the runaway slave Onesimus, who had robbed his master before departing. On his flight, Onesimus encountered Paul, who told him about Christ. In the process of Onesimus's conversion, a warm filial bond developed between the two. In his letter to Philemon, which Onesimus hand delivered, Paul says he is returning his "very heart." It is clear that Onesimus has been an extraordinary help to Paul. Paul sends the converted slave back to his master with the hope that he will receive him as a Christian brother, suggesting that Paul would welcome Onesimus back as a free person who could resume helping him in jail.

In some cases, the remainder of the story of a New Testament saint's life is undocumented tradition. For Onesimus, we have some reliable written records that may continue his story. In the second century, Ignatius of Antioch (October 17) wrote a letter to the church at Ephesus in which he praises Onesimus as an outstanding bishop. It is possible that as bishop Onesimus helped to collect Paul's letters and had them published in Ephesus.

Paul also states that he sent Onesimus with Tychicus to deliver his letter to the Colossian church. Paul calls both men "beloved brothers."

Finan of Lindisfarne (d. 661)
❧ Respectful faith

On the beautiful island of Iona, Finan served as an Irish bishop and abbot in the seventh century. Well-educated and far-sighted, he involved himself in the political process of Northumbria, England. Finan maintained respect for Celtic customs and resisted exchanging them for the religious patterns of other cultures. He became bishop of Lindisfarne and worked untiringly for the evangelization of Northumbria. Finan helped to establish monasteries in Gilling, Tynemouth, and Whitby. He also sent missionaries into East Anglia.

FEBRUARY 18
Theotonius (1086–1166)
❧ *Leadership*

Portugal was a newly established kingdom in the twelfth century when Theotonius returned from a pilgrimage to the Holy Land. The political leaders of Portugal appreciated his special abilities and encouraged him to become bishop. He refused, and instead devoted himself to ministry for the poor. Today, Portuguese Christians have a high regard for Theotonius.

Following a second trip to the Holy Land, Theotonius came back to Portugal and helped establish a monastery at Coimbra. This project received significant financial support from King Alphonsus and Queen Mafalda. In spite of her strong support for the Monastery of the Holy Cross, the queen's request to visit the enclosure was never granted.

Theotonius became abbot of the monastery, living his remaining thirty years there. He was eighty when he died in 1166

FEBRUARY 19
Boniface of Lausanne (d. 1265)
❧ *Personal burden*

Some of us do not achieve impressive goals or make a great name for ourselves, and yet we live a thoroughly Christian life in what some have called "quiet desperation." A saintly example of this is Boniface, who began life in Brussels, Belgium. His schoolteachers were nuns at La Cambre. When he became seventeen, they sent him to the University of Paris for higher education. He turned out to be an excellent student and remained in Paris for seven years as a popular teacher of Christian doctrine. Personal conflicts among the faculty and students resulted in a boycott of his classes.

Rather than continue the struggle, Boniface moved to Cologne and began to teach in the cathedral school. Two years later he became the bishop of Lausanne. He accepted the post with enthusiasm and devoted himself to the task. As has been true of so many who labor for Christ, Boniface ran into years of opposition and misunderstanding. Exasperated, he publicly expressed his poor opinion of the clergy who worked with him. Opposition intensified, and Emperor Frederick II also began to work against Boniface. An unruly group of men ambushed and seriously wounded him in 1239. Weak and completely discouraged, he resigned his post as bishop and returned to Brussels and the nuns at La Cambre. He lived his remaining years at the abbey, dying in 1265.

FEBRUARY 20

Eucherius of Orléans (d. ? 738)

❦ *Heavy responsibility*

Eucherius recognized the brevity of human life and focused on eternity. An eighth-century Frenchman with a Christian background, Eucherius left home in 714 and entered a Benedictine abbey in Normandy. He followed an exceptional life of quiet prayer for seven years, and became bishop of Orléans. He was only twenty-five and did not want to depart from the abbey to take the role of bishop, but after a reluctant beginning, he turned out to be a respected and helpful leader.

Charles Martel, a powerful politician, supported his military campaigns against invading Arabs with money taken from the church's treasury. When Bishop Eucherius objected to the practice, he was consequently arrested. In 737, Charles had him exiled to Cologne, Germany, and then to a fort near Liege, Belgium.

Eucherius maintained a humble and accepting attitude that impressed the people watching over him in Liege. With no obvious reason to keep him in prison, they turned him over to the monks at the abbey of St. Truiden, where he lived quietly until his death.

FEBRUARY 21

Peter Damian (1007–72)
✒ *Quiet service*

Orphaned as a young child in Ravenna, Italy, Peter became the ward of an older brother who was abusive and uncaring. Another brother, named Damian, recognized his plight and took him to his own home, changing the course of his life. Damian treated him affectionately and saw to it that he received a good education. Later in life, he expressed his gratitude by taking this loving brother's name.

In 1035, Peter became a Benedictine monk. He joined an austere group at the monastery of Fonte Avellana who were applying the reforms of Romuald (June 19). Eight years later, the monks elected Peter abbot of the monastery. As their leader, he practiced what we now call "tough love," being kind and forgiving when appropriate, but strict and demanding when necessary. His writings reveal a strong disapproval of any kind of laxity among monks.

In 1057 Peter Damian became a bishop and took a leading role in reforming religious life in Germany and France. Always remaining a monk in the core of his being, he asked to be relieved of his wider responsibilities and returned to the quiet and solitude of his monastery. Inside its walls, he busied his hands with woodcraft and writing highly regarded Latin poems and hymns, while sustaining a life of prayer that was interrupted a few times by the need to settle ecclesiastical conflicts outside.

He died in seclusion with his monks at the monastery, but respect for him was widespread. Dante wrote Peter Damian into the seventh heaven of his *Divine Comedy*.

FEBRUARY 22

Margaret of Cortona (1247–97)
✒ *New life*

Margaret began her life on a little farm in Tuscany. Her mother died while she was still a child, and her stepmother took little interest in her. She became involved with a young cavalier from Montepulciano, living openly with him as his mistress for nine years and bearing him a son. When her lover was murdered during his travels, Margaret took her boy and returned home, begging her father to give her another chance. Responding to his second wife's opinion, he refused to take them in.

Margaret had heard that Franciscan friars were compassionate toward sinners. In desperation, she took her son to Cortona to seek their help. Two women there, Marinana and Raneria, recognized Margaret as someone in trouble and offered to help. After hearing her story, they took mother and son to their home.

The next three years were a sordid mixture of hope and despair as Margaret struggled, trying to begin a new way of life. She left the home of her two friends, and began to live in a small cottage while taking care of the sickly poor. At last, she experienced a religious awakening and the Franciscans accepted her.

Around 1289 Margaret began to have vivid moments of inspiration. Feeling guilty about her past, she did everything imaginable to make amends. Her nights were nearly sleepless as she prayed and meditated. When sleep overtook her, she would rest on the bare ground. She subsisted on the simplest plain food and wore uncomfortable clothes that made her bleed. She died at the age of fifty, having given the second half of her years to acts of penance for the first half.

FEBRUARY 23

Polycarp (ca. 69– ca. 155)

☙ *Faithful courage*

The story of Polycarp's heroic martyrdom has stirred Christians since the first century. He was introduced to Christ by the original disciples who were companions of Jesus. Church tradition maintains that the apostle John (December 27) was involved in Polycarp's conversion. When Ignatius of Antioch (October 17) passed through Smyrna as a prisoner on his way to execution in Rome, Polycarp kissed his chains.

Polycarp

Polycarp was an experienced and beloved bishop who, at the age of eighty-six, became a victim of the anti-Christian movement that was sweeping though the Roman Empire. The Romans arrested him in 155. We know about his death because his church in Smyrna wrote and circulated an account of it. Except for the New Testament, this is the oldest report of Christian martyrdom in existence. Because of its great value, a condensed modernization follows:

At Caesar's festival several Christians were forced to fight wild beasts. The crowd grew restless and cried out for Polycarp. For a few days Polycarp moved from place to place outside the city, always praying for the churches throughout the world. A tortured servant revealed Polycarp's location, and mounted police hurried to make an arrest. Late in the day they found Polycarp in an upper room of a cottage. He could have escaped, but he refused, saying, "God's will be done." He came downstairs and talked with the police, who were surprised to find such an old man. Polycarp ordered food and drink for them because it was well past suppertime. He then asked for an hour alone for prayer. They gave him permission and he remained in prayer for two hours. The Roman police were sorry they had come to arrest such a venerable old man.

After Polycarp had prayed for everyone he knew, and for the Church, they put him on a donkey and led him into the city. Polycarp's father attempted to persuade him to save himself by saying "Lord Caesar" and offering incense. He refused to listen and the police led him roughly into the stadium. The crowd made a deafening roar when they saw him enter.

The proconsul asked him if he were truly Polycarp. When he affirmed that he was, the proconsul began to dissuade him. "Have respect for your age. Swear by Caesar. Denounce Christianity. Curse Christ and I will release you."

Polycarp replied, "I have served him for eighty-six years and he has done me no wrong. How can I blaspheme my king who saved me?"

The proconsul continued to plead with Polycarp, who answered, "Hear plainly that I am a Christian. If you are willing to learn our doctrine, give me a day to teach you."

The proconsul said, "Persuade the people."

"I think you would be a worthy student. Christianity teaches respect for civil authorities. But I will not attempt to defend myself against this unruly mob."

"I have wild animals! If you do not repent, I will throw you to them."

"Send for them. We are not permitted to repent from better to worse."

"If you are not afraid of the beasts, I will have you burned."

"You threaten me with fire that burns for a little while. You don't know about the fire of judgment that is to come. Don't wait. Do what you will." Polycarp was full of courage and joy as he spoke.

The proconsul sent his herald into the stadium to announce three times, "Polycarp admits he is a Christian." The residents of Smyrna cried out in a rage, "This is the teacher of Asia, the father of Christians, the destroyer of our gods."

The crowd rapidly gathered wood from the workshops and baths. They were going to nail Polycarp to a stake, but he said, "Let me be as I am. God will keep me here without the nails."

They lit the fire, but the flames took the shape of a vaulted chamber, like a ship's sail full of wind. It made a wall around Polycarp who was unharmed, like bread baking in an oven, or gold being refined. The executioner stabbed him in the heart with a lance, and so much blood gushed out that it extinguished the flames, and the crowd marveled.

FEBRUARY 24

Montanus and Lucius (d. 259)

❦ Courageous martyrs

In the case of these third-century martyrs we have a trustworthy and uncontested report. Two letters from the saints themselves record their suffering in prison, and other written accounts come from the pens of people who were present when they were martyred.

The Emperor Valerian severely persecuted the young Christian Church. Montanus and Lucius were among eight or ten Christians arrested in 259 and placed in a filthy dungeon among other prisoners. They remained in this inhumane circumstance for months, sometimes without food or water.

When led outside to the place of execution, each had an opportunity to utter last words. Lucius was in poor health and quiet by nature. With nothing to say, he died first. Montanus remained strong and repeatedly quoted a verse from Exodus: "Whoever sacrifices to any god other than the LORD must be destroyed." He criticized Christian heretics and urged believers to be courageous. He spoke his final prayer loud enough for everyone to hear. The Romans beheaded all of them, one by one.

FEBRUARY 25

Tarasius (d. 806)

❧ Sacred and secular

One of the less well-known saints, Tarasius lived in the second half of the eighth century. He was secretary of state for the ten-year-old emperor Constantine VI and his mother, the Empress Irene. While working for the government, Tarasius managed to live a thoroughly religious life. In 784 he reluctantly became patriarch of the Church and began a program to reinstate the value of icons and other images.

Tarasius, though the example of his life was exemplary, fell into disrepute for being associated with Constantine, who divorced his wife and married one of her maids. Though Tarasius did counsel the emperor against the action, other religious leaders thought he was too lenient. In fact, he lost the support of Constantine and had a difficult time during the remainder of his reign.

Tarasius died of natural causes in 806, having devoted twenty-one years to full-time Christian ministry.

FEBRUARY 26
Paula Montal (1799–1889)
❦ *Good example*

When she was only ten, Paula's Spanish father died. To make enough money to educate her younger brothers, she began making lace with her mother. The turn of the nineteenth century was a troubled era in Spanish history, but Paula lived in peace, making the best of her circumstances.

In 1829, Paula opened a school helping girls earn a living by teaching them lace making. In the process, she also taught them the basics of Christianity. She commented, "I want to save families by teaching children the love of God." Her work spread throughout the world.

Paula lived for nine decades. Those at her bedside recalled her last words: "Mother, my mother."

FEBRUARY 27
Francis (Gabriel) Possenti (1838–62)
❦ *Turning away*

Here is a saint who as a teenager earned the nickname *Il Damerino*, "the Lady's Man." His friends in Assisi, Italy, observed his great interest in fine clothes, theater, and dancing. Handsome and popular, he was the life of the party. When two serious illnesses threatened his life, he vowed to enter a monastery. Both times, after recovering, he changed his mind.

Still, life as *Il Damerino* was not satisfying. He had a deep hunger in his soul for the things of God, and partying became tiresome and dull. When a religious procession passed through the streets Francis saw the processioners carrying a picture of the "Sorrowful Mother," Mary. An inner voice said, "Francis, the world is not for you anymore." This was a life-changing event.

Entering a Passionist monastery at the age of eighteen, he exchanged his given name for Gabriel of the Sorrowful Mother. Humility and obedience became driving forces in his life. But the thing others noticed most about him was his cheerfulness. Even in the monastery he was enjoyable to be around.

Tuberculosis took Gabriel's life when he was only twenty-four. Great numbers of people continue to visit his shrine.

FEBRUARY 28

Romanus and Lupicinus (d. ? 460)

⚐*Spiritual seeking*

Romanus was thirty-five when he went alone into the forested Jura Mountains on the border of France and Switzerland. He took with him Cassian's *Lives of the Desert Fathers,* some seeds, and a few garden tools. In a remote spot where the Bienne and the Alière rivers come together, Romanus began a life that somewhat parallels that of David Thoreau at Walden Pond. He filled his days with reading, observing nature, gardening, and prayer. Most of his visitors were woodland creatures and an infrequent hunter. With the passage of time other similarly inclined religious individuals began to camp near him. One of them was his brother, Lupicinus. Eventually their sister and some other women also arrived.

The two brothers decided to build monasteries to accommodate the growing crowd. Their monks devoted much time to manual labor, wore primitive clothing and wooden shoes, and subsisted on a simple diet.

Romanus died about the year 460, and Lupicinus lived another twenty years.

MARCH 1

David of Wales (d. ca. 600)

⚐ *Simple living*

David (or Dewi, or Dafydd) is our first Welsh saint. He lived in the sixth century and very little is known about him. As a monk, he was nicknamed "Aquaticus" because he preferred water to wine or beer. He devoted himself to acts of mercy and stringent personal austerities.

David founded a monastery at Mynyw where the brothers lived in extreme simplicity and prayed constantly, even while working. Unnecessary talking was discouraged, and rather than harnessing animals, tey used their own muscles to pull the plow.

Shakespeare notes a curious and unexplained tradition on St. David's Day that prompts the Welsh people to wear leeks or daffodils.

MARCH 2

Teresa Verzeri (1801–52)
Fresh interpretation

The early nineteenth century was a time of social and religious unrest in Italy. The recent French revolution had sent shudders of new enlightenment through all of Europe. It was in these stimulating times that Teresa Verzeri was born.

As a youngster, Teresa entered the Benedictine Monastery in Bergamo. When she was thirty, she helped found the Institute of the Daughters of the Sacred Heart of Jesus. Her desire was to interpret Christianity in a new way for a new time. People were looking for rational explanations regarding matters of faith, but Teresa wanted them to rediscover, rather, a loving and trusting relationship with God. To accomplish this, she built schools and educated a wide spectrum of society, focusing on this approach of love and trust in God.

Overworked, Teresa Verzeri was only fifty-one when she died. Her mission continues today on four continents. The Daughters of the Sacred Heart of Jesus have a ministry for street children in Central Africa, a mission for the poor in India and in the Amazon jungle in Brazil, and a ministry for abused women in the suburbs of Rome.

MARCH 3

Katherine Drexel (1858–1955)

❧*Dedication of Resources*

Sometimes a person who inherits a fortune finds a way to get rid of all of it by helping others. Katherine Drexel was born to a wealthy Philadelphia banking family. At a young age, though, it became clear to her that no amount of money would protect anyone from suffering and death.

When she vacationed with her family in the western United States she observed the pitiful living conditions on the reservations for Native Americans. She was strongly motivated to do something to help.

While traveling in Europe, Katherine asked Pope Leo XIII to send more missionaries to the United States. She was startled when he asked, "Why don't you become a missionary?" Returning home, she did exactly that.

In 1913, she used her inheritance to establish the "Sisters of the Blessed Sacrament." She spoke openly against injustice and racial discrimination. She worked tirelessly for the educational and spiritual needs of American minorities. Ignoring personal risk, she traveled widely before the years of convenient transportation. She opened the first mission school for Native Americans in New Mexico in 1894. Additional schools for Native Americans west of the Mississippi and schools for blacks in the South soon followed.

Eventually known as "Mother Drexel," she established Xavier University in New Orleans in 1915. This was the first black university in America. When the Second World War began she had set up black schools in thirteen states and fifty mission schools for Native Americans in sixteen states. Segregationists opposed much of her work and burned one school she built in Pennsylvania.

When she was seventy-six, she had a cerebral hemorrhage and needed to retire from active administration. Her prayer-saturated life continued until she was ninety-seven. When she died in Philadelphia in 1955, her pallbearers represented several races.

MARCH 4

Casimir of Poland (1458–84)

Brevity of life

Called "the Peacemaker," Casimir was born to royalty in 1458. The Polish prince responded positively to religious instruction as a child. He began to pray fervently early in life and seemed conscious of the presence of God. He was a cheerful and pleasant young man. Expressing his faith, Casimir began works of charity for the poor while still in his youth.

After a futile attempt to lead an army as a teenager, Casimir determined that war was a waste of effort and resources. He devoted the remainder of his short life to study, meditation, and prayer while sometimes functioning briefly as viceroy in Poland when his father was out of the country. Never married, he died of tuberculosis in his early twenties. At his request, he was buried with a copy of his favorite hymn beneath his head.

MARCH 5

Adrian and Eubulus (d. 308)

Martyrs

Corrupting power has always produced ruthless persons of authority. Responsible to no one, political leaders in all times and places have acted in shameless ways that often go unreported. Adrian and Eubulus became victims of such a leader.

Diocletian, after distinguished service in the army, became Roman Emperor in 284. An autocrat, he viewed the Christian Church as an organization that he could not control. Early in the fourth century, Diocletian's persecution of Christians opened the way for his governors in distant places to disregard the human rights of anyone professing faith in Christ.

Two young men became innocent victims of this persecution: Adrian and Eubulus. They departed their home in Magantia to visit the Christians in Caesarea. Guards stopped them at the city gate and asked what they were doing. Naively, they told the truth.

The guards seized them and carried them to the governor, who had them tortured and put in line to be thrown to the lions. Two days later, the Caesareans held a public festival. Adrian was the first casualty. A lion clawed and chewed him, but did not kill him. The crowd expressed boredom and Adrian was murdered with a sword.

Eubulus soon received the same treatment, except this time there was an offer of mercy if he would make a sacrifice to pagan idols. Eubulus preferred to die. He became the last Caesarean martyr in a persecution that had lasted twelve years under three Roman governors.

MARCH 6

Colette (1381–1447)

Determination

A carpenter's daughter, Colette Boilet was born in Picardy, France. She had a natural inclination for prayer and meditation. Both of her parents died when Colette was seventeen. Though not the sort of person one might expect to do such a task, she became interested in revitalizing the barefoot "Poor Clares." After a personal struggle, living eight years as a Franciscan hermit, Colette accepted the assignment. She wrote, "I dedicate myself in health, in illness, in my life, in my death, in all my desires, in all my deeds so that I may never work again except for your glory, for the salvation of souls, and toward the reform for which you have chosen me."

Though she met with resistance, Colette successfully strengthened the order, establishing new convents in France, Flanders, and Savoy. A visionary, Colette once saw a multitude of souls falling away from God. They reminded her of snowflakes in a winter storm. She began to pray daily for lost sinners. By personally guiding individuals, Colette managed to bring many back into a life of faith.

MARCH 7

Angela of the Cross (1846–1931)

✍*Prayer and labor*

The cook and the laundress who worked in the convent of the Trinitarian Fathers in Seville, Spain, had fourteen children, eight of whom died early. They named the one born in 1846 "Maria of the Angels" and called her "Angelita." Her parents set excellent examples of morality and piety.

Angelita had only a modest amount of formal education and as a young girl went to work in a shoe shop. Even the atmosphere of this place contributed to her religious stimulation and growth. The employees gathered daily to pray and read the lives of the saints. At sixteen, Angelita came under the sensitive spiritual direction of Jose Torres Padilla.

By the time she was nineteen, Angelita was sure she wanted to commit herself to a religious life. She applied to the Carmelites in Santa Cruz, but they refused to accept her because of her poor health. Meanwhile, a cholera epidemic was spreading in Seville, and her spiritual director encouraged her to start caring for its needy victims.

In her early twenties, still in poor health, Angelita applied again to enter a convent. The Daughters of Charity of Seville accepted her in 1868. Unable to find any relief from her illness, she soon had to leave the convent and return to the shoe shop. Here her prayer life deepened.

During a time of prayer in 1871, Angelita perceived an empty cross in front of the chapel's crucifix. She interpreted this to mean that God was asking her to accept the empty cross, to "be poor with the poor in order to bring them to Christ."

Continuing to support herself at the shoe shop, she organized a community with three other women and began a vital ministry to the poor. The "Sisters of the Company of the Cross" rented a room in Seville and devoted all of their spare time to the contemplative life. It was their policy that the poor and the dying could always interrupt their time of prayer and silence. Others began to call Angelita, "Mother Angela of the Cross," and more affectionately, "Mother of the Poor." The sisters thought of themselves as "angels" who were available to give loving assistance to those who would have been overlooked by the world.

When she died, there were twenty-three convents of the Sisters in Spain.

John of God (1495–1550)

✍ *Repentence*

John was a Portuguese soldier who experienced a life-changing conversion. At the age of about forty, he was overwhelmed with a desire to give his life to God. The advice he received was to look for God in ordinary daily life.

On a visit to neighboring Spain, John responded to a sermon by John of Avila (May 10). In response, he decided to repent of his sins by a public demonstration of self-flagellation. This resulted in his arrest and confinement in an institution for the mentally ill.

John of Avila heard of his misfortune and went to visit him. Knowing the prisoner was misguided rather than insane, John advised him to begin caring for the needy rather than punishing himself. This quieting influence of John of Avila made a dramatic difference.

John of God opened a house to take care of sick indigents. He worked tirelessly, with the utmost devotion, for his patients, and his attractive devotion generated support. Benefactors contributed funds to finance his ministry. When the archbishop of Granada summoned John after hearing complaints that his hospital was open to prostitutes and tramps, John replied, "The Son of man came for sinners, and we must seek their conversion. I would be unfaithful to my vocation if I neglect this. I don't know of any bad person in my hospital other than myself." The archbishop became one of John's most ardent supporters.

Falling ill after rescuing a drowning man from a flooded river, John of God died on his knees before the altar in his hospital's chapel on March 8, 1550.

MARCH 9

Frances of Rome (1384–1440)

⚜ *Christian service*

Frances listened to her parents rather than her heart. At the age of thirteen she married Lorenzo de' Ponziani and began housekeeping in Rome. It was 1397, and though she would have preferred to become a nun, she became a good wife, bearing Lorenzo three children.

Her sister-in-law shared her interest in prayer and Christian service to others. Their husbands encouraged them to be active among the poor with acts of faith and charity. Frances ministered to the victims of epidemics and wars. In 1409, Lorenzo was exiled for political reasons. When he returned, a broken man, five years later, Frances cared for him. Adding to their grief, the plague killed two of their three children.

Frances, who had been born to Roman aristocracy, sold all her possessions to raise funds for caring for the sick. She organized a society of Roman women to help her ministry of self-denial and service. Her husband died after they had enjoyed forty years of happy marriage. Frances lived her remaining years with her community. Her life reminds us that not all of us are expected to live a holy life in a specifically religious setting. We may serve God in the ordinary tasks of daily living.

MARCH 10

John Ogilvie (ca. 1580–1615)

⚜ *Stressful times*

At the turn of the seventeenth century, many Scottish families were a mixture of Catholic and Presbyterian. John Ogilvie grew up Presbyterian. During this time, as a student in France, he enjoyed participating in the heated religious discussions of his day. These intellectual debates among Protestants and Catholics permeated academic life. By the time John was seventeen he had decided to be Catholic. More than a decade later, in 1610, he became a Jesuit priest.

John Ogilvie returned to Scotland as a missionary, but found the political stresses at home extremely confining. For their personal safety, most Catholics kept their faith a secret. Church and state issues had become matters of life and death in Great Britain.

In Edinburgh, Ogilvie tutored the son of William Sinclair and visited Catholics in prison. In the cruel environment of his time and place, James I had him arrested and tortured, and placed him on trial for high treason. Ogilvie declared his allegiance to the king, but refused to grant spiritual authority to worldly power. The result was his condemnation. He was given an opportunity to recant, but he refused. His death was by hanging.

MARCH 11

Maximilian (d. 295)

Standing firm

Today we would call Maximilian a "conscientious objector." In 295 a Roman proconsul sailed to Algeria to recruit soldiers for the legion stationed in that area. Most were volunteers, but there was an obligation of service for sons of veterans. Maximilian was twenty-one when his father presented him to the recruiter. Tall and strong, he appeared to be an excellent candidate for the army. Unfortunately, pagan ceremonies were an integral part of Roman military life, and Maximilian did not think a Christian should participate. Over his objection, he was measured (5'10") and then handed a soldier's badge.

A trustworthy document faithfully records the conversation that took place. A modern paraphrase of a portion of it follows.

He said, "My army is the army of God, and I cannot fight for this world. I won't do it."

The proconsul asked him why he was being so stubborn. "What has put these ideas into your head?"

"My conscience and the One who has called me."

The Roman turned to Maximilian's father. "Speak to your son!"

His father replied, "He knows what he believes. He should do what he thinks is best for him."

The proconsul spoke sharply to Maximilian. "Agree to serve. Take the military seal."

"I will not accept the seal. I already have the seal of Christ my God. Your seal is worthless. I cannot wear a piece of lead around my neck after I have received the saving sign of Jesus Christ my Lord, the Son of the living God."

After threatening the punishment of death again, the proconsul attempted to reason with Maximilian. "Military service is a proper thing for young men. There are soldiers who are Christian who serve as bodyguards to our leaders."

"They know what is best for them. I am a Christian and my conscience forbids me to serve in your army."

"Then I will send you to your Christ right now."

"I can think of nothing better. I shall not perish, and if I do depart from this world, my soul shall live with Christ, my Lord."

Maximilian's name was struck from the roll and he was condemned for disloyalty. As the guards were preparing him for execution, he encouraged his companions to be brave and instructed his father to give his new clothes to the executioner.

MARCH 12
Luigi Orione (1872–1940)
❧ *Sharing gifts*

Some of us get a great start in life because of positive religious influences. Luigi Orione was born in 1872 to a devoutly religious Italian mother. By the time he was ten, the example and guidance of his community's excellent priests had given him a strong desire for a religious vocation. Until he was thirteen, he worked with his father, paving streets.

Luigi's teen years were a mixture of formal studies and hard work. He supported himself as a custodian at the cathedral in Tortona. Confident that God was directing him to become a priest, he kept his eye on that goal while growing into adulthood. By the age of twenty he began to teach and care for others.

Luigi Orione received ordination in 1895. The Sons of Divine Providence which he founded began extended missionary work in Brazil in 1913. He understood that God was an essential participant in his work, and he practiced a life of steady prayer. He established an extensive network of schools, churches, shrines, and homes for the poor and needy. Respected for his mature insight and good judgment, Orione was often responsible for resolving difficult community and ecclesiastical problems.

Broadcast radio was becoming popular, and Luigi Orione was one of the first to use it effectively for religion. He also had a printing press and published magazines and brochures.

Heart attacks ended his life in San Remo, Italy, on March 12, 1940.

MARCH 13

Euphrasia (380–420)

✎ *Faith amid uncongenial circumstances*

Fifth-century Constantinople was a difficult time and place for a young girl born into the imperial family. Euphrasia's father died while she was an infant. The emperor Theodosius then took the child and her mother into his care. When she was five Theodosius arranged for Euphrasia to marry the son of a wealthy senator, delaying the wedding itself until she grew up.

When she was seven, her mother took her to their family's Egyptian property. In Egypt she was attracted to a religious community. There, she declined the marriage arrangement that had been made when she was a girl, and transferred to the emperor her fortune, specifying that it be used for charitable purposes. She remained in the convent until she died at the age of thirty. An ancient biographer records that Euphrasia possessed extraordinary meekness and humility.

Leobin (d. ca. 556)

❦*Inspiration and strength*

In the early years of Christianity, there was a sharp separation between the rich and the poor. Saints emerged from both nobility and peasantry. It is worth noting that great minds and spirits are present across the full spectrum of economic status. This was true in the sixth century, and it remains true today.

Leobin worked among peasant-saints in French agricultural fields as a child. Full of intellectual curiosity and a desire to learn, Leobin began menial labor at a monastery. He worked all day and studied at night. When the monks complained that his bright lamp was interfering with their sleep, Leobin constructed a screen to shade it from them. With continuous self-directed education, he made remarkable progress and became respected for his religious knowledge.

Leobin eventually spent five years in an abbey near Lyons. Strife between France and Burgundy brought this to an end. The monastery was raided, and the monks fled for their lives. Only Leobin and an old man remained. The raiders were looking for hidden booty to plunder and interrogated the old man, who referred them to Leobin. Because Leobin told them nothing, they resorted to torture, performing horribly painful and inhumane acts. Discovering nothing, the raiders left Leobin for dead.

Leobin survived, recovered, and lived a quiet life, much of it as a hermit. Ultimately, he became bishop of Chartres and participated in councils, leading the church through various reforms. His death occurred on March 14 in about the year 556, after a protracted illness.

MARCH 15
Louise de Marillac (1591–1660)
✐Caring for the poor

Louise de Marillac was born in France and lost her mother early. Her father took care of her and began her education at home. He died when she was only fifteen. To survive, she married Antony Le Gras, who was a secretary to the queen. It turned out to be a happy marriage, and she bore him a son, Michel. Sadly, her husband also succumbed to illness and Louise became a widow.

One of the great meetings of souls occurred in 1623 when Louise accepted Vincent de Paul (September 27) as her spiritual director. Vincent was responsible for the establishment of a variety of charitable organizations. Louise, determined not to marry again, began to work with the sick and impoverished at one of his projects in the slums of Paris.

Both Louise and Vincent soon realized that the work was greater than could be accomplished by part-time volunteers. They organized a community of women who devoted themselves full time to caring for the poor. They called themselves Daughters of Charity. Vincent conceived of them as a secular community whose members wore ordinary clothing. "Your convent will be the infirmary; your cell, a rented room; your chapel, the parish church; your cloister, the city streets and hospital wards; your enclosure, obedience; your grill, the fear of God; your veil, holy modesty." In fact, the Daughters of Charity became a recognized religious congregation in spite of the fact that they lived and worked outside of a typical enclosure.

Their purpose was service to the poor. This involved practical nursing in their homes, caring for neglected children, and managing life with abusive spouses. They were to look for Christ in the faces of the indigent. The call of any needy person would take them away from their times of prayer. Turning from worship to serving the poor, they would be going "from God to God."

Thousands joined the ranks of the Daughters of Charity. Louise de Marillac was a respected and inspired leader who left an organization that has flourished for centuries beyond her death in 1660.

MARCH 16
Abraham Kidunaia (d. ca. 366)
✎*Bonds of faith*

Abraham Kidunaia was a runaway groom. His wealthy Mesopotamian parents arranged marriage for him, but he slipped away on his wedding day and became a desert hermit. When his family found him he was deeply absorbed in prayer, living in a small cell with minimal possessions. He resisted their pleading to return home. When he inherited his father's great wealth, he asked a friend to distribute all of it to the poor. He kept a bowl, a sleeping mat, and a goatskin cloak for himself.

On rare occasions, Abraham Kidunaia exchanged his solitude for service to others. Once he accepted the challenge of leading a nearby pagan community to Christ. He was not welcomed at Beth Kiduna, however, and the villagers severely beat him for meddling in their lives. On a return visit, he spoke openly, accusing them of idolatry and pointing out their need for salvation. The result was that they nearly killed him by throwing stones at him. Not easily discouraged, Abraham continued his mission to the recalcitrant community for three years, receiving nothing but insults and abuse until the day arrived when they asked to be baptized and became devoted Christians. After teaching them for a year, Abraham returned to his hermit's cell.

Abraham's niece Mary became an orphan when she was seven. He constructed a cell next to his own and began to care for her. She lived in the same environment of prayer and monastic discipline.

Some consider the report spurious, but the legend is that when Mary was twenty, a man pretending to be a monk raped Mary. She felt polluted and ashamed and did not want to tell her uncle about it. Running away to Troas, she found shelter in a brothel.

Two years later Abraham Kidunaia, still ignorant of what had happened, discovered her location. Dressing himself in a soldier's uniform, he rode a borrowed horse to the brothel. The sight of his niece, dressed and painted like a harlot, devastated him. He pretended to seek her services until they were alone.

When she recognized who he was she became speechless. Abraham asked, "Why don't you speak to me, my heart? Haven't I come to take you home, my child? Your sin is upon me, my daughter. On the Day of Judgment I will give an account of it for you to the Lord. I am the one responsible for this."

Mary protested that her sin was too great for her to think of returning to her old life with him, but Abraham continued reassuring her of God's mercy. "Your sins might seem like mountains to you, but God's mercy is on all he has made. If sparks could set the ocean on fire, then your sins might defile the purity of God. Sin is only a part of being human. It happened to you very quickly. Now God will help you to come out of it even more quickly. God does not will the death of sinners. He wants them to live.'"

Their conversation lasted well into the night. Her uncle's great love finally changed her mind. "If you know of any penance I can do, tell me, and I will do it. You go first and I will kiss your footprints as I follow. You have cared enough about me to come down into this pit of filth in order to bring me out." She wept at his feet the remainder of the night.

The next day Abraham and Mary returned to their cells in the desert. Her prayers became even more ardent. Abraham survived ten years after their reunion, dying at the age of seventy.

MARCH 17

Patrick (? 390– ? 461)

❦ Saint of the Emerald Isle

People of Irish descent in many parts of the world celebrate St. Patrick's Day enthusiastically. The wearing of green clothing is observed on that day by many who have nothing to do with Ireland and have little knowledge of Patrick's achievements. About the only thing most people can cite is the fiction that he chased all the snakes off the Emerald Isle.

Patrick was the son of a fourth-century, Roman civil servant on the west coast of Britain. When he was sixteen, raiders kidnapped him and sold him as a slave in Ireland, where he became an unwilling and unpaid shepherd for six years. During the lonely hours of tending sheep and herding cattle in the desolate hills of the north, Patrick became devout, spending much time in prayer and meditation.

Escaping Ireland on board a sailing ship, Patrick found his family and began to study for the priesthood in Gaul. For fifteen years he lived in a monastery. Ireland remained on his mind though, and visionary dreams convinced him his purpose in life was to return to the Irish people and preach the gospel. Only a few of the Irish people had become Christian by 432. Working with other missionaries against great difficulties, Patrick preached in remote portions of the island where the gospel had never been proclaimed. God's love replaced natural resentment. Pagan druids and even a few Christians opposed his missionary activity, but Patrick's preaching produced great results.

Patrick baptized thousands, ordained hundreds of Irish clergy, and founded several monasteries. He set up a system of churches whereby the Irish would keep faith alive and revitalize the Church in Europe during the Dark Ages.

MARCH 18

Cyril of Jerusalem (ca. 315–86)

Doctrinal diplomacy

When Cyril became a bishop in 348, a heresy called "Arianism," which denied the divinity of Jesus, was widespread in the Roman Empire. An enormous power struggle threatened to split the Church. The controversy divided ecclesiastical leadership, and individuals took firm stands on one side or the other. Compromise was out of the question. Each side considered itself correct and the other wrong. Affirming one's faith meant condemning another's viewpoint.

Cyril, born in Jerusalem, had a diplomatic and conciliatory nature. He became a target of serious accusations that bordered on slander. Some of his enemies accused him of selling church property to give alms to the poor. In the Arian debate, each side thought he was too sympathetic with the other. As a result, sixteen of his thirty-five years as a bishop were lived in exile.

Only one of his books survives, a collection of instructions for new Christians who were candidates for baptism. Cyril's book provides one of the earliest statements of Christian theology we possess. In it, he attempts to express a positive faith, and insists on the relationship of faith and action, insisting that "Pious doctrine is not acceptable to God without good works."

MARCH 19

Joseph (first century)

ℐ *Faithful support*

The carpenter Joseph is a familiar figure in the Christmas story. Joseph was engaged to Mary, who would bear our Lord. Neighbors knew Jesus as "the carpenter's son." While there are many biblical references to Joseph that confirm the contemporary belief that he was Jesus' father, there is no record of anything he ever said. Matthew and Luke, the only Gospels that tell us anything about the childhood of Jesus, clearly express that while others "supposed" Joseph to be his father, they themselves affirm the Virgin Birth.

The Gospel of Matthew tells us that Joseph received in a dream a divine revelation regarding the birth of Jesus. Though one imagines the inner conflict and emotions Joseph and Mary must have experienced, the New Testament account does not record any hesitation. The important thing noted in the Gospels is that Joseph responded to God as obediently as Mary. He accepted his place in the divine drama.

In all of the birth and infancy scenes, Joseph is present. We wish we could know more about the relationship of the boy Jesus to the man Joseph. Certainly Joseph and Mary must have shared an awe of this child. The Gospels make it clear that Jesus grew up in an ordinary home, accepted the discipline of his parents, and remained obedient to them.

The last time we hear anything about Joseph is the account of Jesus' visit to the Jerusalem temple at the age of twelve. Scholars assume Joseph died before Jesus began his public ministry. It is entirely possible that Jesus took over the responsibilities of Joseph's carpentry business in those unmentioned years before his baptism in the Jordan by John.

It is a great tribute to Joseph that Jesus spoke of God in terms of a father. Though human fatherhood is but a dim reflection of God's caring love, it is a starting place for comprehending the love of our Father who is in heaven.

MARCH 20

Maria Josefa (1842–1912)

✍ *Charity in depth*

Maria was unusually sensitive to the poor and the sick, and had a natural inclination to meditation and prayer. Born in Vitoria, Spain, she was the eldest daughter of Bernabé Sancho and Petra de Guerra. At the age of fifteen, she went to Madrid to live with relatives while she completed her education. By the age of eighteen, she wanted to enter a full-time religious vocation.

After brief experimentation, Maria founded the Institute of the Servants of Jesus of Charity and directed it for forty-one years. Nursing the sick in a contemplative context gripped her thoughts. "Do not believe, sisters, that caring for the sick consists only in giving them medicine and food. There is another kind of care you should never forget—that of the heart which seeks to adapt to the suffering person, going to meet his needs." By the time of her death in 1912, forty-three houses of charity were open with more than one thousand sisters hard at work. The work of the Institute of the Servants of Jesus continues today in many countries around the world.

MARCH 21

Benedetta Cambiagio (1791–1858)
❦Faithful parenting

Benedetta was a pioneer in providing high-quality education for young women. With her husband's help, she founded a school and a religious congregation in Italy. She was ahead of her time in promoting the right of women to complete an education.

Benedetta had a mystical experience at the age of twenty that left her with a compelling desire to pray and to live a life consecrated to God. In 1818, she and her husband, Giovanni Frassinello, agreed that they should live chastely, "as brother and sister," and take care of Benedetta's younger sister, Maria, who was dying from intestinal cancer. They began what is now called "a supernatural parenthood unique in the history of the Church." They worked together to promote the human and Christian formation of poor and abandoned girls. By including practical skills such as cooking and sewing, they tried to transform students into "models of Christian life" who would establish Christian families.

MARCH 22

Deogratias (d. 457)
❦Leadership in difficult times

The destruction of the Roman Empire was partly the work of the Vandals. Their devastation extended across the Mediterranean Sea to North Africa, resulting in the breakdown of Christian leadership. When Deogratias became bishop of Carthage in 456, there had been no bishop there for fourteen years.

At first, Deogratias received enthusiastic support from most of the people in the area, whether or not they were Christian. Within a year, though, assassins made several attempts on his life.

Deogratias will always be remembered for selling church art and equipment to raise funds for ransoming and taking care of slaves imported to North Africa from Rome by the Vandal leader Genseric. Deogratias did everything he could to keep families together. Deogratias converted his two largest basilicas, *Fausti* and *Novarum,* into accommodations for displaced refugees. As time permitted, he helped in the sick wards.

Part of the population of Carthage quickly turned against him, making serious threats against his life. Exhausted by only a year of labor as the bishop of Carthage, Deogratias died a natural death at home in 457. Because it was likely that people looking for relics would rob his grave, he was buried in a secret place. The Vandals would not allow another bishop in Carthage for another twenty-three years.

MARCH 23
Turibius of Mongrovejo (1538–1606)
✺ *Missionary success*

The archbishop of Lima, Peru, began his adult life as a Spanish lawyer. Outstanding in the legal profession, he became a professor of law at the University of Salamanca. In 1580, the archbishopric of Lima became vacant, and people in positions of authority thought Turibius was the perfect choice for the position in Spain's New World colony. He resisted because as a layman he was ineligible. A good lawyer knows the rules. Church leaders eliminated his handicap by ordaining him a priest and bishop, and then sent him to Peru.

In the sixteenth century, Lima was geographically isolated and morally lax. Peru stretched out four hundred miles along the coast, with spurs running inland among the peaks of the Andes. Travel was extremely difficult, and the behavior of the Spanish conquerors toward the native population was atrocious. An enormous task faced Turibius. He began by carefully learning the languages spoken in his territory and devoted years to visiting the various communities. Listening became as important as speaking. He visited every section of his vast territory. If threatened by marauders or faced with difficult physical obstacles, he would make comments such as, "Christ came from heaven to save us and we ought not to fear danger for his glory." As bishop, he denounced the exploitation of the Peruvians by Spanish nobles and clergy. Against opposition, he imposed reforms. In 1591 Turibius organized the first seminary in the Western Hemisphere.

At the age of sixty-eight, he became seriously ill but continued hard work to the very end. Making out his will, he gave his personal belongings to his servants and all the rest of his property to benefit the poor. He died on March 23, 1606, as those around him sang Psalm 122, "I was glad when they said to me, 'Let us go to the house of the LORD.'"

MARCH 24

Irenaeus of Sirmium (d. 304)

❦ *Inner strength*

There are several notable early Christians named Irenaeus. This day's saint is Irenaeus of Sirmium, a community in modern Serbia, about forty miles west of Belgrade, that today carries the name Mitrovica.

Irenaeus became a martyr early in the fourth century. As a young man, remembered in contemporary biography as handsome, Irenaeus became a religious prisoner during the Diocletian persecution of the Church. His captors insisted that he offer a sacrifice to pagan gods, torturing him on the rack when he refused. His family tearfully begged him to cooperate with the officials in order to save his life, but he remained resolute.

A second public trial resulted in a death sentence. He was beheaded and his body thrown into the river.

MARCH 25
Lucy Filippini (1672–1732)
❧ *Attractive teaching*

Lucy Filippini was born in Tuscany, about sixty miles from Rome. Orphaned early in life, she became a serious student while still quite young. Soon, she was an outstanding popular teacher, with more children coming to her than she could accommodate. They called her the *Maestra santa*, the holy schoolmistress. Something about her healthy spirit and common sense appealed to others.

Her health began to fail in 1726. Interestingly, she died on the exact day she had predicted: March 25, 1732.

MARCH 26
Braulio of Saragossa (ca. 585–651)
❧ *Prayer and simplicity*

Of Spanish saints, Braulio is one of the best known. A pastor and writer, he became a monk in the year 610 and bishop of his hometown, Saragossa, in 631. He participated in the third, fourth, and fifth Councils of Toledo.

Prayer occupied much of every day and night. Braulio avoided pomp and luxury, preferring simple clothes and plain, simple food. He was a caring pastor and notable for his liberality to the poor.

Toward the end of his life, failing eyesight hampered his studies. When he knew his last day had come, he used it to recite psalms.

John of Egypt (d. 394)

✥Restrained living

Like Joseph, John of Egypt was a carpenter. He was born in Lycopolis, which is now the Egyptian city of Asyut. Probably the best-known saint of Christian Egypt, John of Lycopolis withdrew to the desert of the nearby mountains. He carved three little cells in the stone at the top of a steep hill. One became his bedroom; another, his living room; and the third, his oratory. He shut himself in with a wall, receiving food through a little window. Five days a week he conversed only with God. On weekends, he would talk with men (but not with women) about spiritual matters. He never ate until sunset, and then he confined his diet to dried fruit and vegetables. He declined bread or anything cooked. This diet sustained him from his fortieth to his ninetieth year. So many came to visit him that it became necessary to construct a guesthouse for them. John's followers took care of the management of this establishment.

He was a respected prophet. He seemed able to read people's minds and souls, exposing the secret sins of his visitors. He also predicted the outcome of a military conflict. In 394 he perceived his approaching death, shut his window on the world, and gave orders that no one should bother him for three days. He died peacefully, on his knees at prayer. Archaeologists rediscovered John's cell above and beyond the popular tourist monuments in Asyut in 1901.

MARCH 28
Tutilo (d. ca. 915)
❦*Dedicated gifts*

A monk in Switzerland, Tutilo apparently was a universal genius, a polymorph. Remembered as extraordinarily handsome, this strong man had a large frame. Eloquent and quick-witted, he was a painter, sculptor, architect, metalworker, mechanic, poet, orator, and passionate musician who played and taught a wide variety of instruments at the abbey school.

King Charles admired Tutilo and thought it was a pity that such a genius was secluded in a monastery. Tutilo avoided the limelight and appeared in public reluctantly. A few of his works of art and four musical compositions remain. After his death, he was buried in a chapel that took his name.

MARCH 29
Rupert of Salzburg (d. ca. 717)
❦*Civilizing with faith*

Most of today's visitors to Salzburg, Austria, think of Mozart. In Mozart's day, of course, the medieval stone fortress located above the town was already an ancient relic. Few realize that the Duke of Bavaria gave a missionary named Rupert a ruined town that was then called Iuvavum. Rupert rebuilt Iuvavum and named it Salzburg for its salt mines and fortress.

Rupert was an effective Christian evangelist who worked hard at civilizing his converts. He encouraged the development of the salt mines and commerce up and down the Salzach River.

MARCH 30
Leonard Murialdo (1828–1900)
Service to Christ

An assiduous student, Leonard Murialdo continued his studies long beyond his ordination as a priest. Leonard had a great interest in the education of poor young men, and for thirty-seven years he directed a men's college in Turin. There he emphasized music, theater, and gymnastics. For young men in trouble with the law he established agricultural centers. Social justice became one of the Church's important concerns under his leadership.

MARCH 31
Guy of Pomposa (d. 1046)
Simplicity

Guy (also known as Guido, Guion, Wido, Witen and Wit), began life near Ravenna in the eleventh century. To please his parents, he dressed impeccably. But at a religious event in Ravenna, he saw the vanity of his garments, stripped them off and gave them to some indigents. Then he put on the shabbiest clothes imaginable, and in the spirit of simplicity he sought a religious life and lived for a while on a little island with a religious hermit.

He rose to high office in the Church and became the prior of St. Severus at Ravenna and abbot of Pomposa. Many novice monks were attracted to him, making it necessary to build another monastery to accommodate them. He delegated the business administration to others and gave most of his attention to prayer and spiritual direction. Nearing the end of his life, Guy endured fierce and unjustified persecution by the bishop of Ravenna.

APRIL 1
Hugh of Grenoble (1053–1132)
Solitude and productivity

Being religious in a secular world is not easy. Consider St. Hugh, bishop of Grenoble, France, who grew up in a home that placed a high value on prayer and almsgiving. From his earliest years, Hugh exhibited a spiritual sensitivity that some interpreted as shyness. Always modest and courteous to others, he never made a display of his intelligence and thorough education.

At the age of twenty-five, Hugh became bishop of Grenoble. For two years he engaged in a serious struggle against the moral laxity among clergy, but resigned his post because he felt ineffective in this position. Others thought he had been making excellent progress, but Hugh could only think about what he had not accomplished. Discouraged, he became a Benedictine monk and retreated from the world of ecclesiastical responsibilities.

After Hugh had spent only a short time at the monastery, his superiors insisted that he return to Grenoble and continue his leadership of the ministry there. He performed with distinction, maintaining a close relationship with his people, even visiting monks in hermitages, lingering for spiritual conversation and doing menial chores. His desire for solitude never ceased.

Hugh had an outstanding ability to speak in public. Though he distrusted himself, his efforts at reform were successful and his people began to practice religion in fresh, new ways.

Part of the work of the bishop of Grenoble involved taking care of the community's infrastructure. Hugh managed road and bridge maintenance, built hospitals, raised taxes, and created a farmer's market. He applied himself to the details of this civil work as diligently as he did to his religious vocation.

A significant relationship developed between Hugh and the founder of the Carthusians, Bruno (October 6). Bruno taught at Reims when Hugh was a student there. His desire for religious solitude was as strong as Hugh's, and he sought it at Grenoble. Together, they began to build the splendid monastery of the

Grande Chartreuse. Hugh had his own cell in the new monastery and frequently turned aside from his responsibilities for a time of quietness and prayer. Such a life can become addictive, and once Bruno insisted that Hugh return to his responsibilities as bishop of Grenoble.

Painful illness plagued his final years, but he never complained. As he neared death, he recited the Lord's Prayer and the Psalms continuously. At the age of seventy-nine, Hugh died, surrounded by Carthusian monks in the monastery he had helped found.

APRIL 2

Francis of Paola (1416–1507)
❦Dedicated life

Born in southern Italy in 1416, Francis was an answer to the prayers of his childless parents. They had vowed to dedicate any son born to them to the honor of St. Francis of Assisi (October 4), whose name they gave him when he was born. They did their best to give their son a solid introduction to faith in Christ. When he became twelve, they kept their vow by sending Francis to live a year among friars.

As a teenager, Francis of Paola took a trip to Rome with his parents. The big city's decadence and lavishness disturbed him. Repulsed, he determined to live quietly in the country, away from the hustle and bustle of commerce and society. Wanting to live after the example of Francis of Assisi, he began living in a cave outside of Paola and scrupulously practiced fasting and penance.

Others came to join him. In 1436 they took the name "Hermits of Brother Francis of Assisi." Residents in the area, impressed by their dedication to poverty and simplicity, got together and built them a church and a residence. They were officially recognized as a monastic order in 1474, and other houses were opened in southern Italy and Sicily.

Against his personal desires, Francis accepted an invitation to visit the king of France in 1483. He traveled from Italy barefoot, refusing plush accommodations, and praying most of the way. A most unusual guest in the French court, he fasted rather than feasted, never wore shoes, and used a board for a bed. French authorities were impressed with his sincerity and integrity, and opened the way for him to establish houses in France, Spain, and Germany.

Francis never returned home. He died in France on Good Friday, April 2, 1507.

APRIL 3

Richard of Chichester (1197–1253)

In the world

Life in England at the end of the twelfth century had hardships for Richard, who lost his parents early. But somehow, Richard avoided serious mistakes and became an excellent scholar and teacher at Oxford, becoming chancellor of the university. With excellent administrative skills, he moved higher until he was defending the Church against King Henry III and sought refuge in France from the king's wrath.

Returning to England, Richard became Bishop of Chichester, but Henry III refused to accept him, nominating a rival. The pope ruled in favor of Richard, and in a fit of pique, the king confiscated all of his property. King Henry III decreed that no one should even give the new bishop shelter. So Richard became a stranger among his own people. Living with one of his priests, he did the best he could by visiting on foot. After about two years of this punishment, the king changed his policy, and Richard began to function at full capacity in his position as bishop.

Lovingly open to everyone, both stern and merciful to sinners, generous to anyone in need, and a great conductor of business, Richard was an outstanding example of a bishop. Under his guidance, both religious professionals and ordinary church members sharpened their knowledge and behavior.

Richard is the author of the well-known prayer that concludes: "May I know thee more clearly, love thee more dearly, and follow thee more nearly, day by day."

He was in Dover when he became seriously ill and died on April 3, 1253.

APRIL 4

Isidore of Seville (ca. 560–636)

❧Conscientious living

Our task in this life is to do the best we can with what we have, without becoming discouraged when we fail to achieve greatness. The Spanish bishop and scholar Isidore lived a life precisely along those lines. The idea occurred to him as he sat in the woods, weary with trying to measure up to his older brother's standards. He noticed how water had worn down a stone, one drop at a time. Instead of learning everything instantly, he would learn gradually, steadily, never giving up. In this way, Isidore became the most learned person of his time, an authority on a wide range of subjects including theology, Scripture, biography, history, geography, astronomy, and grammar. Many manuscript copies of his works survive. We do not know much about Isidore's early life other than that he was born in Spain about the year 565. He followed his brother as bishop of Seville around 600. His own manuscripts reveal a high standard of conduct for bishops, but we have no contemporary reports regarding his personal behavior.

The product of his pen has earned him great respect for centuries. Not only does he provide us with encyclopedic knowledge from his time and place, he also reveals a spiritual alertness. He urged clergy to pray and read Scripture. "The more conscientious one is in becoming familiar with the sacred writings, the richer an understanding one will draw from them. As with the earth, the more it is cultivated, the more abundant is its harvest."

APRIL 5

Vincent Ferrer (ca. 1350–1419)

✌A house divided

Saints do not always agree with each other, and saints can hold misguided notions about important subjects. So it was that Vincent Ferrer, who lived in Spain through the turn of the fifteenth century as a Dominican priest, became entangled in the theological controversies of his day. The Great Schism was a period of almost forty years (1378–1417) when the Church had two popes, each claiming to be the legitimate leader. Vincent supported Clement VII, the French candidate. Urban VI had many good supporters, including Catherine of Siena (April 29). Most scholars today think Catherine made the better choice.

Some of Vincent's surviving books and sermons reveal that he unfortunately lived in harmony with the prejudices of his time and place. His large treatise against the alleged deceit of Jews is a prime example.

Vincent was an appealing Christian who attracted large crowds of listeners when he spoke in public. He lived an austere life and had little regard for his own holiness. In a treatise on the spiritual life, he gave himself low scores: "I am a plague-spot in soul and body; everything in me reeks of corruption because of the abomination of my sins and injustice."

By 1409, there were *three* rival popes, and near the end of his life, Vincent made a great personal effort to help end the divisiveness of the Great Schism. At a special church council meeting in 1414, Vincent attempted to convince one of the three, Benedict, to resign. His famous "dry bones" sermon before a large gathering of bishops and nobles condemned human pride and pointed to the necessity of Christian unity. All of these efforts failed. Vincent then persuaded King Ferdinand of Aragon to cease his financial and political support for Benedict. This worked, and Benedict resigned. The council was then able to restore unity.

APRIL 6

Prudentius Galindo (d. 861)

❦*Guiding light*

Prudentius, a prolific writer, grew up in an affluent Spanish family. About 843 he became bishop of Troyes, located southeast of Paris.

Prudentius played an important role in a theological controversy concerning predestination. Gottschalk, a monk, taught that Christ died only for a minority, the "elect," while most of us were doomed to hell from all eternity. This is the enduring theological dilemma known as "double predestination." Hincmar, bishop of Reims, had Gottschalk excommunicated, thrown into prison, and tortured for his published ideas. Prudentius wrote the bishop, stating that Gottschalk's punishment was too severe, and that Augustine (August 28) had written something similar. Later, Prudentius prepared a book refuting John Scotus Erigena, who was the source of much of Gottschalk's thinking.

Prudentius took an active part in the various councils that deliberated the complex theological issues, but the ravages of time and health gradually reduced his effectiveness. He died on April 6, 861.

APRIL 7

John Baptist de La Salle (1651–1719)

❦*Fulfilling a vision*

Why not teach children in their native dialect rather than in academic Latin? Why not teach them to be good Christians as they are learning their lessons? The answers to these questions were obvious to John Baptist de La Salle, and the results for seventeenth-century underprivileged French children were dramatic.

As a seminary student in Paris, John Baptist de La Salle taught some poor children a basic knowledge of Christianity. Adrien Nyel, a nonprofessional who was opening schools for the poor in Rouen, approached him in 1679 with a request for help in establishing a new school in Reims. Financial support already existed, and John Baptist's function would be administrative. In retrospect, he said that he would not have accepted the opportunity if he had known the results, but that with the "eyes of faith" he could see God's purpose. An unremarkable student himself, he became a leading educator.

Eager students swamped the new school at Reims. He quickly needed more teachers, and more money. Soon enough, he needed to build more schools, and the quality of teacher training cried out for serious evaluation. John Baptist de La Salle overcame his personal reticence and opened his home as a school for teachers of the poor. He lived with them, taught them, and prayed with them. His family and community responded negatively to this activity, requiring John Baptist to rent a cheap house and move in with his teachers. Calling themselves "Brothers of the Christian Schools," their reputation for excellence began to spread. Requests for more schools poured in.

While a story like this may thrill and inspire readers today, it was not only hard work, but also a heartache for John Baptist de La Salle. His family never supported his ministry and continually antagonized him. Some who joined with the Brothers of Christian Schools soon dropped out. Others were jealous and considered the new schools a threat to their own security. They forced some of his schools to close, and John Baptist had to work through the courts to get them open again. Other schools had poor leadership and discipline problems.

No one had attempted any work like this in France before John Baptist de La Salle. Since the work lacked official recognition by the Church, and no existing category fit a group of unordained men devoted to teaching the poor, he perceived the necessity of drawing up a Rule similar to those followed at monasteries. He used familiar language to express novel ideas. "The first effect of faith is to attach us strongly to the knowledge, the love, and the imitation of Jesus Christ and to union with him." All teaching is "for the glory of God, with the intention of pleasing him, through the movement of the Holy Spirit." The Brothers are "ambassadors of Christ to the young. Teachers must, in St. Paul's phrase, 'put on Christ' so that they can radiate him more effectively." John Baptist worked on his Rule for twenty-five years, revising it several times. Approval of the rule was granted after his death.

APRIL 8

Julie Billiart (1751–1816)
❧ *Overcoming handicaps*

Marie Rose Julie Billiart began life in Picardy, France. Her parents had a small shop and did some farming. The family fell into difficult times in 1767, and Julie worked hard to help earn enough for them to survive. Julie was on her way to a religious vocation when a sudden paralysis confined her to bed. Under a doctor's care, she only became worse, experiencing severe pain. An invalid at thirty, she determined to become a Christian witness even without the ability to move her arms and legs. People came to her for spiritual guidance, and she taught children from her bed.

Caught up in the French Revolution, Julie got into serious trouble by sheltering priests in her home and being a friend of aristocrats. Others had to spirit her away to Compiègne when there were threats made against her life. Impassioned revolutionaries chased Julie from hiding place to hiding place. She asked, "Dear Lord, will you not find a corner in paradise for me? There is no room for me on earth." Her extreme stress resulted for a while in the loss of her ability to speak.

Following these trying times, her voice gradually returned and she established the Institute of Notre Dame for the education of poor children and the training of female teachers. After being an invalid for twenty-two years, Julie suddenly regained the ability to walk and began long journeys to develop and unite the Institute. She made sweeping changes in nineteenth-century religious life. Sisters needed to have the freedom to leave their enclosures in order to teach the public. Thorough preparation for class became an act of self-discipline. She wrote, "We have the most difficult vocations because we must live an interior life while doing external work."

On her deathbed in 1816, Julie Billiart asked a Sister to read a favorite page from *The Imitation of Christ.* "If you willingly carry the cross, the cross will carry you, and bring you to that desirable place where there will be no end."

APRIL 9

Waldetrude (d. ca. 688)

Religious in the world

Waldetrude grew up among saints. Her parents, sister, husband, and children are all canonized saints. Waldetrude successfully lived an austere solitary life without enclosure in an abbey. Many turned to her for spiritual direction. Eventually, she founded a convent at Chateaulieu in a part of France that is now inside the boundary of Belgium. Here, she acquired a reputation for charity, healing, and mercy. She died about 688, and her remains are still preserved in a fifteenth-century church built near her convent.

APRIL 10

Magdalen of Canossa (1774–1835)

Helping others

Five-year-old Maddalena Gabriella di Canossa lost her wealthy Italian father and saw her mother run away with another man, leaving five children to care for themselves. Growing up became a misery, complicated by serious illness and an insensitive French governess.

As she approached her twenties, Magdalen began to care for poor girls in her community. Relatives tried to dissuade her, but she replied, "Should the fact that I was born a marquess prevent me from serving Jesus Christ in his poor?" She wanted to reduce the poverty and improve the morals of the people around her. She helped hospital patients and the homebound, gave religious literature to local churches, organized retreats, worked with girls in trouble, and handed out money and food to the poor at her door. In 1808,

Magdalen opened a girl's school in an abandoned monastery. This evolved into the Congregation of the Daughters of Charity.

Magdalen had some mystical experiences that she attempted to describe in her personal *Memoirs*. Like most other saints, she found that words were inadequate. "I felt at a certain point as if I were enraptured in God. I saw God within me like a luminous sun. This absorption in the Divine Presence made me unable to stay on my feet. I had to lean against something. The strength of heavenly joy was almost suffocating."

Many of her writings have survived her death.

APRIL 11

Stanislaus Szczepanowsky (ca. 1030–79)
❧ Conflict

Born in Poland, Stanislaus became bishop of Cracow when he was a little over forty. For a while, the new bishop had the support of King Boleslaus II, but they soon had a serious disagreement.

Though the true nature of the argument is now clouded, the king did not behave in the manner Stanislaus demanded. The bishop then excommunicated the sovereign.

Infuriated, King Boleslaus ordered his guards to kill Bishop Stanislaus, who sought refuge in St. Michael's Chapel. The guards were not willing to violate the sanctity of the chapel, so the angry king himself dashed in and murdered Stanislaus with a sword. The king soon lost his throne, but the Polish people continue to venerate Stanislaus.

APRIL 12

Teresa of Los Andes (1900–20)
❧ Saintly influence

Teresa of Los Andes presents an outstanding example of the influence one saint may have upon another. When, in her mid-teens,

Juanita Fernández Solar read *Story of a Soul* by Thérèse of Lisieux (October 1), she decided she wanted to become a Carmelite nun. Her diary records her thoughts: "I belong to God. He created me and is my beginning and my end. If I am to become entirely his, I must do his will. If as my Father he knows the present, the past, and the future, why don't I abandon myself to him with complete confidence? From now on I put myself in your divine hands. Do what you like with me."

After Juanita read the biographies of Teresa of Avila (October 15) and Elizabeth of the Trinity (November 8), her determination to become a Carmelite increased. At the age of nineteen, she joined the Carmelites at Los Andes, Chile, saying she wanted "to learn how to love and how to suffer."

The Carmelites at Los Andes lived in extremely primitive conditions. Taking the name of Teresa, she welcomed the strict observance required of her as well as the simplicity of her new life. Love, service, prayer, and suffering dominated her religious thought and activity. In this environment, she felt as though she had found heaven on earth.

She became ill with typhoid fever and died. Today, she is one of South America's most beloved saints.

APRIL 13

Martin I (d. 655)

✍ *Taking a stand*

Details regarding the early life of the last pope to suffer martyrdom, Martin I, are lost. We know he became pope in 649 and became embroiled in religious and political controversy.

The controversy involved an early heresy known as "Monothelitism" which held that Christ did not make human choices, but only divine ones. Constans II, the emperor at Constantinople, considered this an excellent doctrine. Martin convened a council in Rome for the purpose of rejecting this false teaching and condemned the emperor's support of it. The emperor responded by becoming angry and hostile. In 653, he sent troops to Rome with orders to arrest Martin. Frail because of poor health, Martin did not resist. Soldiers took him to the Aegean island of Naxos, put him in prison, and began to torture him. He commented in a letter to the Church in Rome, "I have not been given water for a bath in forty-seven days. I am frozen through and wasting away with dysentery. The food they give me is inedible. But God sees all things and I trust in him."

Though Martin was actually condemned to death, the emperor instead exiled him to Crimea, where he died of starvation and abuse.

APRIL 14

Benezet of Avignon (ca. 1163–84)

❦ *Divine purpose*

We use "bridge builder" as a metaphor for an outstanding mediator or reconciler. Benezet was literally a bridge builder. As a shepherd boy from Savoy, he moved to Avignon, France, around 1178. A visionary figure instructed him to build a bridge over the Rhone River. Like Noah, he had difficulty convincing anyone that such a project was his purpose in life, but Benezet eventually received enough support and assistance to begin construction on the bridge.

Benezet died before the completion of the span, but the work continued until the bridge was finished. Later, a construction crew added a small chapel to the design of the bridge and reburied Benezet's body inside it. His remains rested quietly there for almost five hundred years. A catastrophic flood in 1669 destroyed the bridge and washed the saint's coffin downstream. When searchers recovered it, they were startled to see that his body had not decayed. A verse in the sixteenth Psalm that Peter (June 29) quoted in his Pentecost sermon says that God will not allow his holy one to "see corruption." In the early years of Christianity, an incorrupt body was often a factor in the declaration of sainthood. Modern medicine acknowledges that sometimes a human body will not decompose because its fat becomes wax in response to moisture. Doctors label this tissue phenomenon *adipocere*.

APRIL 15

Damien de Veuster (1840–89)

✎Loving service

Faraway places have always chanted a siren song to adventurous people. This is how it was for Damien de Veuster. After hearing about the Hawaiian Islands, he could not rest in Belgium. There were spiritual needs among the residents of those fabled islands, and the twenty-three-year-old priest received permission to sail in 1863. He arrived in Honolulu after a five-month voyage and began a decade of mission work on the island of Maui.

Hawaii had no resistance to European diseases. Smallpox, tuberculosis, measles, and other illnesses took a heavy toll on the resident population. Their numbers were reduced from about three hundred thousand to fifty thousand. While Damien was at work, leprosy broke out. American and British traders were concerned enough about the new epidemic of an incurable disease to persuade local authorities to banish all lepers to the island of Molokai, which soon gained the name "Devil's Island."

Medical inspectors and armed soldiers came to Maui with instructions to enforce the removal of lepers. Families turned to Damien for help. They wanted to care for their own at home. Damien attempted to reason with the visiting authorities, but no one would listen to him. The tears and sobs of Hawaiian families torn apart because of an imported disease deeply moved him. Rather than remain on Maui, he volunteered to minister to the lepers at Molokai. Damien understood it would be a one-way trip.

It is not easy for us to imagine life in a nineteenth-century leper colony. Boat crews were too terrified by the disease to actually tie up at a pier. They stopped offshore and made their passengers jump in the water and swim the remaining distance through the pounding surf. Those who survived walked onto the beach of a lawless island of misery and hopelessness. The lepers had to fight to survive, the strong taking advantage of the weak.

There were about eight hundred lepers on Molokai when Damien stepped on shore in 1873. He attempted to bring some order to chaos by organizing many funerals and burials in a place he called a "living cemetery." He encouraged the lepers to grow gardens in order to improve their meager diet. He engineered an irrigation system, built simple huts and a church, using the assistance of the able-bodied. Visiting doctors would bring medicines, but they would not get near the lepers. Damien tended to the needs of the miserable members of his flock with his own hands. "If I cannot cure them as our Savior did, at least I can comfort them." He turned a human jungle into a civilized community.

In 1885, Damien recognized the symptoms of leprosy on his own skin. For a quarter of a century, he had ministered quietly without recognition. Now he suddenly became a celebrity. Newspapers and magazines found a sensational story in the brave self-denial of a priest from Belgium. News quickly spread around the world, and Damien became a target for criticism and suspicion as detractors asked what the autocratic leader was doing with the contributions that came to him. He wrote, "If I didn't have the continual presence of the divine Master in my poor chapel I could not persevere in my decision to share the lot of the lepers." Robert Louis Stevenson, author of *Treasure Island,* wrote a powerful defense of Father Damien.

Compassionate people did all they could to help, but it was too late for the leper colony on Molokai. Damien died on April 15, 1889. All of us will die of something. Damien died of love.

APRIL 16

Benedict Joseph Labre (1748–83)
✍Spiritual seeking

The phrase "a fool for Christ" describes Benedict Joseph Labre, a rare Western example of a religious wanderer. Born in southern

France and reared by an uncle who was a priest, he made up his mind by age twelve to give his life to God. The Trappists rejected him when he was eighteen because of his youth. The Carthusians and the Cistercians also refused to accept him. Benedict decided he would let the world be his cloister and began a journey by foot that took him thousands of miles across Europe to shrines and churches.

Benedict continued his not-so-aimless wandering for several years, neglecting to take care of personal hygiene and wearing rags. This naturally caused people to avoid him, providing the privacy he wanted for his prayers. He was never a beggar, so when some well-meaning person insisted on giving Benedict alms, he would look for someone needier and pass it on to them. He accepted food, but usually dined on discarded garbage. Well-read, he possessed a solid foundation of knowledge.

His wanderings eventually brought him to Rome, where he slept in the ruins of the Coliseum where so many Christians were martyred. In daylight, Benedict would visit Rome's various churches for extended hours of prayer. His health gave way and he collapsed on the steps of the Madonna dei Monti when he was thirty-five. After a few hours resting in a butcher's house, Benedict died. Children began running through the streets, crying out, "The saint is dead!" His parents learned of his death when they read one of the popular biographies written about the Christian tramp.

APRIL 17

Simeon Barsabae and Companions (d. 341)

✥ Martyrs

Christianity developed out of Judaism, and during the first century after Christ, most of the world did not distinguish between Christian and Jew. Christianity gained independent recognition about the year 100. For the next two hundred years, it became the scapegoat of the Roman Empire, blamed for every political and economic difficulty. The emperor Decius wanted to exterminate all Christians in 250, but his reign ended before he realized his dream.

The most organized and deadly persecution of Christians came under Diocletian, beginning in 303. In 313, an edict of toleration declared Rome's acceptance of the upstart religion, but serious persecution continued in the Persian Empire until the fifth century. Simeon Barsabae and others were caught in these troubled times.

Simeon was bishop of Seleucia-Ctesiphon in central Mesopotamia when Shah Shapur II reigned supreme. In 340, Shapur closed the churches in his realm and increased taxes on anyone admitting they were Christian. Most of Bishop Simeon's people were poor, and he refused to collect the penalizing taxes. Simeon was arrested and taken before the Shah, where he stood firm. After Simeon spent a short time in jail, the Shah ordered executions for Simeon and about a hundred other Christians. The trustworthy written record of eyewitnesses of these martyrdoms still exists.

APRIL 18

Alexander of Alexandria (ca. 250–328)

Doctrinal orthodoxy

Anyone who became a bishop in one of the four great cities of the Roman Empire (Rome, Constantinople, Alexandria, and Antioch) carried the title *patriarch*. In 451, Jerusalem became the fifth city on the list. A patriarch had spiritual oversight of a large geographical area. Alexander became patriarch of Alexandria in 312.

The job was a headache from the very beginning. Another priest, Arius, wanted the position and became antagonistic when he did not get it. His many vicious accusations against Alexander stung and burned. At this time an emotionally charged debate regarding which date should be observed for celebrating Easter raged in the Church. Another debate began when Bishop Melitus of Lycopolis in Egypt strictly opposed any attempt to restore to full communion those who had fallen away during times of persecution.

In addition to all of this, Arius kept the doctrinal pot boiling with his Arian Controversy, which probably began as a way to discredit a rival but grew to historic proportions and became a turning point in church history. At issue were the person and work of Jesus Christ. Speculative theology may not be a popular sport in the world today, but in the early centuries of Christianity, it was vital.

Arius held that Christ was divine, but something of a lesser God who was not united with the eternal Father. For him, Christ was neither fully God nor fully human, but something in between. Alexander, however, believed this was an entirely unsatisfactory description of the nature of Christ.

Alexander attempted to have a gentleman's discussion with Arius regarding these things, but Arius remained uncooperative and continued to split the church along these doctrinal lines. As patriarch, Alexander called an official council of about a hundred bishops from Egypt and Libya. This meeting condemned Arius for presenting heretical ideas. Rather than apologizing and changing his thinking, Arius traveled to Jerusalem and persuaded two influential bishops, both named Eusebius, to support his teaching. A series of letters to various leaders resulted in more support for Arius. Alexander wrote letters of his own and garnered about two hundred and fifty signatures for himself from all over the empire. The controversy was no longer a local struggle.

Emperor Constantine grew concerned that the division could threaten the peace and security of his realm. He instructed both Arius and Alexander to cease their "petty discussions of unintelligible minutiae." Arius continued with the heresy, writing popular songs that drilled people in his doctrine, and seeking more supporters. The arbitrator sent by Constantine to resolve the dispute grew utterly frustrated and recommended an international council meeting.

The ecumenical council, which assembled in Nicea in May of 325, was probably the most important church meeting ever held. Arius presented a creed that failed to garner support. Constantine backed another creed that included some highly technical Greek terminology still enjoyed by today's theological students. In essence, the Caesarean Creed held that Jesus was "begotten, not made." He was "of one essence with the Father." We may consider such detailed wrangling boring church business, but it consumed international public consciousness in the early fourth century. People were utterly distracted by theological discussion. Ask a baker the price of bread, and instead of a price in return, you might hear, "The Son is subordinate to the Father." The popular songs Arius composed were sung and whistled in the streets. Religious arguments often led to blows.

Constantine's concerns were as much political as religious because the issue threatened the unity of both church and state. He wanted a creed that used language acceptable to both Greek-speaking and Latin-speaking citizens. East and West had to agree on terminology in order to preserve the peace. The emperor pressed the council to adopt a creed that is the basis of our present *Nicene Creed*. For the first time, the whole Church had a written standard of orthodoxy. Christ is "of one substance (Greek, *homo-ousios*) with the Father." Only Arius and two bishops refused to sign their consent. Constantine then banished them from the empire.

Exhausted, Alexander returned home after the council meeting. A few months later, he was dead.

APRIL 19

Alphege (ca. 954–1012)

❦ Negotiation

One hundred and fifty years before Thomas Becket (December 29) was murdered in Canterbury Cathedral, another archbishop of Canterbury was violently killed. Alphege lived in England during the years of terror by Danish marauders. At the request of an English king with the delightful name of Ethelred the Unready, Alphege attempted to negotiate peace with the Danish warlords. Not only did he get them to stop their aggressive behavior, but he also converted them to Christianity.

Alphege became archbishop of Canterbury in 1005. Unfortunately, other Danes began invading southern England and in 1010 laid siege to Canterbury. They got the money they wanted, but instead of departing, they entered the city and held Alphege hostage.

The Danes released others they had captured after the payment of a ransom, but they wanted three thousand gold crowns for the freedom of Alphege. When he would not permit his people to pay that much, the Danes murdered him by striking him in the head with an ax. This brutal act horrified higher Danish authorities, and they directed a solemn burial at Canterbury for the man who had become a national hero. Anselm (April 21) held that to die for justice is to die a martyr. A century and a half later, one of the last words Thomas Becket ever spoke was "Alphege."

APRIL 20

Hildegund (d. 1188)

Depending on God

A Christian cross-dresser with a purpose, Hildegund provides us with an astonishing true story. The temptation today is to dismiss her incredible tale as legendary, but her adventures stand up to scrutiny.

Hildegund was the twelfth-century daughter of a German knight or merchant. After her mother's death, she went with her father on a pilgrimage to Jerusalem. For her protection as they traveled through various lands, she dressed like a boy and used the name Joseph. Their journey was successful, but on the way home, her father died. The servant who kept their purse absconded, leaving twelve-year-old Hildegund in Tyre without any money. She continued trying to return to Germany, but many things happened along the way—including her almost being hanged in Verona.

Once back home, Hildegund was still without means to support herself and decided to become a lay "brother" at the Cistercian monastery at Schönau. As Brother Joseph, she began a life of quiet prayer and meditation, dying after a few years in 1188. Only then did anyone discover her secret. A similar story of a woman in male clothing is told of Pelagia (October 8) and others.

APRIL 21

Anselm (ca. 1033–1109)

Intelligence and faith

A great mind and spirit entered the world when Anselm was born in Aosta, a town on the border between Burgundy and Lombardy. He performed well in school and, at about the age of fifteen, decided to become a monk. When this did not turn out to be possible, he sank into a secular life for two years.

From the age of seventeen until he was fifty-nine, Anselm lived in Normandy at the Benedictine abbey of Bec. In the autumn of 1092, while visiting England, Anselm became archbishop of Canterbury, appointed by a sick king who was thought to be on his deathbed. Anselm soon faced an insoluble dilemma.

King William Rufus did not die, and like so many desperate promises made to God under duress, his willingness to have an archbishop at Canterbury evaporated. He wanted its revenues for his own coffers. He restricted Anselm's ability to function and threatened that he would not allow Anselm back into England if he visited the continent. The archbishop wrote, "I saw in England many evils whose correction belonged to me and which I could neither remedy nor, without personal guilt, allow to exist."

Anselm thought it was necessary to leave England in 1097 to visit religious communities in France. King William Rufus died while Anselm was across the English Channel. His successor, Henry I, requested that Anselm return to Canterbury. Henry restored church property and gave Anselm the freedom to conduct church business. Unfortunately, this relationship also deteriorated with the passage of time. Anselm went into exile a second time, an absence that began in December 1103 and continued until August 1106. For a quiet, contemplative monk, Anselm surprised his biographers by using those years to accomplish some impressive political gains and garner popular support. Church administration may not have been Anselm's strongest interest, but he accepted his position as the will of God and worked effectively without complaint. Obedience was an important part of the Benedictine Rule. Anselm said, "When I professed myself a monk I surrendered myself in such a way that thereafter I could not live according to my own will, but only in accordance with obedience either to God or to the Church of God."

Anselm nurtured close personal friendships and was not reluctant to express his emotions. His spirit was warm and tender. The correspondence, prayers, and meditations of Anselm began to circulate while he was still alive. Both public and private readings of his work guided many souls.

Far beyond his considerable achievements in church and state is his work as a theologian. Anselm wrote eleven large treatises. His *Proslogion*, written in 1078, explains that the theologian's task is that of "faith seeking understanding." In his great mind, reason took its place beside mystery. Faith is compatible with intelligence, and we do not have to suspend rational thought to be Christian. At the same time, he wrote, reason alone does not result in understanding. Faith is an essential element in useful theology, and if Scripture clashes with reason, Scripture is correct.

Why God Become Human (Cur Deus Homo) is Anselm's masterpiece. In it, he presents a theory of divine atonement and redemption that was to become the standard for Christian doctrinal ideas for centuries. Rather than quoting authorities and long strings of Bible verses, Anselm's writings present original, sustained, and clear thinking.

APRIL 22

Theodore of Sykeon (d. 613)

❦ Healing and exorcism

Sykeon was a town in Galatia, Asia Minor. Theodore's mother kept an inn at Sykeon that also functioned as a brothel. She hired an extraordinarily good cook who attracted so much business there was no continuing need to earn money with prostitution. This unnamed excellent cook, also a devout Christian, taught Theodore how to pray and encouraged him to attend church. When he grew old enough to be on his own, Theodore became a hermit, living in a cave beside a chapel.

Many visitors began to seek Theodore because he was known as a healer and an exorcist. To recover some solitude he moved up a mountainside and made his home in another cave. This did not work, because vermin overran the place and the lack of cleanliness ruined his health.

Seventh-century expressions of faith puzzle us today. When Theodore returned from a pilgrimage to Jerusalem, he began a life of austerity, living in cages suspended above the floor of a cave. He became a wonder-worker, and people started coming to him again in great numbers. For those who wanted to be his disciples he built a monastery. Then, much to his surprise and dismay, Theodore became bishop of Anastasiopolis. He functioned in this capacity for almost a decade and then resigned in order to spend more time in prayer. Healings and spiritual direction filled the remainder of his life.

APRIL 23
George (d. ca. 300)
✥Strength in Christ

Many great artists have tried their hand at the legend of St. George and the dragon, among them Raphael, Rubens, Donatello, Ucello, and Mantegna. George may well be the most popular saint of all. Christians in both Eastern and Western traditions venerate him. Islam calls him a prophet. George, the dragon slayer and rescuer of a young maiden, was a real person who died for his faith, but the famous fable has no historical basis, and we know next to nothing about his life. The tale about the dragon was included in the *Golden Legend* mentioned in the Introduction. George was a knight from Cappodocia who rode into a town that was being terrorized by a dragon that lived in a nearby swamp. The residents had attempted to kill it, but its fiery and evil-smelling breath discouraged them. To keep the dragon quiet, they provided two sheep each day for its breakfast. Running out of sheep, they resorted to human sacrifice chosen by lot. One day the ruler's own daughter became the victim. She dressed as a bride and went to the swamp to meet her doom. At this point, George arrived and attacked the dragon with his lance. Tying up the wounded monster with the young woman's girdle, George led it into town and said he would kill it if everyone would accept Christ as their Savior. Fifteen thousand people agreed to be baptized, and George dispatched the dragon. Dozens of other outlandish stories about George have circulated since the fifth century. The reforms of 1969 removed George from the universal calendar, but allow this as a day of celebration in various localities.

APRIL 24

Fidelis of Sigmaringen (1577–1622)

❧ Christian service

Sigmaringen was a town in Germany where Mark Rey was born. Mark became a lawyer and took an interest in human rights. They called him "the lawyer of the poor." His inside view of how the world conducts business filled him with disgust.

Mark's brother, George, was a Franciscan friar of the Capuchin Order. With that example nearby, Mark quit his law practice, gave his estate to the poor, and became a Capuchin. He took the name Fidelis and began to combine service to the poor with extended hours of prayer. His book of *Spiritual Exercises* was translated into several languages.

Fidelis led a group of Capuchins to Switzerland in an attempt to persuade people not to follow Calvin and Zwingli into the Protestant Reformation. As Francis de Sales (January 24) would learn, this was an emotionally supercharged issue that carried great risk to life and limb. He signed his last letter, "Brother Fidelis, who will soon be the food of worms." After an attempted assassination while Fidelis was preaching in the church at Seewis, Switzerland, a Protestant offered him safety in his home, but he declined. He attempted to take the road out of Seewis, but about twenty enraged peasants surrounded and murdered him.

APRIL 25

Peter de Betancurt (1626–67)

❧ *Christian mission*

Peter descended from Juan de Betancurt, a Norman conqueror of the Canary Islands. By the time he was born in Tenerife, the glory days were gone, and he grew up a poor shepherd boy. As with David, the Old Testament shepherd, the time alone keeping the small family flock groomed a contemplative soul. Peter's awareness of God grew stronger each day.

Reports from sailors returning from the Americas describing the primitive life of people living there stirred Peter's interest. In 1650, as a freelance Christian missionary, he sailed for Guatemala where one of his relatives worked for the government.

In Cuba, Peter ran out of money. As a strong twenty-three-year-old man, Peter was able to pay for the remainder of his journey by signing on as a deck hand. After landing in Honduras, he walked to Guatemala City. Destitute, he stood in line for food each day at the Franciscan friary. He received much more than bread. Friar Fernando Espino became a lifelong friend and helped Peter find a job in a textile factory. In 1655, Peter became a Franciscan and began to work with African-American slaves, abandoned children, emigrants, and other people in difficulty.

Peter died at the age of forty-one and is remembered as the "St. Francis of the Americas."

APRIL 26

Paschasius Radbert (ca. 790–865)

❧ *Continuing education*

Radbert was an abandoned baby of unknown parentage. Nuns of Notre-Dame at Soissons, France, adopted the foundling near the end of the eighth century. Educated at the monastery of St. Peter, he gained a strong interest in classical literature. Becoming a monk himself, Radbert entered the monastery of Corbie, noted for its outstanding library. With these books at his disposal, he prepared himself to become one of the exceptional theologians of his time. After a brief and unhappy experience as an administrator, he devoted himself to scholarship and writing until his death in 865.

Many of his works survive, the most notable being *De Corpore et Sanguine Domini*. This book, written for the instruction of monks, is the oldest doctrinal treatise on the presence of the body and blood of Christ in the Eucharist. Christ's presence, he said, is real, but there is no way to measure it because it is a spiritual presence.

APRIL 27

Asicus (d. ca. 490)
❦ *Faith in obscurity*

Asicus was an early disciple of St. Patrick (March 17) in Ireland. He became the first bishop of Elphin in County Roscommon. Asicus did not enjoy being a bishop and gave up the position to live a solitary life on an island in Donegal Bay. Fine examples of his work as a coppersmith survive, but there is little record of his life.

APRIL 28

Peter Chanel (1803–40)
❦ *Christian missions*

Active persecution of Christians in the Roman and Persian Empires ended by the fifth century, but hostilities have continued elsewhere through history. The blood of martyrs has been spilled in Ireland, England and Wales, France, Spain, China, Japan, Korea, Vietnam, Cambodia, Mexico, Uganda, the Soviet Union, Albania, and Guinea.

It was Pierre Louis-Marie Chanel, the son of a French peasant farmer, who became the first Christian martyr of the South Pacific. As a member of the missionary Society of Mary, Peter had gone to the tropical islands and landed at random on Futuna, one of the French Iles de Horn, northeast of Fiji. He remained there with another young Marist and a European merchant who could help them with the language.

The trio was initially welcomed, but the islanders had a natural suspicion of their motives. Peter's diary records his difficulty learning the language, the strange customs of the people, and his pastoral visits to the sick. His ministry was a mixture of patience and frustration. "How sorrowful is the lot of a poor missionary who cannot yet preach the truths of salvation!"

Resistance to the missionaries began at the top of the island's political structure. The "king" began to worry about losing his position and influence should Christianity became strongly established. The Europeans already living on Futuna set a poor example, and the islanders did not like their exploitation of the island. French and British gunboats patrolled the area, protecting the alien traders. These gunboats began to harass the islanders who sat for instruction by the missionaries.

The king's son requested baptism, and this set off a furor that eventually took Peter's life. Peter commented, "It does not matter if I am killed. Religion has taken root on the island. It will not be destroyed by my death, since it comes not from men but from God." A group of islanders attacked and killed him. Less than a year later, all the residents of Futuna were baptized Christian.

APRIL 29

Catherine of Siena (1347–80)
Christian mysticism

The twenty-fifth child of an Italian wool-dyer and cloth merchant, Catherine became a lay Dominican at the age of fifteen. She lived during the turbulent fourteenth century that was marred by wars and the Black Death (bubonic plague). It was a time of fear and anxiety, of turmoil and change. The Church was corrupt; decadence, bribery, and faithlessness thrived. Rome had become a dangerous place, and in 1309, the church leadership fled to a palace in Avignon, France.

Catherine had impressive, mystical religious experiences in the midst of the social chaos that surrounded her. Rather than enter a convent, Catherine decided to remain active in the world. "My cell will not be one of stone or wood," she said, "but of self-knowledge." She remained something of a recluse for three years, during which she struggled with doubt, disturbing visions, and inner voices. When she found the courage to laugh aloud, they ceased and Christ appeared to her. She asked him, "Where were you when all of this was happening?" He replied, "I was in your heart." An ancient biography of Catherine reports that she began to have visitations from Christ every day. In 1367, she abandoned her solitude and began a life of service to others. A few years later, Catherine reported an overwhelming experience of union with God. "My heart could bear it no longer. Love became as strong as death."

Now Catherine began a wider public ministry, dictating hundreds of letters to people in positions of church and state responsibility. "I tell you in the name of Christ crucified that you must use your authority to do important things." She wrote her principal book during this period of her life. Mystics ordinarily find human language inadequate for expressing their experiences of the divine. *The Dialogue* between herself and God is exciting, but difficult reading. It is not always easy to follow Catherine's line of thought, but it is obvious that it results from a lively personal faith in a loving God. "Love transforms you into what you love." Though uneducated and barely able to read and write, Catherine is the first woman ever declared a "Doctor of the Church," an eminent and reliable teacher.

Catherine developed quite a reputation as a peacemaker, mediating family feuds. Eventually, she traveled across Italy to negotiate peace among armies at war. She made her way to Pope Gregory XI in Avignon and told him he needed to return to Rome. Impressed by her divinely inspired boldness, the Pope did exactly that.

The Church, unfortunately, continued to deteriorate. Catherine became convinced that she must atone for its sins. Her final mystical vision placed the burden of the church on her back, as though it were a large ship. She collapsed in great pain and lay paralyzed. A few weeks later, when she died at the age of thirty-three, people found peculiar marks on her body: the stigmata representing the wounds of her crucified Lord, and a "wedding band" placed on her finger by her spiritual spouse. Before her death, Catherine was the only one who could perceive these marks.

APRIL 30

Pius V (1504–72)
ᐍ*Faith in action*

Anthony Ghislieri became a Dominican in 1518 and was ordained a priest in 1540. A philosophy and theology professor, he became Pope Pius V in 1565. The church and its leadership had fallen into bad times and needed serious reformation. The Council of Trent made decrees and put reforms in writing, but Pius V was required to enforce them. He worked on this for six years.

There were political stresses. At this time Pope Pius V excommunicated Queen Elizabeth of England, resulting in a torrent of aggression against Catholics. He also struggled against the ambitions of King Philip II of Spain, the Ottoman Empire, and the increasing number of Protestants. He sponsored a fleet of more than two hundred European ships that defeated the Turkish navy in the Battle of Lepanto, thus preventing a Turkish invasion. In this conflict, Cervantes, author of *Don Quixote*, received a wound at sea.

In many ways, the circumstances of his times influenced the ideas and motives of Pius V. Critics point out the negative aspects of his almost fanatical conservative faith. As those who evaluate athletic coaches after a game realize, it is easier to make decisions later, than in the midst of disorder and turmoil.

MAY 1

Philip (first century)

✍Practical enthusiasm

A Jew with a Greek name, Philip grew up on the north end of the Sea of Galilee in a place called "Fish House" (Bethsaida). He may have been named for the Roman tetrarch Philip who had governed the area for a decade and turned Bethsaida into a prosperous international community.

Though he certainly spoke Aramaic, he probably also spoke Greek. He did not grow up in a rigidly orthodox home that resisted change, but as his Greek name suggests, his father was broad-minded and open to new ideas and ways of doing things.

Philip was a faithful Jew who waited expectantly for the promised Messiah from God. With other fishermen, he went down to the Jordan River to hear John the Baptist (August 29). Philip was spiritually prepared to respond to Jesus Christ's invitation, "Follow me."

It was the new apostle Philip who ran breathlessly to Nathanael, saying, "We have found him!" Fresh enthusiasm did not dampen Philip's practicality. Before the miraculous feeding of the five thousand who had gathered to hear Jesus on a Galilean hillside, Philip asked Jesus a very logical question: "How can we buy food for all of these people?" And again, at the Last Supper, Philip listened to Christ talk about returning to his heavenly Father to prepare a place for others. His unimaginative response, "Lord, show us the Father and we will be satisfied," startled Jesus. "Have I been with you so long and yet you do not know me, Philip? He who has seen me has seen the Father. How can you say, 'Show us the Father?'" Philip is not one of the major apostles, but every time he appears in the Gospel record, he is associated with major religious issues.

A letter dated about 195 from Polycrates, bishop of Ephesus, yields information beyond the New Testament narrative: "Philip, also one of the twelve apostles, died in Hierapolis along with his two daughters."

MAY 2
Athanasius (ca. 296–373)
✇*Religious orthodoxy*

The divinity of Jesus consumed the thought and activity of Athanasius, patriarch of Alexandria, Egypt, in the fourth century. Strong challenges to this concept were rampant in the church. Athanasius took a firm and unshakable stand in favor of the doctrine that God was in Christ. The personal costs for him were high. He attended endless church meetings and councils, often traveling great distances. He was politically exiled five times over a thirty-year period, some of the time being spent in the Egyptian desert among hermits.

Athanasius was born to Christian parents near the end of the third century. In 328, he became a bishop and was immediately embroiled in the controversies among Christians of his day. He adamantly supported the summary of faith in the Nicene Creed, and became a target for its opponents. Misunderstandings, lawsuits, and harassment became familiar to Athanasius. In the fourth century, theological questions were also political issues of the greatest importance.

Athanasius prepared the first list of books to be included in the Christian Bible. When Jerome (September 30) translated Holy Scripture into the Latin Vulgate, he accepted the choices of Athanasius as the canonical books. These books, and no others, were included.

A prolific writer, Athanasius wrote many books and treatises that continue to be studied. He died of natural causes in 373..

MAY 3
James the Less (first century)
✇*Supporting role*

Two of Christ's apostles were named James. James the son of Zebedee (July 25) figures prominently in the Gospels. One of the

Marys present at the Crucifixion was the mother of the James called "the less." His father was Alphaeus.

The Gospel of Mark refers to James as "the less," which is sometimes translated into English as "the younger." Some believe that "the less" implies he was a small man, but that is only speculation. A respected dictionary of the Bible lists *five* possible individuals named James in the New Testament and then notes that they "are considered by many to be the same person."

The secular Jewish historian Josephus reports that James was stoned to death in the year 61.

MAY 4

Florian (d. 304)

ℐ*Brave faith*

Apart from legendary material, we know little about Florian. He was a Roman army officer who held an important administrative position in the northern area of modern Austria. During the Diocletian persecution, Florian was a hunted Christian who gave himself up to the governor's soldiers. His *acta* says that Florian made a bold statement of faith and received a Roman scourging. After this he was set on fire and thrown from a bridge into the Enns River, near its junction with the Danube, with a stone around his neck. A woman recovered his body, and others took it to the Augustinian Abbey of St. Florian, which is near Linz.

MAY 5

Hilary of Aries (ca. 400–49)

ℐ *Making a choice*

Hilary grew up a fifth-century pagan in Lorraine, France. Well-educated and affluent, he held a high position in local government when his relative Honoratus (January 16) extended an invitation for him to visit his newly opened monastery in Lérins. What Hilary discovered there appealed to him, but also created a personal struggle. "On the one hand," he wrote, "I felt that the Lord was calling me, while on the other hand the seductions of the world held me back. My will swayed backward and forward, now consenting, now refusing. But in the end, Christ triumphed in me." Hilary asked the monks to baptize him, and he remained at Lérins as a brother.

When Honoratus became archbishop of Arles, he took Hilary with him as his secretary. Upon the death of Honoratus, Hilary, at the age of twenty-nine, replaced him as archbishop. A quarrel with Rome regarding the boundaries and persons of authority in Gaul resulted in accusations that lead to Hilary's excommunication. After a passage of time and a cooling of emotions, Hilary was reinstated. Though the written record of this is sparse, there was never any question about his personal integrity or the quality of his religious devotion.

MAY 6

Petronax (d. ca. 747)

❦ Rebuilding

Petronax was a rebuilder, a restorer. Because of his restoration work, he is called the "second founder" of the abbey of Montecassino. A resident of Brescia, Italy, Petronax responded in the year 717 to a request by Pope Gregory II to visit St. Benedict's (July 11) old monastery that the Lombards had destroyed about a hundred and forty years previously. Petronax found a few solitary hermits residing in the ruins. Recognizing his leadership and organizational ability, they elected Petronax their abbot and began to live as a Benedictine community. The Lombard duke of Beneventum generously contributed funds for restoration of the abbey distroyed by his relatives.

Some notable monks then passed through Montecassino, including Willibald (July 7), bishop of Eichstatt, and Sturmius, founder of the abbey of Fulda. Petronax continued to lead the monastery until his death.

MAY 7

Agostino Roscelli (1818–1902)
✒ *Activity and prayer*

Agostino Roscelli grew up in a poor family that lived in Casarza Ligure, Italy. A quiet child, intelligent and sensitive, Agostino helped take care of the family's sheep. Like many other shepherds of a religious inclination, he found the solitude and silence of the hillsides an excellent setting for a deepening relationship with God.

When he began his studies for the priesthood at Genoa in 1835, he had more faith than cash. Financial constraints almost made it impossible for him to stay in school, but his determination and the support of others sustained him. He was ordained in 1846 and became curate of St. Martin d'Albaro.

Eight years later, Agostino accepted responsibility for pastoral care at the Church of the Consolation. He performed the classical duties of the confessional with a grace that attracted droves of people, young and old. For four or five hours a day, Agostino would sit behind the grate, paying no attention to cold or heat, ignoring fatigue, welcoming everyone who came.

In 1847, Agostino began a twenty-two-year labor as chaplain of an orphanage. The record shows that he baptized more than eight thousand newly born babies and offered a father's guidance to their unmarried teenage mothers. While doing this, Agostino also actively ministered to condemned prisoners. He founded the Institute of Sisters of the Immaculata in 1867 to take care of the women's homes he had established.

Serious attention to prayer provided the basis for busy days. "Prayer was his life. If you wanted to find him you had to look in the chapel." Agostino spent long hours praying, and, like his Lord, sometimes devoted entire nights to prayer. The impression of his left knee can still be seen in his wooden kneeler. Managing to keep out of the glare of publicity, Agostino experienced "a genuine mystical and contemplative life."

He died on May 7, 1902, but his work continues in Italy and Argentina.

MAY 8

Boniface IV (d. 615)

❦ *Christian influence*

An Italian doctor's son, Boniface became pope in 608. He had been a student of Gregory the Great (September 3) as well as a Benedictine monk. Boniface IV will always be remembered for converting the Roman Pantheon into a Christian church, the first transformation of its kind. Boniface IV also gave oversight to the expansion of Christianity into England. He died of natural causes in 615.

MAY 9

Pachomius (ca. 290–346)

❦ *Inspiring example*

Kindness inspired by Christ's example can be a powerful evangelistic tool. Such kindness resulted in the conversion of Pachomius, a Roman military conscript from Egypt. Slated to serve the empire as a galley slave, he was being transported down the Nile River with other drafted men. When they docked at Latopolis, the Christians there were compassionate and helpful. Pachomius always remembered their kindness to strangers. After he had served his time, he returned home and began to study Christianity.

After his baptism, he asked a local Christian hermit, Paloemon, to teach him how to pray and meditate. For a while, they lived together in primitive conditions in the Egyptian desert, devoting much time to prayer and manual labor. Paloemon taught Pachomius how to lay stone and bricks.

His masonry skills came in handy when Pachomius helped to design and build a monastery on the east bank of the Nile in 320. Many others joined him, including his older brother, John. In time, several thousand Egyptian monks were following the "Rules for Monastic Life" that Pachomius had prepared. Jerome (September 30) translated this document into Latin, and it became a model for subsequent Rules. He founded additional monasteries in Egypt, a convent for his sister and other nuns, and built a chapel for shepherds near Thebes.

Pachomius died in an epidemic in 346.

MAY 10

John of Avila (d. 1569)
❦Dedicated life

A Spanish law student, John of Avila became a student of theology and philosophy. The sixteenth-century passion for exploration and discovery excited John, and he planned to leave for the New World after his ordination in 1525. He gave most of his inheritance to the poor and arranged to become a missionary to Mexico. The archbishop of Seville, however, had other ideas for him. For forty years John of Avila was a Christian evangelist in southern Spain's Andalusia. The Moors had ruled this area a new generation needed to hear the gospel. He became popular among the people there, though he did get into some difficulty during the Inquisition. No charge against him had any substance.

John's prolific writing reveals unusual spiritual depth and insight. His works are among Spanish literature's most revered classics. He was a skillful spiritual director, and some well-known saints studied under him: Teresa of Avila, Francis Borgia, John of God, and Louis of Granada.

John was extremely ill during his final fifteen years. He died in 1569 at Montilla.

MAY 11

Francis di Girolamo (1642–1716)
❦Preaching Christ

Francis was the first of eleven children, born in a small Italian village. A precocious child, he began to study at the college of Taranto when he was only sixteen, and then went on to Naples for what we would call graduate courses. He was ordained at Naples in 1666, and after four years of teaching, entered the Society of Jesus. It soon became evident that Francis was a gifted preacher, and although he expressed a desire to become a missionary to Asia, others insisted his best mission was to communicate the gospel in Naples. He accepted the judgment of higher authority as an expression of the will of God. For the next forty years, he gave full energy to public preaching. He often spoke as many as forty times a day on the streets, in public squares, and in the churches of Naples, using brevity and eloquence to reach his hearers. Many conversions resulted from his preaching. Thousands gathered around him on Sundays. He was an imposing figure, and people crowded around him hoping for any kind of personal exchange. When engaging in conversation, Francis was soft spoken, but when he spoke in public, his voice boomed with resonance. A popular preacher, he used any device or object lesson imaginable to catch and hold people's attention. People responded enthusiastically. Though he gave the impression of speaking extemporaneously, the notes he left behind reveal meticulous care in the organization of his thoughts.

Francis di Girolamo was seventy-four when he died, after prolonged suffering, in 1761.

MAY 12

Pancras (d. ? 304)

Extended influence

Little is known about many of the people who populate the catalog of saints. Pancras is one of the few of whom it can be said that we know *nothing*. And yet, he is not a fictional character, and he has achieved widespread popularity. Everything known regarding his life can be expressed in one sentence: *Pancras was a Roman martyr early in the fourth century.*

One untrustworthy biography fills in the gaps of knowledge with a mixture of stock piety and vivid imagination. There could be some truth to the tradition that he was a Phrygian orphan whose uncle took him to Rome, and that he was only fourteen years old when he was beheaded because of his faith in Christ.

The results of his martyrdom are truly remarkable. First, as a sign of things to come, the cemetery where his body was buried was later named after him. His influence continued.

• Gregory the Great (September 3) dedicated a monastery in Rome to Pancras.

• Pope Vitalian sent relics associated with Pancras to the king of Northumbria in the seventh century.

• Augustine of Canterbury (May 27) built his first church in England, naming it after Pancras.

• The Venerable Bede (May 25) included Pancras in his Old English Martyrology.

• Six churches in England were dedicated to Pancras. The one in North London passed along his name to the famous Saint Pancras Railway Station.

MAY 13

Julian of Norwich (1342–1416)

🖋 *Mystical insight*

The Revelations of Divine Love is the first book written by a woman in English. It is one of the great treasures of classical spiritual literature.

> God placed high spiritual delight in my soul. I was completely filled with confidence, and resolutely sustained. I dreaded nothing. It was such a happy spiritual feeling that I was totally at peace. Nothing on earth could have disturbed me.
>
> This lasted only a short time. Returning to myself, I became depressed and was weary of my life. I almost lacked the patience to go on living.

Julian of Norwich lived in dreadful times. Britain and the rest of Europe struggled through the fourteenth century with its wars, outbreaks of plague, religious schisms, and political intrigue. A new expression of spirituality grew among the lay people as they attempted to live a Christian life outside of formal religious communities. While the monasteries struggled with laxity among their members and a continual need for reform, individual Christians nurtured close personal relationships with God.

Julian of Norwich, who probably received the name of the church of St. Julian in Norwich, England, became a lay anchoress. She lived in a cell, built onto the exterior wall of the church, that had a window open to the public and another opening that allowed her to see inside the sanctuary. Julian actually shut herself inside this cell, receiving visitors and food through the public window, and participating in worship through the sanctuary window. With a small cottage garden and the companionship of a cat, Julian devoted her life to meditation and prayer.

Julian's books, *Showings* and *The Revelations of Divine Love,* are among the best of a number of English mystical writings that emerged from the fourteenth century. Her autobiographical references tell us that she was born in 1342 and became seriously ill when she was thirty. Everyone was convinced she would die, but instead, she had a series of visions regarding the passion of Christ and lived to write about them.

> He showed me a little thing about the size of a hazelnut. As I wondered what it could be, the answer came, "It is all that is created." It was so small I wondered how it could survive. In my mind, I heard, "It lasts because God loves it."

> In this tiny object, I saw three truths: God made it, God loves it, and God takes care of it.

> Who is this maker, lover, and sustainer God? I do not have the words to express it. Until I am united with God, I can never have true rest or peace. I can never know until I am held so close to God that there is nothing between us.

Julian confidently assures us of the feminine aspect of God.

> As certainly as God is our father, just as certainly is he our mother. In our father, we have our being; in our mother, we are remade and restored, our fragmented lives are knit

together and made perfect. I am the strength and goodness of fatherhood. I am the wisdom of motherhood. I am the light and grace of holy love. I am the Trinity. I am the unity. I teach you to love. I teach you to desire. I am the reward of all true desire.

This woman, whose actual name is lost forever, makes no reference to the political and ecclesiastical turmoil of her time and place. She is totally occupied with God, and it is with confidence in the love of God that she makes her most famous comment: "All shall be well."

MAY 14

Mary-Dominica Mazzarello (1837–81)
Accomplishment in spite of handicap

Mary grew up on a farm near Mornese, Italy, in the middle of the nineteenth century. She labored hard in her large family's field and vineyard until she was twenty-three. She then contracted typhoid fever and the illness left her feeble, making heavy outdoor work impossible. She turned to dressmaking and did so well at it that she hired others to help her. All this time, her spiritual life was actively growing.

In 1864, John Bosco (January 31) visited Mornese with plans to start a school for boys. This did not work out, but he knew there was also a need for a school for girls. He enlisted Mary-Dominica Mazzarello to found and lead the Salesian Sisters. Today, fifty-four countries have Salesian Sister Schools.

Never fully well after her bout with typhoid fever, she died in 1881 at the age of forty-four. Her grave lies beside Bosco's in Turin.

MAY 15

Isidore the Farmer (1070–1130)
The glory of the commonplace

Isidore cultivated the earth, spread manure, planted seeds, chopped weeds, and harvested crops. He did not build monasteries, found religious orders, write books, attract followers, or influence political leaders. Born in Madrid, Spain, Isidore labored in the soil all his life for a wealthy landowner, John de Vergas. Isidore and his wife, Maria, had one child, a son who died at an early age.

Isidore began most mornings in church. He prayed as he worked the farm, and one report says angels could be seen helping him. He was known to be an extremely generous person, sharing his meals with people poorer than himself. He loved animals, and insisted that they be cared for properly. The tale is told that one winter he and another farmhand were taking corn to the mill. Isidore noticed a flock of birds perched in the trees, cold and hungry. While his companion protested and laughed, Isidore opened his sack and poured about half of the grain on the ground for the birds. When they got to the mill, his bag was still full.

In spite of the miraculous stories circulated about Isidore the farmer, the most significant thing about this saint is the extraordinary ordinariness of his life.

Isidore, who died in 1130, is the patron saint of Madrid.

MAY 16

Brendan the Navigator (? 486–578)

✍ *Spiritual exploration*

Brendan founded numerous monasteries, becoming abbot of Clonfert, Ireland, around 559. Several locations in western Ireland still bear his name. He is famous for his voyage to the "Isles of the Blessed" that may indicate he was one of the earliest arrivals in America. A popular book, *Navigation of Saint Brendan*, began to circulate in the eighth and ninth centuries. While it is almost certainly a romantic novel of a mythical sailor, early copyists loved it and spread its circulation. Today more than a hundred original copies and translations of this Medieval Latin text in many languages remain in existence.

MAY 17

Paschal Baylon (1540–92)
Simplicity

Paschal Baylon, a Spanish peasant shepherd, became a Franciscan lay brother at twenty-one. In this capacity, Paschal functioned as a cook and doorkeeper in several friaries. With a cheerful personality, Paschal took care of the poor and the sick. He had an unusually profound interest in the sacramental elements of communion, and Mass was a central focus of his day.

Paschal went to France as a courier of important ecclesiastical messages. Here, he had an opportunity to argue convincingly with a Protestant minister who did not support the Real Presence in the Eucharist. This was Paschal's favorite doctrinal topic and the source of his deepest personal devotion. Huguenots interrupted his trip on two occasions by harassing and throwing rocks at him. His injuries were a source of discomfort for the remainder of his life.

The return trip to Loreto was uneventful, but he died soon after at the age of fifty-two, leaving behind an indelible reputation for sanctity and simple honesty.

MAY 18

John I (d. 526)
Faith in crisis

From the Italian province of Tuscany, John became bishop of Rome, or pope, in 523. By now, the structure of politics around the Mediterranean had divided the Empire into East and West, with one emperor in Rome and another emperor in Constantinople. The Church was still united geographically, but doctrinal heresies threatened to fragment its membership.

Religious issues in the context of that time had strong political implications. Kings and emperors tinkered with theology. Theodoric the Goth, a German leader, sent John I on a political mission to Justin, the emperor of the East, in an attempt to settle a question of religious doctrine regarding the divinity of Christ. When John and Justin seemed to get along amiably, Theodoric became concerned that they might be scheming against him. Police were waiting for him when John returned home in 526.

Pope John I died in prison, probably as the result of maltreatment. There have been twenty-three popes named John, but John I is the only one ever canonized a saint.

MAY 19

Dunstan (909–88)

✒️*Recovery and restoration*

By 909, when Dunstan was born in Baltonsborough, England, the Danish invasions had destroyed most of the English monasteries. The one at Glastonbury was still limping along, and monks there provided the best education they could for him. Dunstan began his adult life as a royal courtier, but soon returned to Glastonbury and began a private monastic life. He developed skills in metalwork, painting, manuscript illumination, and embroidery.

King Edmund appointed Dunstan abbot of Glastonbury in 943 and gave a generous financial endowment to the monastery. Dunstan began the difficult work of monastic renewal, championing the Benedictine Rule. Working together with Sts. Ethelwold and Oswald, he restored other English monasteries. He became bishop of Worcester in 957 and archbishop of Canterbury in 960.

Dunstan lived an active life until his death in his late seventies. On Ascension Day in 988, he delivered three sermons. He died two days later, having contributed much to England's development in the tenth century.

MAY 20

Bernardino of Siena (1380–1444)

✍*Holy name*

Bernardino degl' Albizzeschi and some friends kept the Siena hospital functioning in 1400 when the plague killed most of the hospital staff. Bernardino had been reared by his aunt. When the epidemic had passed, he cared for this aunt until her death. He heard her repeating the name of Jesus with intense devotion. In later years, the name of Jesus became the central theme of his life. He receives the credit for devising the familiar symbol of the first three Greek letters of Christ's name: IHS.

Bernardino became a Franciscan at the age of twenty-two and was Italy's leading fifteenth-century preaching missionary. He traveled widely on foot in Italy, preaching lengthy sermons to large and eager crowds in the open air. When he began this career his voice was thin and weak, but with continued effort it became resonant and powerful. His subject matter involved practical Christian living and moral choices. He illustrated his sermons with anecdotes and delivered them with forceful and sometimes clownish antics. His audiences were moved to both laughter and tears.

By the time Bernardino turned sixty, his health was failing and he had to travel on a donkey rather than on foot. He made what he felt would be his last visit home to Massas Marittima in 1444. Here he delivered a series of fifty sermons in fifty days. From this small town, he pushed on toward Naples, preaching at every community along the way. He never finished his journey, dying in Aquila on May 20, 1444. Many artistic representations of Bernardino of Siena show him holding up the tablet he used at the conclusion of his sermons inscribed with the letters, IHS.

MAY 21

Andrew Bobola (1592–1657)

❧*Hazards of faith*

Andrew Bobola was a Polish aristocrat who became a Jesuit at Vilnius, Lithuania, in 1611, the year of the publication of the *King James Version* of the Bible. Near the border between the ecclesiastical jurisdiction of Rome and Constantinople, he converted entire communities of Eastern Orthodox Christians to Roman Catholicism. This resulted in opposition and persecution. Children were organized into groups to hound him as he moved around, and they tried to drown out his voice with their cries.

A group of Cossacks finally stopped Andrew's mission. They chased Jesuits from their churches and classrooms. Seizing Bobola, they gave him an opportunity to denounce his faith in 1657. When he did not, the angry and frustrated Cossacks burned, beat, mutilated, and beheaded him. After being transferred to several cities, his remains today are kept in the Jesuit church in Warsaw, Poland.

MAY 22

Rita of Cascia (1381–1457)

❧*Secular and sacred*

Rita's parents, following the social custom of Italy in the fourteenth century, selected a man for her to marry. The husband they chose turned out to be brutally violent. Rita endured the misery of eighteen years of unhappy marriage with a man who was unfaithful to her, and she mothered two sons. Her husband's wild life away from home resulted in his murder.

About 1407, Rita became an Augustinian nun at St. Maria Maddalena at Cascia. An ulcer that appeared in her forehead at Cascia symbolized a mark from the crown of thorns and was attributed to her intense meditation on the Passion of Christ. The open wound did not heal, and her mystical experiences continued for fifteen years. During this time, Rita worked quietly, caring for sick nuns.

She died of tuberculosis.

MAY 23
Petroc (d. ca. 594)
Quietly active

Sources of information vary regarding this famous sixth-century saint from Cornwall. He was born in South Wales and became a founder of monasteries. For a while, he lived as a hermit on Bodmin Moor, building a cell for himself by the river, as well as accommodations for a dozen followers up the hill. Legend holds that animals accepted his presence in the forest without fear.

Petroc's remains were subjected to theft and intrigue. King Henry II settled the dispute regarding the resting place of his bones, most of which were returned to Bodmin. His skull is kept in an exquisitely crafted ivory reliquary that was hidden during the upheaval of the Reformation and rediscovered in the nineteenth century. It remains on display in Bodmin today, and many consider it to be the finest example of its kind in England.

MAY 24
David of Scotland (? 1085–1153)
Primary goals

Recognized as Scotland's greatest king, David was the sixth and youngest son of Malcolm III and Margaret. David became king in 1124, the beginning of more than a decade of atrocious civil wars among various earldoms. Instead of becoming distracted by territorial disputes, David gave his attention to improving Scotland. He replaced Celtic tribal boundaries with a feudal system, invited Normans to set up colonies, established a court system, and developed Edinburgh, Berwick, Perth, and other communities into commercial centers without regard for race and clan. Most important, David reorganized the Christian Church in Scotland, establishing firm ties with Rome.

Contemporaries respected David for his personal piety and exemplary moral standards.

MAY 25

Venerable Bede (673–735)

Sacred scholarship

"I have taken delight always either to study, to teach, or to write," Bede admitted. His long life had no dramatic, history-changing events. His biographers attribute to him none of the miracles, mystical visions, and acts of self-denial that are commonplace among the lives of saints. The example of Bede teaches us that scholarship is also a path to holiness. William of Malmesbury declared that Bede was one of the "most learned and least proud" monks in England.

As a child, Bede lived a quiet, protected monastic life. His parents asked a local abbot to care for his education and development when Bede was seven years old. His home for nearly sixty years was the monastery at Jarrow. He rarely left its confinement and probably never traveled outside of Northumbria, but because of his skillful and protracted research, he garnered a view of the world that few others of his generation could realize.

Bede wrote many books, all of them in Latin, the most popular of which is the *Historia Ecclesiastica Gentis Anglorum (Ecclesiastical History of the English People)*. Bede attempted to present history in the form of a readable narrative, showing how Christianity pulled diverse cultures together into a unified nation. While other monastic histories from his time are dry chronicles with little more than lists of names and dates, Bede's history tells us about some interesting personalities and human interactions.

Bede wrote a stirring passage about the beginning of Christianity in his native Northumbria. King Edwin brought his best advisors together to consider the new religion. One advisor compared human life to the "brief flight of a sparrow through a banquet hall." Under its roof, he said, the bird is safe from the storms outside, but then it flies into the darkness and danger of the unknown outside. We do not know our source, he continued, and we are not confident about our destiny. If Christianity can illumine eternity, then it makes sense to follow it. Each advisor, in turn, agreed that Northumbria should officially recognize Christianity.

Bede became seriously ill in 735, but he kept working at his projects-in-progress, including an Old English translation of the Gospel of John. He dictated the closing verses before he died, singing the *Gloria Patri*. Boniface (June 5) said, "The candle of the Church, lit by the Holy Spirit, has been extinguished."

MAY 26

Philip Neri (1515–95)

Keeping faith alive

The remarkable thing about this saint is his glowing, joyful spirit. Philip Neri influenced others without writing books or founding an order. He laughed and he prayed.

Beginning life in Florence, Italy, Philip experienced a dramatic conversion to Christ as a young man, and began to wander toward Rome. Once there, he tutored a few students in order to support a simple life. He knew he was getting ready for some service to God, which had not yet come into focus.

Sixteenth-century Rome was a disorderly mess. Even the top church leaders were spiritually fragmented. Living among the Romans, Philip conceived his vocation. He would wake the Church in Rome, and he would start immediately.

Philip Neri began with impromptu conversations on street corners. With a natural gift for making friends, he would visit banks and markets talking with strangers, always getting the conversation around to religion. People in the neighborhood began to recognize him and welcome him as he gathered more and more friendly acquaintances. He would converse warmly with people as they walked the streets of Rome.

Philip was ordained in 1550 when he turned thirty-five, and he became one of the most popular priests in the city. He began to lead walking tours of the great basilicas of Rome, tours that attracted hundreds of people. During the tours, he would lead prayers and hymns as well as sing a few popular songs. At lunch, the tour members would picnic.

Using attic space above his church, Philip gathered with groups of laity and a few clergy for evenings of prayer and meditation. These groups were called the Oratorians, and each time they met one of the group would talk about a religious subject and then the others would ask questions and make comments. For modern Christians, familiar with discussion groups of all kinds, Philip's ministry seems comfortable, but in the sixteenth century, it was a radical venture. Asking lay people to speak before a church group seemed rather more Protestant than Catholic. The Inquisition actually investigated Neri, but they found him harmless and the pope endorsed his work.

Philip Neri was a Christian mystic with numerous miracles attributed to him. He often experienced religious ecstasy when he participated in communion. People began to declare him a saint, and Philip coped by becoming a clown. He would shave only one side of his face or wear odd clothing. Practical jokes and roaring laughter were a part of his playful routine. He did not want to be "saintly." But his good-natured fun was nothing more than a reflection of his religious joy.

On May 25, 1595, Philip Neri conducted business as usual, hearing confessions and chatting with visitors. On his way to bed he said, "Last of all, we must die." He did not wake the next morning.

MAY 27

Augustine of Canterbury (d. 604)

❦Ministry among pagans

We must be careful not to confuse this sixth-century bishop of Canterbury with the great Christian theologian of the fourth century. Augustine of Canterbury came to England with a large delegation of monks from a monastery in Rome. Alarming tales of rough seas in the English Channel and wild, savage people on the islands tested their courage. The missionaries arrived in 597.

King Ethelbert, a pagan, welcomed them. In 601, the king asked for baptism. Later, Augustine consulted with King Ethelbert when he drafted the oldest, surviving Anglo-Saxon laws. By the time Augustine died, England was well on its way to Christianization.

MAY 28

Germanus of Paris (ca. 496–576)

❦Christian influence

Germanus was a priest in Autun (Burgundy), France, in the early part of the sixth century. He moved to Paris where he became the bishop and royal chaplain in 555. The royal family had a reputation for being rather profane, and Germanus guided them toward a more dignified life. King Childebert I founded an abbey for him which came to be known as *Saint-Germain-des-Prés*.

Germanus had a deep interest in the lives of the saints and had a reputation for the gift of healing blindness, paralysis, epilepsy, and demon possession. Significantly, many of the people Germanus helped were prisoners or slaves of various races.

Germanus died in Paris. His relics did not survive the French Revolution.

MAY 29

Richard Thirkeld (d. 1583)

✐Martyred for faith

Richard Thirkeld was a "late bloomer" who was ordained as an old man in 1579. He had studied at Queen's College, Oxford, as well as at Douai and Rheims in France. Four years after his ordination, when he visited a Catholic prisoner, he aroused the suspicion of the authorities. They arrested him for the crime of being a priest. After two months in a prison in York, he was sentenced to death in 1583. His execution on May 29 was not a public event because of concern about a popular outcry. Richard Thirkeld, like so many of the era in England, was hanged, drawn, and quartered. Samuel Pepys describes this astonishingly barbaric form of public execution in his diary in the entry under October 13, 1660.

MAY 30

Joan of Arc (1412–31)

✐Inner voices

Joan of Arc is unique among the saints. The same church that declared her a heretic and burned her at the stake in 1431, canonized her in 1920. Her role in making history has made her the subject of literature and popular entertainment. She has been loved and hated, scrutinized and diagnosed.

Joan of Arc heard voices. These were not the "voices" that schizophrenics hear, but those of the Archangel Michael and a pair of unknown women Joan called saints. These mystical voices told her to assist her native France by restoring the dauphin to his throne and driving the English back across the channel. She received these instructions at a time when the situation looked hopeless for the French, so the dauphin accepted her offer to become the commander of his wavering army. The military tactics she conceived reversed the fortunes of the French army, who broke a siege on Orléans. Wearing a soldier's armor and carrying a banner reading

Jesu et Maria, Joan inspired and led French troops in a series of stunning military victories. In 1429, the dauphin became King Charles VII, and the uneducated peasant's daughter lived as part of the royal entourage.

Her good fortune did not continue. In a later conflict, troops from rebellious Burgundy took Joan hostage and sold her to the English. They kept her in prison for a year during which time an ecclesiastical court interrogated her endlessly, looking for a way to accuse her of witchcraft or heresy. Joan's answers demonstrated her solid faith, morality, and intelligence. The court condemned her to death. Dishonest power overwhelmed simple purity, but Joan had stood up against it, refusing to compromise.

On May 30, 1431, nineteen-year-old Joan was burned at the stake in the market place at Rouen. Her remains were thrown into the Seine River. At her family's request, the court opened Joan's case for retrial less than two decades later and pronounced Joan innocent.

In the preface to his play *Saint Joan*, George Bernard Shaw held that Joan was actually the first Protestant martyr. "She was also one of the first apostles of Nationalism, and the first French practitioner of Napoleonic realism in warfare as distinguished from the sporting ransom gambling chivalry of her time. . . . She refused to accept the specific woman's lot, and dressed and fought and lived as men did." Shaw goes on to observe, "If she had been old enough to know the effect she was producing on the men whom she humiliated by being right when they were wrong, and had learned to flatter and manage them, she might have lived as long as Queen Elizabeth.

MAY 31

James Salomone (1231–1314)

✐ *Sacrificial faith*

Venice, Italy's "The Father of the Poor" had no brothers or sisters and lost his parents early. Reared by his grandmother and taught by a Cistercian monk, James Salomone became a Dominican at Santa Maria Celeste. As he walked toward the monastery to begin his life as a Dominican, he began to hand out his money to poor people he met along the way. His intention was to reserve enough cash to purchase some books, but at the gate, he spotted a man who needed clothes. Turning over the remainder of his money, he entered the monastery with an empty purse. For the next sixty-six years, James Salomone lived an exemplary Christian life. People loved him and flocked to him for spiritual direction and healing. He died of cancer.

JUNE 1

Hannibal Di Francia (1851–1927)
Caring in depth

Hannibal was born in Messina, Italy. His aristocratic father died when Hannibal was less than a year and a half old. A gifted and intelligent child, Hannibal gained a strong sense of ministry for the poor people living in the slum district of his hometown. Working with what he called a "spirit of twofold charity," Hannibal both cared for the poor and evangelized them. As he ministered to orphans in his own community, he began to express concern for orphans worldwide. Not only were they without families, they seemed like sheep without a shepherd.

It became clear to Hannibal that the training of priests must include spiritual formation. Without prayer and spiritual training the seminaries would only turn out "artificial priests." He worked with great energy behind the scenes to improve the method and content of theological education.

In 1908 a powerful earthquake hit Messina and left eighty thousand dead. Hannibal immediately began a steadying ministry to help the community "start again from nothing."

Though Hannibal Di Francia died on June 1, 1927, the ministry he organized for the poor and for professional religious leaders continues on all the earth's continents.

JUNE 2
Marcellinus and Peter (d. 304)
ℐPersecuted faith

Here are two Roman Christians whose faith resulted in their martyrdom early in the fourth century. A priest, Marcellinus, and Peter, a low-ranking "exorcist," were arrested during Diocletian's intense persecution of the Church. Marcellinus went to work in prison, strengthening the faith of other Christians behind bars with him and making new converts, including Arthemius, the jailer, and his family.

Roman authorities took Marcellinus and Peter into a forested area and killed them secretly. They wanted their burial place to remain a secret in order to prevent them from becoming examples of faith and courage to others. As it turned out, Christians still speak their names today. Arthemius, the jailer, helped spread the story of their martyrdom. Constantine built a church at the site of their tomb.

JUNE 3
Juan Grande Roman (1546–1600)
ℐAgape

Caring for the poor and the sick is one of the most common saintly ministries. Juan Roman did this with a special twist. This sixteenth-century Spaniard had no financial resources of his own. In his late teen years he began to beg for alms in order to have funds for the care of the elderly poor. He established a makeshift hospital near San Sebastian Church in Jerez for those sick and in great need, the incurables, and people who hesitated to beg for themselves.

He took the name "John the Sinner," devoting himself exclusively to the service of God. He petitioned the Jerez town council for greater support of its street people during an epidemic. All the while, Juan engaged in a private life of devotion and prayer.

Reports of John of God's work (March 8) in Granada reached Juan in Jerez. In 1574, Juan decided to visit and experience the regimen there for himself. What he gleaned in Granada, along with a version of John of God's Rule, helped him in his personal life and at his hospital.

Juan lived in poverty himself as he cared for the poor. He owned few possessions, slept on a mat, and ate a diet of simple food. His ministry expanded to include sick and wounded soldiers. The prostitutes of Jerez also came to him for care. As knowledge of his work spread, others began to help him in his labors.

The spring of 1600 was particularly deadly in Jerez. The plague was destroying the health of many people. Juan cared for its victims with no concern for himself, ultimately becoming infected. Christ's comment about laying down one's life for others indicating the greatest love became very meaningful for him. He lived only a week after contracting the plague, dying on June 3, 1600, in his own hospital. He was buried with a simple ceremony in the hospital's courtyard.

JUNE 4

Francis Caracciolo (1563–1608)

✍ *Active and contemplative*

Born to a wealthy family in southern Italy, he was given the name Ascanio. Ascanio was related to Thomas Aquinas (January 28) through both his mother and his father. He lived the first twenty-two years of his life in the typical sporting way of the children of nobility. Things changed when he contracted an ugly dermatitis that resembled leprosy. Frightened people ostracized and shunned him. During these difficult days as a social outcast, Ascanio vowed that he would give his life to the service of God if he ever recovered. His "leprosy" may have been shingles. Whatever it was, he completely recovered.

Keeping his vow, Ascanio traveled to Naples to prepare for the priesthood. After working a few years with prisoners and those condemned to death, Ascanio received a letter intended for another person with the same first name. The letter was an invitation to become part of a new order of priests hoping to combine active and contemplative styles of life. This appealed to him, and he responded positively to the writer of the letter, Giovanni Agostino Adorno of Genoa. The two of them made a forty-day retreat, after which they prepared a set of rules for the new order. In 1588, they formally began the order of the Minor Clerks Regular and Ascanio took the name of Francis.

Adorno did not live beyond forty years. Francis took his place, but would not permit others to treat him as a superior. He continued to work in the kitchen and performed all the usual housekeeping chores. His behavior became an example of selflessness. One of the rules he had prepared for the order was that no one should ever seek office. Holding office was difficult for him. Francis struggled to cope with internal politics and fend off malicious rumors. In 1607, he asked to be relieved of all administrative responsibility in order to consecrate himself to prayer. He died a year later and the age of forty-four.

JUNE 5

Boniface (ca. 680–754)

❧ Christian outreach

An Anglo-Saxon, Boniface had a strong desire to minister to "those who are of one blood and bone" with him and convert pagan Saxons to Christianity. The Rhineland and Bavaria were already Christian regions, but central Germany had bred some colorful popular religions, and Boniface encountered serious challenges to his missionary activity.

A remarkable "contest" occurred in 723 when Boniface demonstrated his opposition to the worship of trees and other traditions associated with the old Norse gods. He cut down an oak tree dedicated to the god Thor. In the manner of Elijah taking on the prophets of Baal on Mount Carmel, Boniface chopped down the tree in full public view. The crowd held its collective breath, waiting for fire to come down from heaven and consume the sacrilegious visitor from England. But nothing happened, except that Boniface used the wood of the tree to construct a chapel on the very spot where it had stood. Many conversions to Christianity resulted.

In his seventy-ninth year, some who were hostile to Christianity attacked and killed Boniface. The monastery at Fulda has the book he was reading when the attacking tribesmen broke into his tent. It bears the marks of sword cuts, and has blood-like stains on its pages.

JUNE 6

Marcellin Joseph Benoit Champagnat
(1789–1840)

Gaining and sharing education

Being born into a family of devout Christians is a special blessing that sometimes does not bear fruit until long after adolescent declarations of independence and the follies of early adult life. But Marcellin Champagnat skipped sowing wild oats, experiencing a call to Christian ministry at the age of fourteen. A traveling priest encountered the young man in his hometown of Marlhes, France. Impressed with the boy's potential, the priest instilled in Marcellin a desire for formal education and preparation for the priesthood.

After attending a seminary in Verrieres, where his lack of an educational background made progress difficult, Marcellin blossomed into a role of enthusiastic leadership at the seminary of Lyons. He fulfilled his goal of ordination in 1816 at the age of twenty-seven. While conducting a parish ministry, he organized the Little Brothers of Mary, whose specific assignment was the education of rural young people. He defined the Brothers' mission in simple terms. "Make Jesus Christ known and loved."

He opened and then enlarged schools. Experienced church leaders wondered about the judgment of this new and inexperienced priest.

Without serious financial backing and organizational support, his ideas seemed idealistic and destined for the trash heap. Still, neighboring French villages kept asking Marcellin to send his Brothers to them in order to teach their children. By 1825, the Little Brothers of Mary occupied all of his time and attention. He taught his helpers to love and respect children, and to maintain a special concern for the poor, the ungrateful, and the neglected.

Exhausted and sick, Marcellin died at the age of fifty-one.

JUNE 7

Anne of St. Bartholomew (1549–1626)

Serving

Teresa of Avila (October 15) often mentions Anne of St. Bartholomew in her writings. From 1575 to 1582 they were close friends and confidants. Their acquaintance resulted from the fact that Anne grew up near Avila. Both of Anne's parents died when she was ten. Her brothers took care of her until her twentieth birthday. From tending sheep, she went on to enter the Carmelite convent of St. Joseph at Avila in 1570, and became the first lay sister of the newly reformed order. Teresa urged her to become a nun, but she declined because of her lack of an education. Teresa died in Anne's arms. Anne wrote: "The day she died she could not speak. I changed all her linen, headdress, and sleeves. She looked at herself quite satisfied to see herself so clean. Then, turning her eyes on me, she looked at me smilingly, and showed her gratitude by signs."

Anne remained at Avila for six more years. In order to establish a new house for Carmelites in Paris, Anne became one of six women who made the adventurous trip. Once in Paris, in a very natural act, she slipped out of the room when the Princess de Longueville greeted them, and went into the kitchen to prepare food.

JUNE 8
William of York (d. 1154)
Inner strength

After William Fitzherbert served as York Minster's treasurer, King Stephen nominated him archbishop of York in 1140. He had a reputation for being kind, likeable, and gentle, though a minority who supported a rival candidate for the position accused him of using religion for gaining wealth, fooling around with women, and meddling in political affairs. The issue concerning William of York became a fiasco that resulted in tensions between England and Rome, sparked vituperative correspondence, and took a long time to resolve, ultimately with William's deposition.

William sought privacy in Winchester, where he lived six years as a monk until 1153. When his opponents died, he returned to York to serve as bishop. It was not long before he also died; some say he was the victim of poisoning. They buried him in the cathedral, considering him both a victim of injustice and a saint. There is no doubt that William was unwittingly involved in a power struggle for the English throne. It is to his credit that he never expressed any resentment toward his adversaries.

JUNE 9
Columba of Iona (ca. 521–97)
Books and souls

A wandering Scot-Irish monk who started life as the child of a royal family, Columba was a church leader with an unfortunately short temper. A large man with a loud voice, Columba was a striking person who combined his powerful physique with the soul of a poet. He devoted fifteen years of his life to preaching and founding monasteries. An avid scholar, he had a passion for collecting manuscripts.

Columba copied a rare psalter by Jerome (September 30) that a fellow monk, Finnian, had brought back from Rome. When Finnian discovered this, he accused Columba of taking advantage of his generosity and claimed the copy as his own property. The dispute went to King Diarmaid of Ireland, who agreed with Finnian. The judgment handed down by the king is famous: "To every cow her calf, and to every book its son-book."

By nature, Columba did not accept the ruling quietly, and his relationship with King Diarmaid grew poorer with each passing experience. Diarmaid sent soldiers looking for a man, accused of killing one of the king's men during a hurling match, who had now run to Columba for protective asylum. Bursting into Columba's sanctuary, they grabbed the accused man and killed him immediately without trial. Fighting then broke out between Columba's clan and supporters of Diarmaid. Three thousand died in bloody hand-to-hand combat. Whether or not Columba encouraged this combat is an issue that has never been settled, but he accepted responsibility for the bloodshed, saying, "Men lie dead through the pride of a man of peace. I will not rest until I win for God the souls of as many men as have fallen in this battle."

In 593, Columba and twelve monks who were his relatives climbed into a flimsy boat and set out to sea. Unsure of their destination, they landed on the barren island of Iona off the coast of Scotland. Columba founded a monastery on Iona that would become the virtual center of Celtic spirituality. Faithful to his oath, Columba made many missionary journeys across the sea to Scotland, evangelizing many, including King Brude of Inverness.

Columba remained on Iona for more than thirty years, copying manuscripts (some of which are the earliest existing examples of Irish handwriting) and working diligently for his Lord. Life on the island mellowed him and replaced his fiery temper with a calm and gentle spirit.

JUNE 10

Margaret of Scotland (1046–93)

Devout living

Educated in Hungary, Margaret actually grew up in the court of Edward the Confessor (October 13). Her grandfather was King Edmund Ironside of England and her mother was a Hungarian princess. Being one of the last members of the Anglo-Saxon royal family, she was in danger when the Normans invaded England. Margaret attempted to return to Hungary, but became shipwrecked off the Scottish coast. With royalty in her blood, she married King Malcolm III of Scotland in 1070. The first of their eight children became King David I (see May 24), recognized as one of the greatest Scottish kings.

Margaret was devout, loving, and just. Prayer, reading, and needlework for church paraments filled her private hours. She founded the great Benedictine abbey of Dunfermline as a place for the burial of Scottish royalty. Biographers report that Margaret had a positive influence on her husband. The king could not read, but he respected her books and had ornate covers put on them. He recognized that Christ lived in her, and her preferences and moral decisions became his own.

Life was not easy for Margaret, Queen of Scotland. Worn out, she died at the early age of forty-seven.

JUNE 11

Barnabas (first century)

Encouragement

Barnabas is one of those people most of us would enjoy meeting. Though his actual name was Joseph, his revealing Christian nickname, "Barnabas," means "Son of Encouragement." We first hear of him in The Acts of the Apostles when he sold his farm and donated the proceeds to the church, "laying it at the apostles' feet." Barnabas had the courage and understanding to introduce the converted adversary and former threat to the Church, Paul, (June 29) to the Christian community. They still feared Paul as a persecutor, but Barnabas helped establish trust for him. Barnabas became Paul's traveling companion and fellow communicator of the gospel, and the two did effective work together. They established a thriving church in Antioch, the first place where followers of Jesus were called "Christians." This congregation sent Barnabas and Paul abroad on a missionary journey into the northeastern Mediterranean area. Again, the duo met with encouraging responses.

Paul and Barnabas intended to continue their mission, but before they departed, they had a disagreement regarding taking along a young man named John Mark, a cousin of Barnabas. Part of the way through a previous journey John Mark had dropped out of the team. Barnabas let Paul go on with Silas, and took John Mark with him to another destination. The last we hear of Barnabas was when he "sailed away to Cyprus" with his cousin.

JUNE 12

John of Sahagun (1419–79)

❧Speaking out

John began life in the Spanish town of Sahagun. After receiving an education at the Benedictine monastery there, John became a priest. For a while, he served a number of area congregations simultaneously, but then decided to attend the University of Salamanca for four years.

Completing his studies, John began a nine-year pastorate with the parish of St. Sebastian, Salamanca, a city notorious for immoral behavior and crime. John accepted the challenge and gained a reputation as a preacher and spiritual director. On several occasions, John's public pronouncements regarding moral choices resulted in opposition. An impressive document describes an incident that followed a sermon in which he criticized property owners who took advantage of tenants. The infuriated duke of Alba sent two assassins to kill John. When the assassins met their victim, they were unable to follow their instructions. Filled with remorse, they asked his forgiveness.

Gallstones that required surgery interrupted John's ministry for nearly a year. During this time of sickness and convalescence, John joined some Augustinian Friars, and continued to preach in public. He commented, "God alone knows what has passed between God and my soul." In 1479, he correctly sensed that his life was near its end.

JUNE 13

Anthony of Padua (1195–1231)

✑ *Making a difference*

Many saints have performed their most astonishing miracles from beyond the grave. The fascination with relics and shrines is kept alive by the remarkable things that take place among common people. Anthony's popularity as a saint owes much to miracles that many attribute to him. For centuries, people have called on St. Anthony to help them find something lost. The story of a returned personal psalter in answer to Anthony's prayer may have resulted in his status as the patron saint of lost things.

Anthony was a Franciscan friar and priest who knew Francis of Assisi (October 4). Born in Portugal, Anthony studied in France and moved on to northern Italy. His early assignment was simply to take care of a small hospice for lay brothers at Monte Paolo. Anthony served in obscurity with no one suspecting the latent talent filling him to the brim.

Recognition came to Anthony the way orchestra conducting came to an assistant named Leonard Bernstein—he was asked to pinch hit at the last moment. He attended an ordination ceremony of both Dominicans and Franciscans. Each Order expected the other to provide the speaker. When they turned to Anthony, he protested that he was a dishwasher and janitor. Pressed, he agreed to preach an extemporaneous sermon before a gathering that included the bishop and Dominicans who specialized in excellent preaching.

His unprepared sermon began hesitantly, but he soon found his rhythm. He delivered an astonishing and superb Christian message. An early biography states, "He poured forth brilliant and burning words, a flood of divine eloquence." The remarkable depth and understanding of his sermon was clothed in a speaking style that riveted attention. As a result, Francis wrote a letter authorizing him to preach and teach. "I am well pleased that you should read sacred theology to the friars, provided that such study does not quench the spirit of holy prayer and devotion according to our Rule."

Anthony began a preaching mission that took him to most Italian communities. He spoke outdoors, without notes, in the manner of modern day revivalists. The results were life-changing for many. The sound of his voice turned people away from destructive behavior such as gambling and drinking. Criminals reformed and did not return to jail in a repetitive cycle. Enemies kissed and made up. Legislators passed laws against usury. He worked significant wonders among people that go far beyond the legendary material about him.

His preaching took him back to France with similar positive results. Wearing himself out, he died on June 13, 1231, at only thirty-six years of age. His spirit was in harmony with the spirit of Francis. Both loved nature and felt their kinship with it. Both loved Jesus Christ to the highest imaginable degree.

Modern scientists scrutinized Anthony's remains in 1981, confirming the facts that he died at an early age, had a meager diet, worked hard, and possessed a long, thin face with deep-set eyes.

JUNE 14

Methodius of Constantinople (d. 847)

❧ Cherishing art

Iconoclasm, a passionate attempt to remove human images from churches, was active in parts of Europe in the eighth and ninth centuries. Both Judaism and Islam had rules against the artistic representation of people and animals. The plain "cracker box" architecture of early Protestant churches in America played upon

Old Testament law and illustrates an anxiety about statues and paintings fostering superstitious practices.

Methodius of Constantinople became caught up in the ninth-century iconoclasm of the Eastern Church that was led by the emperor Leo V the Armenian. Methodius thought that religious statues and paintings assisted devotion. He believed a picture could help illiterate Christians to understand and visualize religious ideas and events. Much religious art was already part of the inheritance of the Church from previous generations. Consequently, Methodius took a firm stand against the destructive movement. The emperor threw him in jail, where he remained for seven years.

Living conditions during his imprisonment were distressing. The authorities did not place Methodius in a stone dungeon or an iron-barred cage, but rather in a cave-like tomb. They locked two thieves in with him, and one of them died. The decaying corpse was never removed, but left beside the living.

About 828, the authorities thought it was time to release Methodius. Gaunt, pale, bald, and dressed in filthy rags, he came blinking into the sunlight. With gratitude to God for his survival and freedom, he demonstrated that his spirit was not broken. When the new emperor Theophilus continued the purging of religious art, Methodius confronted him with a sharp question. "If an image is so worthless in your sight, why do you condemn the images of Christ but not the veneration given to representations of yourself?"

Theophilus condemned Methodius to a flogging and put him back in prison, this time with a broken jaw. With the help of friends, he escaped jail the first night. The emperor died soon after and iconoclasm became a thing of the past. Within a month, churches in Constantinople had their icons back. The new empress Theodora designated Methodius patriarch of Constantinople, his broken jaw still bandaged, in 842. The immigrant from Sicily had made his mark. Five years later, Methodius died.

JUNE 15

Germaine Cousin (1579–1601)

✒ *Quiet spirituality*

Germaine's life was "of few days and full of trouble." She tended sheep outside the small village of Pibrac, near Toulouse, France. Her mother died giving birth to her, and her father never got over the loss of his wife. Both he and his second wife rejected the child, giving her scant attention and feeding her leftovers and table scraps. Germaine had a swelling in her neck and a paralyzed right arm, possibly the symptoms of tuberculosis, but in that day, the diagnosis was scrofula. She had to sleep under the stairs or out in the stable, and she was never accepted as part of the family.

Germane accepted all of this without complaint. She returned love for hate, smiles for mistreatment. She particularly liked taking care of the sheep because it gave her time alone with God. Her prayer life developed an intensity and depth on the fields under open sky. Here she experienced the nearness of God.

Many days, when the church bells announced Mass, Germaine would push her shepherd's crook into the earth and run to church. She left her sheep in God's hands, and no harm ever came to them. Neighbors began to recognize her spirituality and devotion, but at home, it made no difference. Her stepmother sharply upbraided her for sharing her table scraps with beggars in the streets.

Minor miracles now become a part of Germaine's story. On a cold winter day, her stepmother caught her holding up her apron. Confident that she was taking a missing loaf of bread to the poor, she insisted that Germaine let go of it. Instead of bread, summer flowers tumbled to the ground. Her family gradually began to recognize Germaine's special qualities, but even as they softened their approach to her, she continued to perform her daily chores and sleep under the stairs. They found her there one morning, dead at the age of twenty-two. Her grave at Pibrac became a popular destination for pilgrims.

JUNE 16

Tychon of Amathus (d. ca. 450)

❧ *Laboring in the vineyard*

Limassol, on the island of Cyprus, was known as Amathus in the fifth century. Vine growers in southern Cyprus remember Tychon of Amathus annually.

Tychon was poor. Though he owned the land for a small vineyard, he lacked the capital to purchase grapevines. The story behind his festival relates that he picked up a discarded branch pruned in a neighboring vineyard and rooted it. As he waited for cuttings to sprout, he prayed that God would grant him four favors: that sap would flow in the cutting, that it should be fertile and productive, that its fruit would be sweet, and that it might ripen early. In the years that followed, Tychon's vineyard produced excellent grapes that ripened ahead of the normal harvest.

The annual celebration of St. Tychon's day on June 16, with its blessing of the grapevines, comes well ahead of the normal ripening season on Cyprus. Prayers accompany the squeezing of juice into an ornate chalice from a bunch of immature grapes. Some have questioned the historical existence of Tychon, but most accept that he actually lived in Amathus, where he became a bishop.

JUNE 17

Hypatius of Chalcedon (d. ca. 450)

❧ *Taking a stand*

A number of heresies troubled the early Christian Church. Nestorianism taught that the human and divine natures of Jesus Christ were separate rather than mingled together. Hypatius fiercely opposed Nestorius and his ideas. In fact, he challenged a number of other evils that were creeping into religious life in the fifth century.

People avoided an abandoned monastery near Chalcedon because it had a reputation for being haunted. Hypatius discovered it while looking for a retreat site. Ghosts did not frighten him, and he began a Christian community there. One of his monks Callinicus wrote the biography of Hypatius. Unfortunately, Callinicus had a taste for spooky things, causing objective scholars to question the authenticity of his narrative.

The basic story Callinicus tells is that Hypatius was born in Phrygia. His father, a respected scholar, had high standards of learning and beat Hypatius when he did poorly in his studies. At eighteen, Hypatius ran away to Thrace and became a shepherd. One day when he was singing out on a meadow, a priest heard his pleasant voice and taught him how to chant psalms. Subsequently, Hypatius befriended a retired soldier named Jonas. The two of them became Christian hermits. It was while Hypatius was on one of these lonely retreats of prayer and self-denial that his father found him. All was forgiven and father and son were reconciled. Leaving Jonas in Constantinople, Hypatius returned home and founded his monastery in the deserted "haunted" structure near Chalcedon. From this location, he worked hard to support orthodoxy and to refute Nestorius.

JUNE 18

Amandus of Bordeaux (d. ca. 431)

Fulfilling one's purpose

Amandus grew up in a Christian home and possessed a thorough familiarity with sacred Scripture. The mistakes that trap so many adolescents did not scar his early life. Recognizing his special qualities, Bishop Delphinus of Bordeaux ordained Amandus and put him to work in his own church. When Delphinus died, Amandus became bishop. Eventually, his health and vigor began to fail. Amandus urged the people to elect a younger man to replace him. Severinus accepted the responsibilities of the position, but did not live long, and Amandus had to resume his labor as bishop of Bordeaux.

Interestingly, this information is preserved in the fifth-century correspondence of a Spaniard, Paulinus, who was converted and instructed by Amandus. The two became friends for life.

JUNE 19

Romuald (ca. 951–1027)

✐*Practicing piety*

Romuald was exposed to violence as a child. He saw his father kill a relative in an angry dispute over property. Horrified, he ran to a nearby monastery and began a life of penance and prayer. He disturbed the other monks by his extreme practice of piety, and they asked him to leave. Romuald became convinced of the need for revitalizing monastic life. For the next thirty years, he traveled around Italy, promoting monastic life and setting up hermitages.

Illness prevented a planned mission to Hungary on several occasions. Romuald returned to his struggle with lax monks and the need for monastic reform. His efforts were not entirely welcomed, and the disturbed religious people made false accusations against him. He quietly accepted punishment for a crime he did not commit. When a prince gave Romuald a fine horse, he exchanged it for a donkey, saying he would feel closer to Christ on such a mount.

One of Romuald's disciples was Peter Damian (February 21). Together, they gave a fresh start to the monastery at Fonte Avellana and founded another one at Camaldoli in 1012. Here, Romuald put strict practice of the Benedictine Rule into effect. Silence pervaded the atmosphere and fasts were severe. Some described Romuald as harsh. When he died in his cell in 1027, he was alone.

JUNE 20

Alban (third or fourth century)

✐*Caring and sheltering*

The Venerable Bede (May 25) wrote an important history of the English church. In it, he tells the story of Alban, a prominent citizen who lived under the Roman occupation in the third century. Alban was not a Christian when he gave shelter to a priest fleeing for his life during a time of persecution. Impressed by the demeanor and behavior of his guest, Alban asked the priest to instruct and baptize him. He then decided to help the priest escape by exchanging clothes with him. The Roman soldiers arrested Alban and took him before a judge. When the judge discovered Alban was not a priest even though he was dressed like one, he became angry. "You have concealed a sacrilegious rebel rather than turn him over to my soldiers. I shall have you punished with his tortures." Alban acknowledged that he had become a Christian and accepted the sentence. He was flogged and beheaded in public, a common practice in Roman Britain.

JUNE 21

Osanna of Mantua (1449–1505)

Spiritual insight

Osanna had a mystical experience when she was five years old. While walking beside a river, she felt herself swept up into heaven, and a voice told her "life and death consist in loving God." This ecstatic experience influenced the rest of her life. It was the first of many. Some of her visions included traditional religious imagery, sometimes seeing Christ as a crucified child. Other mystic moments were sublime and beyond description. She attempted to keep these experiences a secret, but they would occur at unpredictable and awkward times.

Osanna (Hosanna) was born to wealthy parents in Mantua, Italy. Like most parents, they prayed that she would find a suitable husband. They were dismayed when she announced that she would rather join the Dominicans than marry. Because of her steadfast determination, they eventually agreed.

Continuing to live at home with her large family, Osanna acquired a reputation for holiness. She would spend hours in her room, praying silently, and was often at church. One of her relatives was the duke of Mantua. He began to turn to her for spiritual direction, and then for guidance in political matters. Her prayer life laid a foundation for an active ministry to the sick, the poor, and the afflicted. With her political connections, Osanna found ways to help many victims of injustice. Her life, given to serving others, corroborates her spiritual vision.

Thomas More (1478–1535)
❧*Sacred intelligence*

Utopia is a common word in most vocabularies, but few are familiar with Thomas More's book published in 1516. An English translation of that famous title would be: *Nowhere*. More's Latin text combines religious discussion with social teaching, political commentary, jokes, puns, and literary contrivances that make it an extraordinary work. Thomas More pretends to recount a tale he heard about a happy island in the New World where people did not have the many problems of life together that plagued Europe. The familiar struggle for power and money did not exist in Utopia. Instead of using gold for currency, the Utopians made useful things with it, such as chamber pots. They had only a few simple laws and needed no lawyers. Religious tolerance accepted any creed other than atheism and the denial of human immortality. A sentence from five centuries ago seems contemporary: "No prayers are used except those anyone may speak boldly without offending any sect."

Thomas More grew up in a prominent judge's home. At fifteen, Thomas attended Oxford and became engrossed in classical literature. His father pulled him out because he did not want his son to become a poorly paid scholar. He put him in London's law school instead.

In 1499, at the age of twenty-one, More met Erasmus, and they became close friends. Both enjoyed a fine sense of humor and a disdain for scholasticism. More said that such studies were about as valuable as milking a he-goat into a sieve. Both More and Erasmus loved the Church and wanted to see it reformed without upheaval. They did not want to see it split apart by hasty reasoning and futile disputes.

More considered becoming a priest, but did not. For quite some time he wore a horsehair shirt next to his skin that was coarse enough to cause blood to show through his outer garments.

Erasmus wrote the most reliable character profile of Thomas More. He reports that More was careless in dress and formality, that he was abstemious in food and drink, that he was cheerful with quick humor and a ready smile, inclined to jokes and pranks, and that his home was a place of laughter. "All the birds in Chelsea came to him to be fed." More was twice a faithful husband, a loving father to his children, an excellent public speaker, and exceptionally generous to others. Erasmus asks, "What did Nature ever create milder, sweeter, and happier than the genius of Thomas More?"

Thomas More was active in Parliament, eventually appointed to the council of Henry VIII. In 1529, he became Lord Chancellor of England. The authorities burned Protestants at the stake during these years, and More did not see any inconsistency between his part in this and his ideas of religious tolerance in *Utopia*. He vigorously opposed William Tyndale and his translation of the Bible into English. But when the king appointed himself "Protector and Supreme Head of the Church," Thomas More considered Henry VIII the most dangerous heretic of them all, and More's ethical and political position regarding the annulment of the king's marriage to Catherine of Aragon resulted in his being sent as a prisoner to the infamous Tower of London. He remained there among vermin for fifteen months, cold, hungry, and pressured by his family to change his mind.

Unjustly convicted of treason, Thomas More went to the scaffold in 1535. He bubbled with humor even then. The construction of the platform was rickety, and More said to an attendant, "I pray you, Mr. Lieutenant, see me safe up, and for my coming down let me shift for myself." He then hugged the executioner, who had asked for forgiveness. After asking the spectators to pray for the Church and for the king, he recited Psalm 51 and placed his head upon the block. He moved his long gray beard out from under his chin. "It is a pity to cut anything that has not committed treason." He was fifty-seven years old.

JUNE 23

Mary of Oignies (d. 1213)

❧ *Virtuous living*

Mary lived the simplicity and austerity of a Franciscan before there were any Franciscans. She grew up in Belgium, the daughter of wealthy parents. They forced her into marriage to the son of another wealthy family when she was only fourteen. She convinced her husband to respect her virginity and persuaded him to let their home become a hospital for lepers.

Mary's biography comes to us from Cardinal James de Vitry, who was her confessor and disciple. He speaks highly of her virtuous life, but cautions readers that her spiritual life was bizarre. She had what used to be called "the gift of tears," weeping uncontrollably when meditating. "Her steps might be traced in the church . . . by her tears on the pavement." References to the crucifixion of Christ would often cause her to faint.

Many came to visit Mary. In the final five years of her life, she sought solitude at the monastery at Oignies, where she filled her days and nights with prayer. She died at the age of thirty-eight in 1213.

JUNE 24

Bartholomew of Farne (d. ca. 1193)

Prayer and work

A simple hermit living on the Farne islands off the Northumbrian coast, Bartholomew began life with the Scandinavian name Tostig. Because his twelfth-century playmates made fun of his odd name, he began to call himself William. Searching for his ancestral roots, he traveled to Norway for an education and became a priest.

Returning to England, he went to Durham to become a monk and received yet another name, Bartholomew. He then went to the Inner Farne Island, planning to occupy an ancient cell. Unfortunately, another hermit already called the cell home and resented Bartholomew's arrival. The lack of welcome was palpable, and eventually the other hermit left the island. Later, as the island became "crowded," Bartholomew himself departed occasionally in disgust because of tangles with other personalities. Bartholomew insisted on wearing clothes made of ram skins that he never permitted anyone to wash until they became stiff with dirt and sweat. His motto: "The dirtier the body, the cleaner the soul." The other monks at Durham commented wryly, "Bartholomew makes the island fragrant with his virtues." He remained in the Farne Islands for forty-two years, cheerfully enjoying fishing, keeping a pet bird, and receiving guests, but mostly engaging in prayer and manual labor.

JUNE 25

Prosper of Aquitaine (ca. 390–456)

✐ *Literary conversation*

We know more about Prosper's ideas than his life. His correspondence with Augustine (August 28) led to significant treatises from both saints. Augustine published his understanding that most of us will be damned because grace through Jesus Christ is required for salvation. Prosper read Augustine's *Concerning Predestination* and wrote a response he called *De vocatione omnium gentium,* insisting that Scripture teaches that God's grace is a gift and that God's mercy extends to everyone. Prosper also became involved in other religious disputes, usually taking a more moderate approach in his search for answers.

The writings of Prosper also include poetry. *De ingratis* (*About those Without Grace*) is a lengthy poem dealing with the problem of God's grace and human free will. In the pages of his well-known *Chronicle* he reviews the history of the world and theological controversies from the beginning of creation to the overrunning of Rome by Vandals in 455.

Prosper's death took place while he was working in Rome.

JUNE 26

Josemaria Escrivá de Balaguer (1902–75)
✒️Sacred secularity

Josemaria was a master of Christian living who reached heights of contemplation with continuous prayer. Born in Spain, he became a priest in 1925 and began serving a rural parish. Two years later, he moved to Madrid and studied for a doctorate in civil law. In Madrid, he met people from many occupations and conceived a mission to help bring spiritual depth to ordinary secular work. People, he claimed, could follow Christ and find holiness in daily life. God's Work (*Opus Dei*) began in 1928 during a personal retreat. The effort began to spread across Spain under his direction. Josemaria believed that every aspect of life could be an offering to God. If a person cultivated a deep devotional life, then that individual could discover sanctity in secular work. With enough prayer, everything can "lead us to God, feeding our constant contact with Him, from morning till night. Every kind of work can become prayer."

With a desire to give his idea worldwide opportunities, Josemaria Escrivá began working from Rome in 1946. Suffering diabetes, struggling to find financial backing, and facing the many difficulties of organizing the expansion of *Opus Dei*, he maintained a cheerful attitude, saying, "True virtue is not sad or disagreeable, but pleasantly cheerful."

After fifty years of priesthood, Josemaria prayed, "I am still like a faltering child. I am just beginning, beginning again, as I do each day in my interior life. And it will be so to the end of my days: always beginning again." He died of cardiac arrest on June 26, 1975. The man who insisted that the earth is a pathway to heaven was gone, but he left an organization that continued to grow and to transfigure common life.

JUNE 27

Cyril of Alexandria (ca. 376–444)

✒️*Diplomatic correction*

The nephew of the Bishop of Alexandria, Egypt, filled his uncle's position in 412. At the time, Alexandria was a center of vitally alive Christian activity and growth. Cyril had strong opinions and became a controversial theologian who made impulsive decisions, violently defending what he considered right thinking. If a congregation seemed less than supportive, he closed it. He drove Jews out of Alexandria and confiscated their property. He quarreled with civil authorities and antagonized local religious people. He fought lingering paganism in Egypt in bloody contests. We can learn from this saint that even those with flaws and weaknesses may live a life of holiness. God can change human personality. Cyril is an answer to the question that Nicodemus asked Jesus: We *can* be born again.

With time, Cyril controlled his hair-trigger temper and took a position of leadership in defeating Nestorianism. The heresy's leader, Nestorius, became archbishop of Constantinople in 428. He taught that Christ combined two natures, human and divine, but that there was no union of the two. Jesus' human body was merely the temple of the divine spirit. Mary gave birth to Jesus, but not to the eternally existing Word mentioned in the opening of the Gospel of John. She was Christ-bearing rather than God-bearing. Cyril of Alexandria disagreed, saying that Nestorianism made mockery of the Incarnation and destroyed the doctrine of redemption. His argument was sent to Rome where Nestorius was condemned. This ultimately led to a division with the new Nestorian Church. The issue is still a matter of debate. Was Cyril of Alexandria defending essential Christian doctrine? Would diplomacy and patience have prevented the schism?

JUNE 28

Irenaeus (ca. 130– ca. 200)

✒ *Clear thinking*

Irenaeus is one of the most important thinkers in the early Christian Church. He was our first systematic theologian. We know little about his personal life other than that he was Greek. It is certain that the youthful Irenaeus met Polycarp (February 23). He wrote that he could point to the very spot where Polycarp sat when he taught. Irenaeus had heard "the accounts Polycarp gave of his conversation with John and with another who had seen the Lord."

Irenaeus moved on to the Roman outpost of Lyons in Gaul and then visited Rome. While he was in Rome, the church in Lyons suffered vicious persecution under emperor Marcus Aurelius, and the bishop there, Pothinus, became a martyr. Upon his return to Lyons, Irenaeus became bishop to fill the vacant position.

Gnosticism was another of the heresies that threatened the early church. The five books Irenaeus wrote refuting the Gnostics provide our best insight into his mind. Gnosticism was an eclectic faith, combining gleanings from Greek philosophy, mythology, and pagan rites overlaid with a veneer of Christianity. The Gnostics believed that the only ones saved are those with secret religious knowledge. Only freedom from the physical world allows us to enter into the spiritual realm. Their occultism and pride were the secret to their popularity. When people become Gnostic, Irenaeus wrote, they become "puffed up with conceit and self-importance . . . with the majestic air of a cock, they go strutting about—as if they have already embraced their angel."

To oppose the Gnostics, Irenaeus produced the concept of apostolic succession. This traced true Christian doctrine back to the original apostles. It was important to have an authoritative check against new religious ideas, he claimed. There was nothing inherently evil about God's creation. Human sin is the source of its corruption, he said, not as the Gnostics claimed, evil in itself. Following the publication of Irenaeus's books, Gnosticism lost its appeal and was no longer a challenge to Christianity.

Irenaeus remained a gentle person who honestly cared for the spiritual well-being of his opponents..

JUNE 29
Peter and Paul (first century)
✌*Leadership*

Peter was the first apostle to respond to the call of Jesus Christ. At the time, his name was Simon, and he was a commercial fisherman. The record states simply that Simon "left everything and followed him." Our Lord named him *Petros,* "Rock." Like other working people of his day, Peter lacked formal education.

Peter was uninhibited, impulsive, and demonstrative. He often spoke and acted before he thought. It was Peter who jumped into the Sea of Galilee that stormy night when Jesus came toward the boat he was in, walking on water. Only Peter spoke to Jesus during the Transfiguration of our Lord, offering to build booths for holy dignitaries. The Gospel excuses him by noting, "He did not know what to say." After the Resurrection, while in a boat Peter recognized Jesus walking on the shore of the Sea of Galilee, tore off his clothes, and swam ashore to be with the risen Lord.

A personality like Peter's, guided more by feeling than by thought, is capable of both great ecstatic heights and great depths of despair—mood swings. When Jesus told the apostles that he would go to Jerusalem and "suffer many things," Peter was quick to blurt out, "God forbid, Lord! This shall never happen to you." Jesus rebuked him with the famous words, "Get behind me, Satan. You are a hindrance to me. You are not on the side of God, but of men." What a downfall!

When Jesus washed the feet of his disciples, Peter protested, "You shall never wash my feet!" Jesus replied, "If I do not wash you, you have no part in me." Peter quickly went to the opposite extreme, "Lord, not only my feet but also my hands and my head." It was like Peter to be downcast one moment and enthusiastic the next, only to become depressed again. His bitter tears when the rooster crowed the morning of Jesus' arrest gives us one of the most touching moments in all of Scripture.

One thing emerges from the Gospel accounts of Simon Peter. He represented all of the disciples as their leader. He was one of three who were with Jesus at the profoundest spiritual moments. He certainly became important in the early days of the Christian Church. Significant changes happened to Peter after the resurrection of Christ. He developed strength and stability. His sermon on the day of Pentecost pulled Christianity into a new and powerful dynamic. Bold courage replaced his hiding in the shadows and denying his Lord. Peter played a vital part in fostering the growth of Christianity from an obscure Jewish sect into a worldwide religion. When he baptized Cornelius, he set a precedent that Gentiles could become Christians, and he persuaded a church council to open doors for the welcome of non-Jews. "God shows no partiality," he said.

There are no additional reports about Peter after that council meeting. There is a suggestion in a letter by Clement of Rome that he was in Rome at the end of his life and "suffered many outrages."

Irenaeus (June 28) calls the Church at Rome "the greatest and most ancient Church, founded by the two glorious apostles, Peter and Paul." Irenaeus had been a student of Polycarp (February 23) who knew John (December 27). This story passed along by word of mouth from the earliest days of the Church.

Peter and Paul are often mentioned in the same breath, and both are assigned to this day. The conversion of Paul is celebrated on January 25, where you may read more about his contributions to the Church. The two great Christians were quite different. Paul was a highly educated intellectual, a Jewish Roman citizen who was outside the group that knew Jesus. Paul never held any authority in the Jerusalem Church, but he had a leading role in the development of Christian theology. The writers and councils that defined Christian doctrine turned to Paul's writing for guidance.

A bronze medal from the first half of the second century provides a rare example of how Peter and Paul looked. The relief portraits are probably based on actual memory and have been models for later artists. The bronze representation of Peter shows a muscular, thickset man with a curly beard. Paul is thin and bald with a long head and a small beard. His eyes are set deeply in his face.

The death and burial of these two inspired church leaders remains a matter of tradition, intense study, and debate. It is likely that both were martyred for their faith.

JUNE 30

First Roman Martyrs (first century)

✇*Sharing Christ's suffering*

After Christ's resurrection, Christianity rapidly spread throughout the Roman Empire. It only took a few decades for the church to take root in the capital city. At first, the Romans could not distinguish between Christians and Jews. They tolerated Christians as another sect of Judaism, which seemed beyond comprehension to the Roman mind. Tacitus, the Roman historian, wrote, "Among the Jews all things are profane that we hold sacred; on the other hand they regard as permissible what seems to us immoral."

Nero began serious persecution of Christians in Rome after the great fire in 64, and accused them of arson. Vivid descriptions by Tacitus record the humiliation and agonizing deaths of those first Roman martyrs. Because Peter and Paul were among the many anonymous victims, this day commemorates the others who also died. Tacitus comments, "Despite their guilt as Christians and the ruthless punishment they deserved, the victims were pitied. For it was felt that they were being sacrificed to one man's brutality rather than to the national interest."

JULY 1

Oliver Plunket (1629–81)

✇*Brave faith*

Irish judges refused to hear the case against Oliver Plunket, a priest who was ordained in Rome in 1654. Oliver had been a professor of theology and was archbishop of Armagh, Ireland. Opponents brought absurd charges against Plunket during an Irish politico-religious upheaval. The authorities arrested him and took him to London for a more objective trial.

He summarized the accusations against him in a letter from jail: *My accusers swore that I had seventy thousand men in Ireland to promote the Catholic cause, that I had the harbor of Carlingford ready to bring in the French, and that I levied monies upon the clergy in Ireland for their maintenance—such romances as would not be believed by any jury in Ireland.* Because there was no evidence against him, the court in London dismissed his case. A hastily arranged second trial found him guilty of "propagating the Catholic religion."

Oliver Plunket had no fear of death and wanted to be an encouraging example for others. *Christ by his fears and passion merited for me to be without fear. I daily expect to be brought to the place of execution, where my bowels are to be cut out and burned before my face, and then my head to be cut off, etc. Which death I embrace willingly.* He was hanged, drawn, and quartered on July 1, 1681, at Tyburn, the principal location in London for public executions.

JULY 2

John Francis Regis (1597–1640)

❦*Dedicated service*

John Francis Regis spent most of his life in and around Fontcouverte, France. After attending school at Béziers, John determined to become a Jesuit and entered Toulouse as a novice in 1616. Before the process was complete, the plague ravaged his community, but he escaped by retreating to a rural area.

In 1630, he finally became an ordained priest and, with a fellow priest, began to care for victims of the plague. When his coworker died, John went to Pamiers as a teacher, and began missionary activity in the area around Montpellier. This region was under Huguenot control, and to protect themselves many Catholics abandoned their unpopular religious affiliation. John Francis Regis devoted the remainder of his life to guiding inactive members back into Catholicism, and to working among the poor and neglected.

John died of pneumonia in 1640 after exposure to harsh conditions while conducting his ministry.

JULY 3
Anatolius of Alexandria (d. 283)
Respected leadership

Anatolius was humble and deeply religious; he was an outstanding scholar, teacher, and writer. As head of a school in Alexandria, Egypt, he devoted himself to educating others as well as himself. Jerome (September 30) heaped praise upon Anatolius for his books.

When Romans laid siege to Alexandria during the rebellion of 263, innocent civilians starved along with those who were opposing Roman occupation. Anatolius negotiated the freedom of women and children, the sick and the elderly. Saving many lives, Anatolius received accolades as a peacemaker. One unexpected result of his success was that the city's noncombatants no longer exhausted supplies, and the rebels were able to continue their resistance for a long time. When they ultimately lost, Anatolius had few friends on either side and had to leave Alexandria.

Traveling to Palestine, Anatolius settled in Caesarea where he was welcomed with open arms. On his way to a meeting in Antioch, he passed through Laodicea, in Asia Minor. Church leaders in Laodicea were familiar with the writing of Anatolius and asked him to become their next bishop. He agreed and served them for fifteen years, dying a natural death in 283.

Elizabeth of Portugal (1271–1336)

❧*Peaceful arbitration*

The Spanish and Portuguese usually call Elizabeth "Isabella." She was the daughter of King Peter III of Aragon, a kingdom in modern Spain. For political reasons, Elizabeth married King Denis of Portugal when she was twelve years old. They had two children, Alonzo and Constance, but King Denis turned out to be an uncaring and unfaithful husband and father. Their relationship became a public scandal.

Queen Elizabeth kept a regular schedule of prayer, morning and evening. She provided food and lodging for the poor and for travelers on pilgrimages. Her son, Alonzo, angered by the rule of his father, wanted to lead a rebellion against King Denis, but Elizabeth calmed the passions between father and son. People began to call her "the peacemaker." She once used her ability as a negotiator on personal and rational levels when she prevented a war between Portugal and Castile.

King Denis became seriously ill in 1324, and Elizabeth took an interest in his care, praying for his conversion and never leaving his room, except to attend church. During this long illness, the king repented of his immoral life and asked Elizabeth to forgive him. When he died the next year she became a lay Franciscan, living the final eleven years of her life in a little house she built near the Poor Clare convent she had founded years before at Coimbra. This allowed her to retain control of the royal treasury rather than turn it over to her son, Alonzo, who would have spent it foolishly instead of using it to help the people of Portugal. She loved her son, but she also understood his character. By remaining a layperson, Elizabeth did not take a vow of complete poverty, but only a vow of simplicity.

Elizabeth emerged into the world of power politics on several occasions, usually arbitrating struggles involving her relatives.

JULY 5

Anthony Zaccaria (1502–39)

❦Wholeness

Anthony studied medicine at Padua University and started a practice in Cremona, Italy, his hometown. He became a secular priest, or deacon, in 1528, because he observed that human illness had both a physical and a spiritual dimension.

Anthony Zaccaria founded the Clerks Regular of St. Paul in 1530. They became known as the "Barnabites" because they worked out of St. Barnabas Church in Milan. The priests in the order vowed to "regenerate and revive the love of divine worship and a properly Christian way of life by frequent preaching and faithful ministry of the sacraments." They emphasized Pauline doctrine and the Eucharist.

Renewal of the Church is a never-ending task, and Anthony devoted himself to the challenge in an era of laxity and abuse. Unfortunately, Anthony wore himself out in his service to Christ, shortening his life to thirty-six years. He died at home in Cremona.

JULY 6

Maria Goretti (1890–1902)

❦Innocence

Sexual assault is not a subject many religious people want to discuss, but it is more prevalent than we may imagine. The story of Maria Goretti, tragic as it is, serves a double task as a reminder and an inspiration.

Maria was the child of Italian peasants, born near Ancona. Not a bright child, she was nonetheless cheerful and devout. Her father died when she was ten, and her mother went out to work, leaving Maria at home to do housekeeping.

An eighteen-year-old neighbor, Alessandro Serenelli, began to make advances toward her. Maria's disinterest frustrated Alessandro to the point that he attempted to force her into submission, threatening her with a knife. She fought him with all her strength, but he repeatedly stabbed her during the struggle. Maria was hospitalized, but after forgiving Alessandro and expressing concern for her family, she died the next day. Her story does not end here, however.

Alessandro received a lengthy jail sentence. Eight years after he murdered Maria, he had a dream in which he saw Maria picking flowers to give him. The dream was vivid and disturbing. Alessandro, who had been hostile and unrepentant, became a convert to Christianity. When he was released from prison twenty-seven years later, Alessandro was a changed man.

His first act upon receiving freedom was to visit Maria's mother and beg her forgiveness. On Christmas Day, 1937, Alessandro and Maria's mother received communion together. He was standing with a quarter million people in St. Peter's Square when Maria became a canonized saint in 1950.

JULY 7

Willibald (ca. 700–81)

❦ *Faithful service*

From Wessex, England, Willibald became familiar with monastic life at an early age and joined his brother on a lengthy journey to Rome, Jerusalem, and Constantinople in 722. The written narrative of his visits to sites associated with Jesus Christ was the first travelogue written in Anglo-Saxon. In 730, he moved into the Italian Montecassino monastery that Petronax (May 6) had renovated, and remained there for a decade.

At the request of Boniface (June 5), Willibald went to Germany where he was ordained and became bishop of Eichstätt in 742. He served as bishop there for forty-five years, dying a natural death in 781. His shrine may be visited in Eichstätt Cathedral.

JULY 8

Aquila and Priscilla (first century)

❦Working together

Husband and wife, Aquila and Priscilla were companions of Paul (June 29) in Corinth and Ephesus. Aquila was a Jew, but Priscilla may have been Roman. They both have Latin names, suggesting a connection with Rome. Like Paul, they earned a living as professional tentmakers. Some have guessed that Aquila may have earlier subcontracted work to Paul. Aquila and Priscilla's home was certainly spacious enough to accommodate guests. They labored together with Paul now, not as tentmakers, but as evangelists and Christian teachers.

After a court hearing, Paul left Corinth for Ephesus, taking Aquila and Priscilla with him. When Paul continued on to Jerusalem, this holy couple remained to minister in Ephesus. They encountered Apollos, from Alexandria, an intelligent Christian who knew little of doctrines such as baptism. Aquila and Priscilla taught Apollos the essentials of Christian doctrine. We cannot be sure of the circumstances, but Paul wrote in his Roman letter that Aquila and Priscilla took great risks for him.

There is evidence in Christian tradition that Priscilla was more active and capable than her husband. The order of their paired names reverses over time. A few biblical scholars have even suggested that she may be the author of the book of Hebrews.

JULY 9

Pauline (1865–1942)

❦Suffering service

Pauline was born near Trent, Italy. Her parents named her Amabile Wisenteiner, and took her to Brazil when she was ten years old. Jesuit missionaries there welcomed the immigrant family and helped form much of her early spiritual development. When she was fifteen, she moved into a cottage near the chapel of St. George at Vigolo, Brazil, to provide nursing care for a woman dying of cancer.

The Jesuits made it clear that there was a great need for such services in the community. In response, Amabile and two of her friends, Virginia and Teresa, founded the Little Sisters of the Immaculate Conception in 1895. Amabile now took the religious name, "Pauline of the Suffering Heart of Jesus."

Though troubled by some internal ecclesiastical maneuvering and leadership struggles, Pauline said, "The presence of God is so intimate to me that it seems impossible to lose it. Such presence gives my soul a joy which I cannot describe." In 1938 she began to experience complications of diabetes that led to the amputation of a finger, and then her right arm. Pauline was totally blind during the last months of her life. She died July 9, 1942, in Sao Paulo. She became the first canonized saint in Brazil.

JULY 10
John of Dukla (1414–84)
Preaching ministry

John's birthplace, Dukla, is near Tarnow, Poland. As a young man, he lived as a hermit near his hometown, but joined the Conventual Franciscans at Lemberg (now in Ukraine) in 1440. He served as a preacher and local superior until he joined the Observant Franciscans in 1463. Polish people called this group "Bernardines."

With great patience and love, John devoted himself to preaching and ministering to German congregations for the remainder of his life. He continued to speak from the pulpit even after losing his eyesight. Political boundary changes in that part of Europe through the next five centuries delayed the canonization of John of Dukla until 1997.

JULY 11
Benedict of Nursia (ca. 480–550)
Prayer and work

A balanced life includes a mixture of prayer, study, work, community activity, and relaxation. Benedict of Nursia demonstrates a life in harmony with God and the world. Few have left a mark as indelible as he did when he wrote the Benedictine Rule.

Benedict grew up in a distinguished Italian family. His sister was St. Scholastica (February 10). A limited amount of detail exists regarding Benedict's life. A famous biography written about him by Gregory the Great (September 3) is the prime source for biographical material.

Gregory tells us that Benedict began his education in Rome, but the moral laxity of other students there became unbearably offensive to him. Benedict quit school, gave up his family inheritance, and actively began a quest for God. Withdrawing to a cave at Subiaco, Benedict sought peace and quiet. Others on similar quests were gradually attracted to him and pulled him into leadership of a monastic community in the area. The monks there quickly objected to Benedict's stern discipline and tried, according to Gregory, to put poison in his wine. Benedict miraculously escaped and returned to the solitude of his cave.

Yet others continued to turn to Benedict for guidance. Because of his striking insights into human nature, others credited him with the ability to read minds and souls. Monasticism appealed to him, and he was enthusiastic about hermits or monks living together in a community where they could share prayer and labor. He eventually organized twelve such communities on a small scale. In 529, Benedict founded the famous monastery of Montecassino. His sister, Scholastica, also opened a religious community for women in that vicinity.

The Benedictine Rule he devised puts emphasis on *ora et labora* (prayer and work). Severe acts of self-discipline were discouraged. As strict as he was, Benedict was gentle and flexible. Self-discipline, he thought, was internal rather than external. The Benedictine Rule emphasizes this, providing a truly workable plan of organized life in cooperative community. Competitive holiness had no place among religious people who were equals and humbly committed to the strength of the group. A modern coach would say he promoted teamwork.

The fact that the Benedictine Rule is beautifully balanced, avoids extremes, and is designed for ordinary people rather than a heroic few, allowed it to grow as the pattern for monastic life throughout Europe and beyond. Ever since Benedict's time, quiet groups of Benedictine monks have lived orderly and productive lives amid a crumbling civilization.

When Benedict died he was buried beside his saintly sister.

JULY 12
Veronica (first century)
☙ *Compassion*

Veronica is not mentioned anywhere in the New Testament. The story about Veronica is a pious legend that can be traced back to the fourth or fifth century Gospel of Nicodemus. Some attempts have been made to identify her with the nameless women of the Gospels, but it is likely that she is named for the miracle associated with her. *Vera icon* means "true image," and the story goes that she was standing beside the *Via Dolorosa* as Jesus fell under the weight of his cross on the way to Golgotha. With a tender gesture, she wiped his face with her veil. Later, she noticed that the cloth she used bore a distinct picture of his facial features. The story of Veronica made its way into the Stations of the Cross, a devotional practice that, during the Lenten season that, helps penitents imagine themselves a part of Christ's passion.

Veronica's legend does not indicate that she was a disciple of Jesus. She simply responded sympathetically to a suffering man. She had no idea who the criminal being executed might be, discovering his identity in the miraculous icon on her veil.

JULY 13
Henry II (973–1024)
☙ *Influence of Christ*

Henry, the last of the Saxon emperors, was born in Bavaria, Germany. The pope crowned him in 1014. As Henry struggled to bring order and strength to Germany, he also worked to reform and to reorganize the Christian Church. He built a cathedral in Bamberg, and established monasteries. The Rule of Benedict (July 11) appealed to him and he enthusiastically supported it because he received a miraculous cure at the monastery of Montecassino in Italy.

Henry died, a splendid example of a Christian political leader, in 1024.

JULY 14

Camillus de Lellis (1550–1614)

❧ Changing things

The mother of Camillus was a mature sixty when he was born. Everyone considered her pregnancy a miracle. She went into labor while she was attending public worship in Bocchianico in Abruzzi, Italy, and decided that she would walk to a nearby stable and provide her child with a manger of straw for his first cradle, like someone else she knew of. Certainly, this infant of her maturity was a holy child and destined to become a saint.

How many holy women have watched in despair as their children grew up to make poor choices for themselves? Camillus developed a nasty temper and a fondness for gambling. A good fighter six-and-a-half feet tall, he joined the Venetian army and set out with his father to battle the Turks. A painful sore on his leg (that never healed) took him out of action and put him in San Giacamo Hospital in Rome. While receiving treatment, Camillus worked as an orderly to help pay bills. His quick temper annoyed the hospital staff, and they quickly returned him to the military.

His addiction to gambling and alcohol became his downfall. He lost everything, even the shirt off his back, and had to take a job as a laborer for a Capuchin religious community. This environment triggered a suppressed awareness of God, and he determined that he would change his behavior. He tried to become a Capuchin friar when construction at the church was completed two years later, but the problem with his leg made that impossible.

Returning to San Giacamo, Camillus worked feverishly to redeem his reputation as he cared for the patients there. Our modern idea of a hospital is not appropriate when we consider the conditions of a sixteenth-century medical facility in Italy. Often, such hospitals were filthy places. No one really expected much of a cure. The poorly trained staff had little medical knowledge. They were tough people, and mistreatment of patients was commonplace. Camillus decided it was time to show the sick and dying some love and respect. He saw Christ in each hospital patient. He began a program of good nutrition for the sick, and he encouraged fresh air, sunshine, cleanliness, and the isolation of infectious patients. The results appeared to be miraculous. Camillus became the hospital's superintendent.

Camillus became a priest in 1584. On the advice of his advisor, Philip Neri (May 26), he founded a congregation of male nurses. The "Clerks Regular of a Good Death, Ministers to the Sick" vowed to serve the sick in hospitals, homes, and prisons. Some of these "Camillans" served on the battlefields of Hungary and Croatia at the turn of the seventeenth century, becomimg the first military medics in history. Many sacrificed their own lives while caring for people with communicable diseases.

In spite of his own chronic and painful illness, Camillus continued to give personal attention to the sick until his own death at Genoa in 1614. By then, he had received enough contributions to build eight hospitals and to found fifteen houses of his order. His mother would have needed to live until she was one hundred and twenty-four to see how his life turned out. We have no record of the time of her death, but we can hope that she at least lived to see him turn to a better life at San Giacamo.

JULY 15

Bonaventure (ca. 1218–74)

Following and leading

According to legend, Francis of Assisi (October 4) named Bonaventure. Actually, his name was Giovanni di Fidanza. He became seriously ill when he was four years old, and his parents took him to the famous saint for possible healing. When the boy's health returned, Francis exclaimed "*Buona ventura*" (good fortune).

Bonaventure entered the Franciscan Order in 1238 and rose to a position of leadership. It is difficult to imagine that Franciscans should have internal rivalries and opposition, but that was the case when Bonaventure joined them. Francis had died a decade earlier, and the Franciscans had split into factions. One group called themselves "Spirituals," because they wanted to maintain the kind of poverty Francis practiced, and felt little need for centralized authority. Another group wanted to tone down the austerities and take a more casual approach. Bonaventure worked hard to pull both extremes toward an agreeable middle. His achievement was significant enough for him to attract the label of "second founder" of the Franciscans.

Bonaventure's writing fills a nine-volume collection today. His work includes two biographies of St. Francis. Bonaventure does not report that he actually knew the saint, but he does provide the source for the legend of his healing. "When I was a boy, as I still vividly remember, I was snatched from the jaws of death by his invocation and merits."

Bonaventure's *The Mind's Journey into God* attempts to express the experience of Francis in the form and language of philosophy

"*Happiness is the enjoyment of the highest good. Because the highest good is above us, we must rise above ourselves before we can be happy. This is a spiritual rather than a physical ascent, and we cannot rise above ourselves unless we are lifted by a power greater than ourselves.*"

The Tree of Life is a small devotional guidebook that leads readers in a meditation on the life of Christ. *The experiences of Jesus*, he writes, *are like the branches of a tree from which we can pluck valuable fruit, such as humility, holiness, patience, and faithfulness.* Bonaventure prayed, *Good Jesus, even though I do not deserve it, grant me the ability to ponder your experiences in my mind. I was not present at the cross, but let me ponder the hour of your passion even as it was felt by your mother and the penitent Magdalene.*

There is a wonderful moment a year before Bonaventure's death that tells us as much about his personal character as any other single event. In 1273, Pope Gregory X appointed him cardinal-bishop of Albano. When the delegation arrived to deliver his red hat and other accoutrements of the office, Bonaventure was in the friary kitchen, washing dishes. He kept the astonished legates waiting until he finished his turn at kitchen duty. His working principle: "Religion is doing ordinary things perfectly." If we cannot do great things, we can do regular things in a great way.

JULY 16

Eustathius of Antioch (d. ca. 335)

Opposition

Eustathius became bishop of Beroea, Syria, in 270. He grew up in Pamphylia, but other than that, we know little of his early life. After fifty-three years as bishop, Eustathius accepted an appointment as the patriarch of Antioch. In that capacity, he attended the famous Council of Nicea where he joined others in opposing the heretical teachings of Arius.

Unfortunately, the Arians gained control of the church at Antioch and deposed Eustathius. He died about 335, an exile in Thrace. The struggle for the control of power and doctrine at Antioch continued for years after his death.

JULY 17

Pavol Gojdic (1888–1960)

Courageous faith

Prešov is located among impressive, snow-covered mountains in East Slovakia. Peter Gojdic was born near this city in 1888, the son of a Greek-Catholic priest. In 1907, he began his study of theology at Prešov before finishing at Budapest in 1911 and being ordained. For a while, he served as an assistant parish priest in his father's church.

He made his vows in the Order of St. Basil the Great at Cernecia Hora in 1922, taking the name of Pavol. He said, "With God's help, I want to be a father to orphans, a support for the poor, and a consoler to the afflicted." He became bishop of Prešov in 1927.

Pavol's accomplishments in Prešov were impressive. He built orphanages, founded the Greek-Catholic school, established new parishes, and used the printing press effectively in promoting the work of the Church. In 1946, he was confirmed as bishop of Czechoslovakia.

When the Communists seized power in 1948, they began serious suppression of the Greek-Catholic Church. For political reasons, they wanted to eliminate all relationship with Rome. Bishop Gojdic refused to cooperate with the plan, turning down offers of political preferential treatment. Like so many others through history, he firmly declared, "I will not deny my faith. Do not even come to me." The Communist Party responded by banning the Greek-Catholic Church in 1950 and putting Pavol in jail. A trial, designed for public display, convicted him of treason the next year. The authorities sentenced him to life without possibility of parole, stripped him of all civil rights, and began years of abusive treatment. Pavol was told that he would be released from prison if he would agree to become patriarch of the Orthodox church of Czechoslovakia. He replied that his conscience would not permit it. Pavol remained in jail, and the difficult conditions continued to weaken his health. His final months on earth were spent in the prison hospital at Leopoldov, where he died on July 17, 1960. He was buried in the prison cemetery under a plain marker bearing only the number 681. In 1968, his body was exhumed and reburied. In 1990, his relics were placed in the chapel of the Greek-Catholic Cathedral of St. John the Baptist in Prešov. He was beatified in 2001, and the process for canonization continues.

JULY 18

Philastrius (d. ? 387)

❧ *Gentleness*

After beginning his life in Spain, Philastrius moved to Italy, where he accepted an appointment as bishop of Brescia. His tenure came during the height of the Arian heresy contest regarding the nature and work of Christ. His book refuting Arianism still exists. He also prepared a complete listing of heresies that had plagued the first three centuries of church doctrine. Augustine (August 28) met Philastrius in Milan about 383 and mentions him in one of his books. His death occurred late in the fourth century. The bishop who followed Philastrius praised him for his "modesty, quietness, and gentleness toward others."

JULY 19

Macrina the Younger (ca. 327–79)

❧ *Christian influence*

Macrina is an example of the value of religious family life. Her parents became canonized saints, as did two of her brothers Gregory the Great (January 2) and St. Peter of Sebatea. Another of Macrina's brothers St. Gregory of Nyssa wrote a memoir of their life together, recalling his older sister's sterling faith and devotion.

Macrina was born early in the fourth century in Caesarea. When she was twelve, her parents betrothed her to a young man who died before the wedding day. Macrina declared herself a widow and did not encourage other young men to take interest in her. She persuaded her widowed mother to live a simple life rather than enjoying the luxury of their inheritance. When her mother died, Macrina turned their family estate into a convent for women of all social classes.

Her brother Gregory returned home in 379 to discover Macrina ill and confined to the boards she used as a bed. Brother and sister conversed at length on life and death. She amazed the great theologian with the profundity of her insight into spiritual matters. Her comments seemed to him to be "more than human." He stayed with her until she died, hearing her prayer: *O God everlasting, towards whom I have directed myself from my mother's womb, send a shining angel to lead me to the place of refreshment where restful waters flow near the bosom of the holy fathers. May I be found before you once I have put off my body. May my soul be received into your hands, blameless and spotless, as an offering before you.*

After her death Gregory the Great conducted Macrina's funeral.

JULY 20

Aurelius of Carthage (d. 429)
❦*Strength of faith*

No one is sure where or when Aurelius was born. His story begins for us around 388 when he was bishop of Carthage. As head of the Church in North Africa, he probably had as many as five hundred local bishops under his direction.

St. Augustine (August 28) was a friend and confident of Aurelius. Their conversations regarding Christian doctrine no doubt contributed to the opposition Aurelius directed toward various heresies that were troubling the church early in the fifth century. Some of his doctrinal opponents behaved violently, causing Aurelius to call in civil authorities against them. He died in his maturity. Contemporaries heaped praise upon his character and actions.

JULY 21

Laurence of Brindisi (1559–1619)
❦*Valuable scholarship*

Laurence of Brindisi was a Capuchin priest who was an outstanding Bible student and preacher. Both of his parents died soon after he was born in Brindisi, Italy. When Laurence grew up, his uncle arranged for him to attend the College of St. Mark in Venice. He went on to study at the University of Padua and demonstrated a natural ability to learn languages. Laurence received his ordination at the age of twenty-three in Venice.

Laurence's linguistic skills led him to intense study of the Scriptures in their original texts, where he derived insights that many scholars before him had missed. With his natural facility for Hebrew, he began to preach to the Jewish communities in Italy with favorable response. Laurence also attempted a mission for the Lutherans.

As chaplain of the imperial army fighting the Turks in Hungary, Laurence made some tactical suggestions that turned out to be successful. We are told that he led troops into battle, carrying a crucifix. Understanding that the best solutions were not the result of military conflict, Laurence was also a successful negotiator and peacemaker.

On a diplomatic mission to Spain, he contracted a serious illness and died in Lisbon.

JULY 22
Mary Magdalene (first century)
ℐDevotion to Christ

Mary Magdalene was the first person to see the risen Lord. She had been in front of the group of women who discovered the empty tomb.

Mary Magdalene was one of the most prominent of the women who followed Jesus in his itinerant ministry and contributed to his support. Though some have suggested it, there is absolutely *no* evidence that she had ever been a prostitute. This notion probably goes back to a suggestion by Gregory the Great (September 3) who thought she could possibly be identified with the unnamed woman who washed Christ's feet with her tears and dried them with her hair. Writers of fiction and songs have seized upon the false idea for years with the result that popular imagination simply accepts it as a fact. The Bible does *not* say Calvary was a hill, that there were three magi, or that Mary Magdalene was a prostitute.

Her name implies that she was from Magdala, a small village on the western shore of the Sea of Galilee. Magdala was a prosperous fishing, boat building, and trading center. "Mary" was, and remains, an often-used name for women. There are many Marys in the New Testament. By adding "Magdalene" to her name, the writers made it clear which Mary they meant.

She did have some problems before she met Jesus. The Gospel of Luke tells us that "seven demons" had gone out of her. Interpreting that phrase has led to much uninformed discussion. All we can conclude is that she probably had some kind of chronic difficulty.

The essence of Mary Magdalene's importance as a saint is that Christ could depend upon her devoted support. She accompanied him to Jerusalem when he returned there for the last time. She stood at the cross. She went to the tomb. The first words the risen Lord spoke were to her. Distracted by grief, she thought he was the gardener. Mary did not recognize him until he spoke her name.

JULY 23

Bridget of Sweden (1303–73)

Activity and contemplation

Bridget had mystical experiences from childhood. Like Teresa of Avila (October 15), she blended both contemplation and activity into an extraordinarily productive life. When she was fourteen, Bridget married Ulf Gudmarsson, a Swedish nobleman. They had eight children who demonstrate that the influence of parents and home do not always determine the development of each child's personality and character. One of their daughters Katherine of Vadstena became a canonized saint. A son Charles was notorious for his mistakes and poor choices, the source of much parental grief.

In 1335, Bridget became lady-in-waiting to the Queen of Sweden. For her work with the royal family, the king gave her some land and empty buildings she could use as a convent. When Ulf died in 1344, Bridget founded the religious Order for the Holy Savior at Vadstena.

Bridget moved to Rome and began to care for the poor and the sick while writing down the substance of her mystical experiences. Her religious order was in financial difficulty, but she labored on.

A shipwreck on a voyage to Jerusalem, combined with the news of her son's tragic death, damaged her health. She died in 1373, soon after returning to Rome. Her daughter, Katherine, continued her work with what became known as the Brigettine Order. Today there are twelve Brigettine nunneries around the world.

JULY 24

Christina of Tuscany/Tyre (fourth century?)

✑ *Religious imagination*

Several women by the name of Christina share this day. We include them here to illustrate a recurring problem historians have with stories of saints from the early centuries of Christianity.

The account Christina *Mirabilis* (which means *Astonishing*) is full of legendary thirteenth-century mystical phenomena, such as her sitting up in her casket and then flying to the rafters of the church.

The stories of two fourth-century Christinas blend in a mix that is impossible to separate. Christina of Tuscany and Christina of Tyre (Phoenicia) share similar life experiences. Scholars consider Christina of Tyre to be essentially a fictional character, while Christina of Tuscany was probably an actual martyr with an existing burial place and shrine. The accounts of the torture and suffering of these two Christinas are graphic and called "unlikely" by scholars. Specialists in the written *acta* of saints reach the conclusion that early hagiographers inflated existing stories of several other women martyrs to give fresh excitement to Christina. This sort of popular religious fiction continues to be produced in our time. Some of it is honest, and some of it leads to false expectations.

JULY 25
James (first century)
✎ *Close to Christ*

James worked together with his brother John, his father Zebedee, and the brothers Peter and Andrew in the fishing trade. This was serious business with considerable investment in time and equipment. When the catch was good, they preserved the fish in salt and sold them far from home.

James responded to Christ's call and became one of two apostles with this name. This James played a part in that special trio of friends who accompanied Jesus in the greatest of spiritual moments—the healing of Peter's mother-in-law, the resuscitation of the daughter of Jairus, the Mount of Transfiguration, the night of agonizing prayer in the Garden of Gethsemane. Along with Peter and John, James was clearly a special friend of Christ.

The book of Acts records that he was the first apostolic martyr, that King Herod Agrippa had James, the brother of John, killed with the sword to please the Jewish opponents of Christianity.

JULY 26
Titus Brandsma (1881–1942)
✎ *Faith oppressed*

The Nazi invasion of Holland in 1940 produced much discussion in churches regarding organized resistance to the Germans. As in every religious debate, people stood on two sides of the issue. There were those who thought Catholics should cooperate with the Nazi occupation in any way that preserved and enhanced the security of Christians. Others felt that the Nazi regime was an unmitigated evil that should be fought against without compromise.

Titus Brandsma, a Dutch Carmelite priest and theology professor, stood at the forefront of the group that opposed the Nazis. Because he was a journalist who wrote for several publications, his views were familiar to many. He called the political climate in

Germany "the new paganism" and sharply criticized the persecution of Jews.

A German directive issued in 1941 forbade any Jewish student from attending Catholic schools in Holland. Titus Brandsma, president of the Association of Catholic Secondary Schools, openly expressed his dismay. When the Nazis declared that all newspapers must print Nazi propaganda, Brandsma personally explained to each editor why the Catholic press could not agree to do that.

A month later, the Nazis arrested Titus Brandsma. A few months later, he was sent to the concentration camp at Dachau, along with twenty-seven hundred other clergy. The inhumane conditions and cruel treatment did not make him bitter. Those who saw him there, and survived to report it, say that he continued his prayer and meditation. Someone heard him summarize the prisoners' situation this way: "We are in a dark tunnel that we must pass through. Somewhere at the end shines the eternal light."

Never in robust health, Titus Brandsma became quite ill at Dachau. The guards sent him to the concentration camp's hospital, the location of infamous medical experiments. They killed Titus with an injection of acid. In 1985, Titus Brandsma became the first Nazi victim to be listed as a martyr.

JULY 27

Panteleon (d. ca. 305)

✍*Martyred for faith*

Panteleon, whose name implies that he cared for everyone, was a fourth-century Christian physician whose practice included meeting the health needs of the Roman Emperor. As he grew up, he turned away from the religion his mother had taught him and began to live a wild bachelor's life. His conscience drove him back to Christianity, and legend says that he converted his pagan father. He was generous with the poor, treating them medically without asking payment for his services, and he achieved some of his cures through prayer.

When the Diocletian persecution of the church began, colleagues turned in Panteleon as a known Christian. The Roman authorities arrested and tortured him. There is a story that he proposed and won a contest in court to see who could heal a paralytic. Regardless of this miracle, Panteleon was sentenced to die. He was nailed to a tree and beheaded around the year 305.

It is worth noting that a reliquary said to contain his dried blood is kept in a church at Ravello. Like the blood of Januarius (September 19), it is reported to liquefy on special days.

JULY 28

Samson (d. 565)

❦ *Christian mission*

This saint is not the Old Testament strong man, but a Welsh monk who lived in the sixth century. Scholars do not place much confidence in the biography written nearly two hundred years after his death.

Samson was a disciple of Illtyd (November 6) who became abbot of the monastery on Caldey Island. He became one of the leading British missionaries of his time, a wandering Celtic monk-bishop.

Samson died around 565, and remains a popular saint in Brittany and Wales.

JULY 29

Olaf Tryggvason (995–1030)

❦ *Spreading the Gospel*

This patron saint of Norway was its king from 1016 to 1029. As a young man Olaf was a pirate and a fighter, but while traveling in France, he became a Christian and helped Ethelred II of England resist the Danes in 1013. When the excellent fighter and eloquent speaker returned to Norway, he seized the throne and performed better than any other Norwegian leader before him. He brought peace, security, and dependable law-enforcement to his land.

Olaf's primary interest was in Christianizing Norway, and to help him in this effort, he invited English missionaries to work in his land. Using both persuasion and force, he pushed for conversions and conformity. An inevitable backlash of resistance led to his deposition and exile in 1029. With Swedish backing, he attempted a return the next year, but was killed at Stiklestad on July 29, 1030.

A spring of water with alleged healing properties emerged from the soil near his grave. Grimkell, an English bishop who had assisted Olaf in his Christianizing efforts, built a chapel there and declared him a saint

JULY 30

Maria de Jesús Sacramentado Venegas de la Torre (1868–1959)

❧Dedication to Christ

Maria was born in Mexico, the youngest of twelve children. Her family encouraged participation in church activities, and by the time she was fifteen she was busily engaged in teaching Christianity to neighbors as well as in taking care of the poor.

In 1905, Maria made a retreat at San Sebastián Analco, Guadalajara. Here her call to a religious life became certain, and she entered the Daughters of the Sacred Heart the same year. By 1922, she was taking an active role in leadership and making impressive improvements to every aspect of the community's circumstances. Her life became an inspiring example of love and humility. She died in 1959.

JULY 31

Ignatius of Loyola (1491–1556)

❧Enduring influence

We read the lives of saints because they are a source of inspiration and encouragement. It was reading about them that completely changed Ignatius of Loyola's life. He became one of the greatest saints of the sixteenth century.

Ignatius had received a serious leg wound and back injury from cannon fire in battle, and spent time recovering from repeated surgeries in his family's castle. To fill the time, he read a Spanish translation by Goberto Vagad of *The Golden Legend*. These stories of great saints caught his attention, possibly because the saints' action based on faith resonated with the code of honor and chivalry that he had learned as a young knight. During his long convalescence, Iñigo López de Loyola began to think it would be a great honor to be a knight for the glory of God. He made up his mind to improve his behavior and to follow the example of the saints.

The cannon ball that broke his leg left him deformed and limping for the rest of his life. The first physician to set his broken leg did a poor job. It had to be broken again and reset. When he was able to walk again, he went to the Catalonian shrine of Our Lady at Montserrat. In the manner of knights in romantic tales, Ignatius spent the night there in a vigil. The next morning he exchanged his fine clothes for the sackcloth of a nearby pilgrim and placed his sword and dagger on the altar. The next day he began several months of solitude and meditation, experiencing mystical religious episodes.

The Gospel narratives of Christ fascinated Ignatius, inspiring him to make a pilgrimage to the sites mentioned in them. His desire to become a priest grew steadily, but he did not have the necessary education, so he began to study Latin and became a student at the University of Paris. He gathered a group of six friends on that campus into a new religious order, the beginnings of the Society of Jesus, or Jesuits. In 1540, the Jesuits received official recognition from Rome.

Ignatius of Loyola placed himself and his men at the service of the Church, declaring that they were ready to travel even to dangerous territory in order to promote Christianity. The list of martyrs becomes densely populated with Jesuits from this point on.

The Society of Jesus is but one of Ignatius of Loyola's great contributions to the world. Another is his *Spiritual Exercises*, a brilliant and inspired guide to spiritual formation. Countless Christians have used it to deepen their meditation and prayer. Four-week-long retreats continue to be offered following the design Ignatius conceived in 1533. Those who do not have a month available for such a retreat still profit from reading through his book. Thomas Merton said, "The *Spiritual Exercises* are very pedestrian and practical—their chief purpose being to enable all the busy Jesuits to get their minds off their work and back to God with a minimum of wasted time." Merton went on to say that he wished he had been able to go through the *Exercises* under Jesuit supervision, but did it on his own. He studied the rules that were in the book and followed them the best he could. "I never even breathed a word about what I was doing to any priest."

Ignatius writes, "In the same way that strolling, walking, and running exercise the body, spiritual exercises prepare the soul to become free of extravagant attachments and to discover what God wants to accomplish in one's life."

Ignatius of Loyola died suddenly on July 31, 1556. At the time of his death, there were about one thousand Jesuits. At the end of the twentieth century there were twenty-five thousand. Jesuits see their function as complementing rather than replacing the work of parish priests.

AUGUST 1

Alphonsus Liguori (1696–1787)
Dark doubt

Sometimes we fantasize that church work ought to be entirely beautiful and permeated with glowing spirituality. People who participate in the life of a congregation, and the larger organizations that provide oversight, ought to be respectful of each other. A warm glow of Christian cooperation and singleness of purpose should be the defining characteristic of religious life together.

This is not the way it is. The lives of the saints often remind us that being a committed Christian can be a struggle. Even Christ had detractors. Sometimes the source of difficulty is political. Every group of people will experience tension and conflict regardless of the degree of shared love. At other times, stress is the result of an intensely personal agony of soul. The life of many dedicated Christians often involves a combination of both interpersonal and personal stresses.

Alphonsus Liguori is an outstanding example of what it is like to be a church leader. He became a popular preacher in the region surrounding Naples where he had grown up. As with Jesus, "The common people heard him gladly," as Mark's Gospel says. His simple, direct manner of speaking strongly influenced the spirituality and behavior of those who heard him.

In 1732, Alphonsus Liguori organized an order of priests that specialized in preaching to uneducated rural people. He struggled for the remainder of his life trying to win official recognition of this "Congregation of the Holy Redeemer."

His ideas and interpretation of Scripture took a moderate, middle-of-the-road course through the thicket of religious teaching. He believed that Christianity was for everyone. Rather than emphasizing strict adherence to religious laws, he understood that love was the best influence and motivator. Each person is free to follow the dictates of conscience. At the same time, a Christian will carefully apply the details of these principles to every circumstance. Formerly an active lawyer, Alphonsus Liguori was both strict and compassionate.

Respect and controversy resulted from his speaking and writing. He had both strong supporters and vicious opponents. Poor health added to his problems during the final dozen years of his life. He experienced great physical suffering and personal spiritual anguish. Even as he continued the exhausting attempt to win official recognition by both church and state for his congregation, his own people engaged in bitter contentions with each other. After Alphonsus made a clerical error, the order he had founded expelled him, in spite of his illness and increasing blindness.

It was only after his death at the age of ninety that the factions in his congregation ceased their divisive behavior and received official recognition. Their work eventually spread around the world. Posthumously, he became a Doctor of the Church.

AUGUST 2

Eusebius of Vercelli (ca. 283–371)

✒*Expressing belief*

Articulating important aspects of faith is not an easy job. Many simply shrug and express some generality such as, "We are all in different boats going to the same destination." While the details of our private spiritual experience may remain inexpressible, there is great value in being able to state clearly our understanding of the person and work of Christ. The Church's creeds allow us to do that.

Time, place, and culture have always affected the character of basic Christian beliefs. In the early centuries some began to teach astonishing things about Jesus, and they had a popular following. Creedal statements became a way to sift these ideas through a sieve, searching for what is valuable, authentic, and essential, while discarding the misdirected and harmful.

Eusebius of Vercelli helped to guide Christians in the fourth century through a difficult maze of divergent opinions and teachings. Eusebius of Vercelli should not be confused with the more familiar church historian or the several other prominent leaders who shared the same name. His ability as a scholar contributed to the composition of the Athanasian Creed. From 354 until his death in 371, Eusebius of Vercelli devoted himself to issues of accurate Christian doctrine. The emperor Constantine invited him to participate in a gathering of church leaders from all over his empire in an effort to deal with popular heresies such as Arianism, which denied the divinity of Christ. At Milan, in 355, Eusebius declined to sign a condemnation of Athanasius (May 2). As an alternative, he placed the Nicene Creed on the table, insisting that Athanasius should be given a chance to defend himself. He championed the separation of church and state, believing that the secular power should not direct religious decisions. The resulting confusion exasperated Constantine, and he threatened to execute them all. He banished the assembled bishops. Eusebius was exiled to Palestine. One of his surviving letters records the distressing treatment he received there.

Eusebius died a natural death, but some consider him a martyr because of his persecution and suffering.

AUGUST 3

Lydia (first century)

ℳMartyred for faith

The missionary journeys of Paul took him to Philippi, a community in what is now Greece. A single reference in the New Testament book of Acts describes all we know about a woman who lived there.

On the Sabbath we went outside the city gate to the river, where we expected to find a place of prayer. We sat down and began to speak to the women who had gathered there. One of those listening was a woman named Lydia, a dealer in purple cloth from the city of Thyatira, who was a worshiper of God. The Lord opened her heart to respond to Paul's message. When she and the members of her household were baptized, she invited us to her home. "If you consider me a believer in the Lord," she said, "come and stay at my house." And she persuaded us.

Lydia marketed purple goods. Because this rare and expensive color is associated with royalty, many commentators conclude that she was wealthy. Others have conceived the possibility that she may have been a common laborer who worked with dyes in a cottage industry. In any event, Lydia and her friends were immigrants from across the Aegean Sea and would have had little respect from the upper class.

Lydia gives us an example of Christian hospitality. After her baptism, she invited Paul and his companions to stay in her home. A possible indicator that she was a woman of wealth is that her house was large enough to comfortably accommodate the missionaries along with her "household." She showed no hesitancy in making these strangers feel at home as though they were part of the family. Welcoming hospitality results from understanding our kinship in Christ. It is on the list of highest Christian virtues.

The Church at Philippi became one of the strongest and healthiest that Paul established. He was clearly fond of this congregation. He addresses his letter to them as "to all the saints in Christ Jesus at Philippi." It was the only stop on his missionary travels where he did not have to work in secular employment to sustain himself. Lydia's courageous hospitality freed him to devote all of his time to his ministry. "I thank my God every time I remember you," Paul wrote in his letter to the Philippians. "In all my prayers for all of you, I always pray with joy because of your partnership in the gospel from the first day until now."

AUGUST 4

John-Baptiste Vianney (1786–1859)

✒Special gifts

Academic standards are necessary, and the proper education of a professional is vital. But sometimes there is good reason to have a little flexibility in order to match the needs of a particularly gifted individual. The machinery that grinds out standardized evaluations may misjudge some outstanding talent that simply will not fit the mold.

John Vianney, a farm boy, grew up in eighteenth-century France. He was a well-behaved, quiet child who enjoyed his experiences with the church. He strongly desired to become a priest. His father needed John to continue helping with farm chores then, and could offer no way to extend John's limited formal education. At the age of twenty he found a way to study at a nearby village. The lessons were not easy. Latin proved extremely difficult for him.

In 1806 John Vianney walked about sixty miles to the shrine of St. Regis (June 16) at La Louvese and prayed that God would help him. He received the courage to continue pursuing his dream, but schoolwork remained a struggle.

After a turbulent experience during Napoleon's military campaigns, John entered the seminary at Lyons. Because instruction was in Latin, he learned very little and failed his examination for the priesthood. With his reputation for being the most devout student at the seminary, the authorities made an exception for him after several years of private tutoring. They ordained him at the age of twenty-nine, commending him to the grace of God, who often has a special work for those who seem to lack academic promise.

The officials assigned John Vianney to a remote village with a small population, but he took his work seriously and had a significant influence among his people. Remaining there for the rest of his life, he became a popular counselor and confessor. He had a special talent for sympathetic listening. Like his Lord, he "needed no one to testify about anyone; for he himself knew what was in everyone," as the Gospel of John says. People came to him in great numbers for spiritual direction. They came from his local community and they came from far away. Beginning about 1830, and continuing for fifteen years, on any given day, over three hundred people met with him. Even the railway provided special tickets for the trip to meet with him at the little village of Ars. He met with people for about twelve hours a day in winter and sixteen or more in summer. His time with each visitor was necessarily limited, but he had a way of touching precisely upon the important point of an individual's religious struggle.

The love of Christ emanated from John Vianney. The French people loved him. Napoleon even sent him the medal of the Legion of Honor, which he declined to accept. During the last two years before his death in 1859, his natural ability for positive conversation attracted thousands who desired even the slightest exchange with him. Sick people sought healing. The devout tried to take a fragment of his cassock. John's response to such activity was, "What misguided devotion!" It should be no surprise that he became the patron saint of parish priests.

AUGUST 5

Mary McKillop (1842–1909)
Enduring misunderstanding

Australia produced its first recognized saint in 1995. Mary McKillop was born in Melbourne to parents who were Scottish immigrants. She founded the Sisters of St. Joseph, whose function was to educate and help the poor. Many young women joined with her in providing rare public services in far-flung areas. She gained Australia's respect and admiration.

She believed that her widespread organization needed independence from each local religious authority in order to work effectively. This, however, did not please the bishops. They abused their positions of power and began to interfere. As necessary as the ministry was, Mary had bypassed their authority.

Mary began to feel the pain of persecution by religious leaders whose vision of the nature of her work was less grand than her own. They complained that she was an insubordinate fanatic. She was discredited, harassed, and slandered. Fund-raising became difficult. She appealed directly to Rome. Pope Pius IX formally approved her organization, but when she returned to Australia, the persecution continued. The bishops continued to seek any cause to dishonor her. Finding none, they falsely accused her of being an alcoholic and of misappropriating funds.

Rome criticized this unauthorized effort, and completely cleared the woman known as Mother Mary of the Cross. Undaunted, the Australian bishops continued their persecution, making one last futile attempt to gain control. Again they were overruled.

These attacks on her character and faith caused Mary much distress, but she quietly accepted them, knowing that God could use the experience to help her grow spiritually. She called her persecutors "instruments in the hands of God . . . most powerful benefactors."

AUGUST 6

Hormisdas (d. 420)

Healing diplomacy

Hormisdas is an example of a relatively obscure individual who held an important position and accomplished significant negotiation under stressful circumstances. There is no record of his personal life.

His father, Justus, gave him the name of the Zoroastrian god of light and goodness.

Hormisdas became pope in 514. His experience before and after this moment is filled with difficult diplomacy. These were years of painful struggle between East and West. Partisans were heatedly contesting important issues of doctrine and church leadership. Fights broke out in the streets among the various factions. Hormisdas is credited with leading the effort that brought peace among Roman and Greek Christians. His negotiating skill certainly classifies him as one of the great referees of all time.

AUGUST 7

Victricius (d. 407)

❧*A matter of conscience*

The early history of the Christian Church contains only a few mentions of a Roman soldier becoming Christian. The Gospel of Matthew records the dramatic confession of faith by a centurion at the foot of the cross: "Surely he was the Son of God!" Perhaps this centurion became a follower of Jesus.

Victricius was a Roman soldier who became a committed Christian early in the fifth century. He believed the teachings of Christ opposed his military service. In an effort to obey his Lord, he laid down his weapons on the parade ground. As a result, the army arrested him and charged him with desertion. He received a painful Roman flogging and nearly gave his life in exchange for this expression of his faith.

Later in life, Victricius became a traveling preacher, and ultimately, bishop of the remote outpost of Rouen. The Christian Church in northern France owes much of its presence to his guidance. Because of his reputation as a peacemaker, Christians in England invited him to come across the channel to mediate their squabbles.

AUGUST 8

Dominic (1170–1221)

❧*Simplicity*

"Whoever governs the passions is master of the world. We must either rule them, or be ruled by them. It is better to be the hammer than the anvil." So spoke the Spaniard Dominic Guzmán. He is one of the few church leaders whose parents from early on encouraged Christian dedication.

In 1203, when Dominic was on a diplomatic mission to southern France, he found the people there taken in by a sub-Christian movement from the East. Spending the night in Toulouse with an adherent of the heretical group, Dominic engaged his host in religious discussion until dawn. He was able to convince him of the value of accurate belief in Christ. Because of this conversation, Dominic's concept of his personal mission began to come together.

He planned to organize a radical new system of outreach, patterned on Christ's words, as he sent out missionaries. "Take nothing for the journey except a staff—no bread, no bag, no money in your belts. Wear sandals but not an extra tunic." Dominic's followers were to win others by example as well as by preaching. Thorough preparation and training were required. On this basis, Dominic founded the Order of Preachers. Today, we know them as the Dominicans.

Dominic met Francis of Assisi (October 4), who developed a similar work across the Alps in Italy. The two shared ideas, and both valued poverty, but they were quite different in personality and approach. Dominic saw poverty as a simplification that provided freedom and mobility. He emphasized education in order to produce competent preachers. Some great Christian thinkers, such as Thomas Aquinas (January 28) and Catherine of Siena (April 29), were Dominicans.

Dominic did not believe in forcing belief and agreement. "You cannot defeat the enemies of the faith like that. Arm yourself with prayer, not a sword."

AUGUST 9
Edith Stein (1891–1942)
❧*Conversion and courage*

Born on Yom Kippur in Breslau, Germany, Edith Stein was the eleventh child of a Jewish family. Her mother was deeply committed to Orthodox Judaism. As many children do when they approach their teen years, Edith declared her independence. Her extraordinary intelligence led her to question traditional faith. She decided she was probably an atheist and focused on philosophy. At the age of fifteen she announced she would not pray again. Her preoccupation was in discovering "the truth." Hearing these declarations brought her mother much grief.

Edith Stein became one of the first women students at the University of Göttingen, and she did outstanding work. Her professor, Edmund Husserl, was impressed with her ability and invited her to assist him at the University of Freiburg. There she received her doctorate at the age of twenty-three.

As Edith approached her third decade she became curious about religion. While visiting a friend in 1921, she discovered the autobiography of Teresa of Avila (October 15). Immersed in it, she read until dawn, devouring every page. "This," she told herself, "is the truth." She received Christian baptism on New Year's Day.

Her mother, of course, was distraught. Edith made a conscientious effort to assure her mother that her acceptance of Christ was not tantamount to rejection of her Jewish origin. Together, they attended the synagogue and read psalms.

In 1933, as Adolph Hitler gained control of Germany, Edith joined the Carmelites at Cologne, determined to share the suffering of Christ. Edith Stein became Sister Teresa Benedicta of the Cross even as the rising darkness of German anti-Semitism became palpable. Laws encouraged religious persecution to a degree never before witnessed in the civilized world. Because she was born a Jew, Edith became one of many victims of a political system that treated people as less than human.

She departed Cologne to spare her Sisters any harm that could result from their associating with her. In the Netherlands at a Carmelite house she wrote *The Knowledge of the Cross*. The Nazis began their occupation of Holland in 1940. Edith, along with all Dutch Jews, was required to wear a Star of David. Eventually the order came that all Christians with Jewish backgrounds who lived in the Netherlands were to be resettled in Poland. Edith and another Carmelite nun of Jewish ancestry were arrested on August 2, 1942. She took her Sister's hand, saying, "Come on—we are on our way to our own people."

After the misery of a detention camp in Holland, Edith began the horrible and inhumane journey experienced by many other Jews. She died in the Auschwitz gas chamber on August 9, 1942, and was officially canonized a saint in 1998.

AUGUST 10

Laurence (d. 258)

✐ Inspiration for legend

Laurence is an example of a saint from the early years of Christianity who has accumulated a large and colorful story contributed by pious imaginations. No one doubts that he was a faithful Christian who died a martyr in Rome in the year 258. His popularity resulted in five Roman basilicas bearing his name, including one that was constructed over his tomb. Great paintings, stained glass, and structures immortalize him in many nations.

Scholars discount the legendary report of his execution, but the story is remarkable and merits retelling. A Roman civil official heard a report that Laurence was selling the church's valuables to help support the poor. Assuming that the church had great wealth, he gave Laurence three days to gather the church's valuables and then to follow the teaching of Jesus by giving to Caesar what was Caesar's.

Laurence brought together Rome's poor and outcast. He assembled this motley crowd in front of the official, presenting them as "the treasure of the church." This resulted in a spontaneous sentence of slow death by roasting on a gridiron. Instead of being in agony, Laurence turned his execution into a joke. After thoroughly broiling on one side, he requested his executioners to turn him so that he might be evenly cooked. Eventually he announced that he was done and they could begin eating. After praying for the conversion of Rome to Christ, Laurence died.

Widespread high regard for Laurence over many centuries points to a powerful and inspiring spirituality.

AUGUST 11

Clare of Assisi (ca. 1194–1253)

✐*Blessed influence*

While Clare will always be associated with Francis of Assisi (October 4), she is a significant and inspiring personality in her own right.

Human society was experiencing remarkable change when Clare was born in Assisi. Rural people were moving into cities. Commerce and property were dominant motivators. Clare's successful family was in the upper social strata. In twelfth-century Italy, the rules and expectations of marriage were different from our own. Girls from wealthy homes were obligated to marry wealthy boys, the oldest child first. Parents often pressured their girls to marry for good business connections. It was not unusual for a girl to mary at age fourteen. For reasons of her own, Clare refused to marry the man chosen for her by her uncle.

Because of the absence of details regarding Clare's early relationship with Francis we can't be sure, but since she lived in sight of the cathedral of San Rufino it is highly probable that she heard him preach. The message of the young man who embraced poverty in the spirit of Christ resonated with her soul. Clare sought an opportunity to discuss this privately with Francis. Their secret conversation sharply focused her strong personal spirituality.

On the night of March 18, 1212, she ran away from home. Francis and his Brothers welcomed her to the Chapel of our Lady of the Angels, about a mile away. Here she exchanged her rich girl's clothes for a sackcloth tunic tied with a rope. She took temporary shelter in a Benedictine convent.

Clare's family and friends tried to talk her out of it. In a moment of high drama, they attempted to drag her away from the altar. After successfully resisting them, she relocated to the nunnery at Mount Subasio. Her fifteen-year-old sister, Agnes (November 16), joined her there. That such young girls were accepted as nuns over family objections can be dismaying to our contemporary society, but society and culture in thirteenth-century Italy were radically different from our own.

The example of Clare's life, the clarity of her mind, and the force of her spirit resulted in abundant and widespread good. Her influence blessed individual lives. Her own mother and the daughter of the king of Bohemia (June 8) also joined with her. She established monasteries in Italy, France, and Germany. Because of the severity of the asceticism practiced by her community, others looked upon them with disdain. The members of her community went barefoot, slept on the ground, were strictly vegetarian, and spoke as little as possible.

Clare's health suffered because of her deprivations. Francis and the bishop of Assisi insisted that she eat a little bread every day and encouraged her to sleep on a straw mattress. As a result she wrote later that "our bodies are not made of brass," encouraging others to take care of themselves by eating and resting in a responsible manner. In fact, she was feeble for the final twenty-eight years of her life, dying on August 11, 1253.

The spiritual legacy of Clare of Assisi endures to the present day. She shines a particularly clear light on the profound possibilities of prayer. Legend reports that her face glowed with cheerfulness after she had spent a time in prayer. G. K. Chesterton has a wonderful page in his biography of Francis that describes a discernable aura glowing around the chapel where the two prayed together. Many consider this first Franciscan woman to be the most faithful of them all.

AUGUST 12

Euplus (d. 304)

❧ *Written on the heart*

An ancient text preserves the story of an enthusiastic early Christian, Euplus, who was martyred in 304. This was a time of persecution by the Roman government.

One day the shouting of a man on the street outside rudely disturbed the quiet of the governor's court at Catania, Sicily. It was Euplus, and he was calling out, "I am a Christian! I am willing to die for being a Christian!" The governor asked his guards to bring him inside.

He was carrying a book of the Gospels when he appeared before the governor, who began to interrogate him.

"Is that your book?"

"You see it in my hand."

"Who has taught you these things?"

"I learned it all from our Lord Jesus Christ, the Son of God."

The governor locked Euplus away in prison for three months and then had him returned for another questioning.

"Do you still have the forbidden writings?"

"I do."

"Where are they?"

"Inside."

"If you still have them, bring them here."

"Inside," Euplus replied, pointing to his heart.

Infuriated, the governor ordered him to be tortured until he agreed to make a sacrifice to the Roman gods. The governor gave Euplus yet another opportunity to recant. Refusing to renounce his faith, he was sentenced to be beheaded.

AUGUST 13

Pontian and Hippolytus (d. ca. 235)

Strength and courage

Many of the saints from the early centuries of the Christian Church surrendered their lives for their faith. Most were common people; some were in positions of responsibility and authority, such as Pontian, Bishop of Rome, or Pope, from 230 to 235. The Roman Emperor banished him to Sardinia, where inhumane treatment and forced labor in the mines destroyed his life.

His successor, Hippolytus, is a puzzle to students of history. We should not identify him with the well-known writer with the same name. His period of leadership was brief. He died a martyr in exile on the same island as Pontian.

When the years of persecution had passed, their remains were returned home and interred with respect.

AUGUST 14

Maximilian Kolbe (1894–1941)

Dying for another

Another victim of Nazi Germany, Maximilian Kolbe is one of the most remarkable saints of modern history. He was born in Poland in 1894 and became a Franciscan monk as a teenager. After being ordained a priest and serving a small parish for several years, Kolbe became the director of one of Poland's great publishing houses. One of his journals had a circulation of 800,000.

When the Nazis invaded Poland in 1939, Kolbe worked diligently to protect many Jewish refugees. The Nazis arrested him and sent him to Auschwitz in 1941. At this notorious death camp, the priest labored to set an example of faith and hope to the other prisoners. When a prisoner escaped, the camp's commandant ordered that ten of the inmates of cellblock 14 be selected for retaliatory punishment. The Nazis would lock them in an underground bunker until they starved to death. One of the randomly selected ten, Franciszek

Gajowniczek, began to weep. "My poor wife and children! I will never see them again!" Kolbe stepped forward and offered to take his place. "I wish to die for that man. I am old; he has a wife and children." When the deputy commandant asked him to identify himself he responded simply, "I am a Catholic priest." The startled commandant let him take Gajowniczek's place.

As his companions began to die in slow agony, Kolbe prayed and sang hymns with them. The next month Kolbe and three others were still alive, having consumed nothing but their own urine. The Nazis gave them lethal injections and cremated them in the death camp's ovens.

In 1982, Maximilian Kolbe was canonized a saint as the surviving Franciszek Gajowniczek looked on. Today, someone continually places flowers in the bunker at Auschwitz.

AUGUST 15
Simplician (d. 400)
Influence of friends

Simplician is an outstanding example of the catalytic effect an individual may have on the development of impressive achievers. A fifth-century priest in Milan, Simplician carefully studied the already ancient Greek writings of Plato. The famous Bishop Ambrose (December 7) was one of Simplician's theological students. Ambrose considered Christian Platonists such as Simplician to be "aristocrats of thought." He recommended the elderly Simplician as his successor.

Augustine (August 28) became a close friend of Simplician, and revealed his spiritual struggles to him. When Augustine commented that he had been reading the works of professor Marius Victorinus, Simplician reported that Victorinus had privately confessed to him, "I want you to know that I am a Christian." Simplician told Augustine he had replied, "I shall never believe it or consider you a Christian until I see you in the Church of Christ." Victorinus laughed, asking, "Do the walls of a church make people

Christians?" Simplician convinced Victorinus to publicly profess his private conviction. This cost Victorinus his job, because Christians were not allowed to teach rhetoric or literature. This narrative profoundly affected Augustine and contributed to his personal conversion.

An important by-product of Augustine's relationship with Simplician was one of Augustine's most important writings: *To Simplician on Diverse Questions*. Some of Augustine's best thoughts on human freedom and the sovereignty of God are found in this work. One life touches others in many positive ways

AUGUST 16

Stephen of Hungary (975–1038)

Establishing the Church

Born into a pagan family, Stephen became a Christian at age ten, and worked to promote Christianity in Hungary when he succeeded his father as duke. On Christmas day, 1001, Stephen became the first king of Hungary. He brutally abolished paganism and built churches and monasteries, leading strong efforts of Christian evangelism. He forbade marriages between Christians and pagans. His goal was a Hungarian national church with a vital Roman connection.

Though he had high goals and the best intentions, things did not go well for Stephen. His son, Emeric, was accidentally killed while hunting. A painful, debilitating illness lingered through his final years. Family members began to scramble to succeed Stephen to the throne. Some of his nephews even plotted to kill him.

Though Stephen enforced ruthless politics in order to unify Hungary, he expressed great tenderness and respect for the poor and needy. Once he attempted to take alms into a slum district while wearing a disguise. Some ruffians assaulted him, stealing his purse. He accepted this royal indignity with humility and a sense of humor, continuing to be openly generous to anyone in need.

AUGUST 17

Joan of the Cross (1666–1736)

❦ *Radical change*

The story of Joan Delanoue's progress from miserly shopkeeper to saint is fascinating. The youngest of twelve children, Joan inherited her mother's little trinket shop near the shrine of Notre Dame des Ardilliers in Saumur, Anjou, France. The sale of crockery and religious objects had barely sustained her large family. As a consequence of the financial insecurity, Joan became miserly and avaricious. She worked long hours, keeping the shop open seven days a week. She rented unfit rooms to pilgrims who visited the shrine. She kept no food in her home so that she could turn beggars away. While it would be impossible for her to ever become rich, she worked determinedly to save every penny possible in her small shop enterprise.

The visit of one scruffy pilgrim in 1693 transformed Joan's life. Frances Souchet seemed to be a religious fanatic who attempted to visit many of the religious shrines. Most first impressions of Frances were negative. She seemed more than a little odd, muttering to herself as she walked. Arriving at Joan's shop, she announced that God had sent her. Joan accommodated the shabbily dressed widow for the night at a greatly reduced fee.

Something about this visit deeply disturbed Joan, changing her pattern of behavior. She began to attend public worship and eventually closed her shop on Sundays. When the eccentric Frances Souchet made a return visit and spoke what she said were messages from God, she had a dramatic effect on Joan. Attempting a radical change in her life, Joan began to support a poor family with six children that had been living in a stable. This led her to help other needy people. In 1698 she was so preoccupied with serving the indigent, she closed her shop. Poor people began to seek her.

Joan's home became a haven for the sick, the elderly, orphans, and the destitute. It became known as Providence House. When Joan expressed anxiety about having enough money to support all the people she had taken in, Frances Souchet assured her, "The king of France won't give you his purse; but the King of kings will always keep his open for you."

A landslide forced Joan and the Providence House to relocate. After a few years of abortive struggle, Joan began an organization that included the welcomed help of others. The Sisters of St. Anne began their work in 1704. With ecclesiastical approval, she became Joan of the Cross, leading forty religious sisters in outstanding charitable work and prayer.

Enduring both physical and spiritual stress, Joan died in 1736 at the age of seventy, beloved by others, and called a saint long before her sainthood became official by the signature of Pope John Paul II in 1982.

AUGUST 18

Alberto Hurtado Cruchaga (1901–52)

Acting on experience

A poor boy who lost his father at the age of four, Alberto decided he wanted to care for others who also knew poverty. After attending the Jesuit College in Santiago, Chile, he became a Jesuit himself. Alberto was ordained in 1933 and began to teach.

In 1944, Alberto began to plan *El Hogar de Cristo*, a shelter for the homeless and abandoned. This developed along the lines of Boys Town in the United States. He also started a Christian labor union known as the Chilean Trade Union Association. Active social service distinguished his ministry. Alberto died of pancreatic cancer in Santiago on August 18, 1952, at the age of fifty-one.

AUGUST 19

John Eudes (1601–80)

Teaching teachers

One of the great Christian ministries is helping other Christians perform their ministry well. John Eudes, a seventeenth-century

French priest, demonstrated this. He was an outstanding speaker, writer, and parish missionary. As he traveled he observed the ineffective ministry of many local clergy. John saw the need for a better-educated clergy and attempted to establish a seminary at Caen. When this met with opposition, he founded the secular Society of Jesus and Mary in 1643 and began to train other parish priests. There are seminaries in Canada and the United States today that have their roots in this French soil.

AUGUST 20

Bernard of Clairvaux (ca. 1090–1153)

Active spirituality

Born to nobility near Dijon, France, Bernard became a major influence in twelfth-century Christianity. He and his five brothers were extraordinarily intelligent and capable. When he became a Cistercian monk in 1112, he is reported to have brought four of his brothers and about thirty of his friends with him. Eventually his youngest brother and his father also joined with him. Bernard's sister remained behind for years, but also entered the religious life as a result of his guidance.

In 1115 Bernard accepted the assignment to establish a new monastery at Clairvaux. This work prospered under his leadership. An outstanding speaker and writer, with an astonishing command of sacred Scripture, Bernard was popular throughout Western Europe. People in positions of sacred and secular authority sought his counsel.

His writings reveal a thoroughly human mixture of character traits. Sometimes assertive, authoritarian, and a little irritable, in other passages he is remorseful, tender, supportive, and caring. Bernard did not hesitate to expose malice and to denounce a lack of common sense in the eminent and mighty. He expressed disgust when he saw unkindness and bigotry in anyone.

Beneath this active and influential exterior lies a profound mysticism. Bernard's prayer experience sustained and nurtured him throughout his busy life.

AUGUST 21

Victoria Rasoamanarivo (1848–94)

Courageous service

In spite of the fact that the London Missionary Society had established a mission in Madagascar three decades before her birth, Victoria was born into paganism. The mission resulted in several thousand converts to Christianity, and in missionaries teaching at least thirty thousand Madagascans to read. As usual, the missionaries were quick to provide translations of the Bible.

A monarchy had ruled Madagascar since the sixteenth century. During Victoria's life, the queen of Madagascar was hostile to Christianity and exiled many of the missionaries. When the queen died in 1861 it became possible for them to return. Jesuit missionaries also set up shop in the country. In 1869 the new queen was baptized a Christian.

Victoria began studying in one of the mission schools and became a Christian convert. Unfortunately, political struggles made being Catholic very difficult in Madagascar. In the popular thinking, Catholicism was connected to French imperialism. King Radama II had a close working relationship with France. He was deposed, and everything associated with France came under fire. Catholic missionaries were asked to leave.

Victoria began a difficult ministry of helping fellow Christians during years of persecution. Exhibiting enormous courage, she defended them in court and in public. Her work helping fellow Christians who were poor and imprisoned nearly exhausted her. She was only forty-six years old when she died.

AUGUST 22

Philip Benizi (1233–85)

Humility

After studying medicine at Paris and Padua, Philip Benizi became a physician in thirteenth-century Florence at the age of nineteen.

Following a natural interest, he became well-read in both the Scriptures and the church fathers. At twenty-one, he abandoned medicine and became a lay member of an austere local religious community. Living in a little cave behind the church, he tended the garden and performed other manual labor from 1255 to 1258.

While conversing on a trip to Siena, Philip surprised his companions with his knowledge of Scripture and church doctrine. He was quickly elevated to positions of greater responsibility, and became one of the foremost preachers in Italy. His talent as an organizer and administrator accomplished more, but more important, he was an outstanding mediator. He is remembered for his role in bringing peaceful resolutions to difficult church conflicts, and for attracting the irreligious into the church.

AUGUST 23

Rose of Lima (1586–1617)

✒*Social service*

The first named saint in the Western Hemisphere was a young woman born to Spanish parents in Lima, Peru. She was such a beautiful baby that her maid said she was "like a rose." The name stuck. Rose, whose real name was Isabel de Flores, remained attractive as she grew up. Her parents took pride in her beauty, and she received many spontaneous comments of admiration from others. Suitors expressed great interest, raising the notion that she might marry well and bring fortune to her family. Her father had lost his moderate wealth through failed speculation in mining.

Rose, however, never married. Taking Catherine of Siena (April 29) as her role model, she dedicated her life totally to God. A handful of reports from four centuries ago create mixed images about her treatment of herself. We know she attempted to damage her attractive complexion by rubbing pepper on her face and lime on her hands. Where do we draw the line between spiritually valuable physical austerity and masochism? Did she suffer from bulimia?

Through needlework and gardening, Rose helped to provide for her family's needs. Moving out of the house into a little hut in the garden, she devoted herself to prayer. She began works of mercy among the poor. A room in her family home became an infirmary where she took care of sick children and the elderly. Some consider her the originator of social service in Peru.

Rose died at the age of thirty-one. By then she was highly regarded by a wide spectrum of society. The crowds that turned out in Lima to show their respect were large, delaying her funeral for several days.

AUGUST 24

Nathanael Bartholomew (first century)

✐ *Without guile*

The New Testament records slight variations in the names of Christ's twelve apostles. The first three Gospels and the Acts of the Apostles mention Bartholomew. Interesting, that's all they do—mention him. They report nothing he said or did. In the first three Gospel accounts, Bartholomew is listed beside the name of Philip. The Gospel of John tells us that Philip brought Nathanael to Jesus. Bartholomew is what we would call a "last name." *Bar* means "son of" and *tholomew* would be the father's name. Given the consistent connection with Philip, the scholars believe the two names may apply to the same individual.

Fortunately, the Gospel of John gives us a rather full picture of Nathanael. We first meet him under a fig tree reading the Scripture, meditating quietly. Christ said Nathanael was without guile, referring to a desirable childlike honesty and openness. This character trait probably prompted his famous question to Philip, "Can anything good come out of Nazareth?"

AUGUST 25
Joseph Calasanz (1557–1648)
❦*Heroic patience*

Joseph Calasanz, a nobleman from Peralta de la Sal, Spain, worked as an ordained priest until a mystical experience confirmed his desire to travel to Rome. Providing a free education for poor and homeless children weighed heavily on him. He resigned his office as vicar general, and with three other priests established *Le Scuole Pie* in 1597.

The school quickly attracted students, and it soon became necessary to relocate and enlarge its facilities to accommodate them. By 1611, the school's enrollment included twelve hundred children. Joseph Calasanz opened other schools, and his organization expanded, receiving recognition as a religious congregation.

At the age of sixty-five, Joseph faced perplexing difficulties. Mario Sozzi, one of the priests in his congregation, gained a position of authority and began to misuse his power. Overbearing and devious, Sozzi brought false charges against Calasanz, claiming that he was criminal and senile. The resulting embarrassment culminated in the loss of the founder's leadership of his schools. Sozzi never suffered any punishment for his misdeeds and died in 1643. Two years later, a formal inquiry reinstated Calasanz, but political intrigue continued. In 1646, his congregation was degraded to a society of priests governed by bishops.

After patiently suffering a quarter of a century of difficult trials, Joseph Calasanz died at the age of ninety.

AUGUST 26
Fillan of Glendochart (eighth century)
❦*Turning aside*

Fillan is one of those saints who is real, but known to us mostly as a legendary figure. An eighth-century Scotsman, Fillan of Glendochart became a popular saint who symbolized endurance, security, and assistance.

One early account of his life indicates that he became a Scots-Irish monk as a young man and lived for years in a simple dwelling near St. Andrew's in Scotland. Soon after accepting an assignment to a position of high ecclesiastical authority, he changed his mind, deciding instead to retreat alone to the hills around Glendochart, in Perthshire. There he worked with others to construct a church.

Fillan's "Quigrich" is a magnificent silver-plated shepherd's crook that is one of the National Museum of Scotland's historical treasures.

AUGUST 27
Monica (332–87)
Intercessory prayer

Appropriately, we recognize Monica and Augustine on consecutive days. Monica was Augustine's mother. Her son in his *Confessions* and other writings reports most of what we know about her. If ever there were someone rewarded by persistent prayer, it is Monica. She is the example of a mother who fervently prayed for her son's conversion, year after exasperating year. Her unfailing pounding at God's door is precisely the kind of prayer commended by Christ in his parable of the importunate widow.

Early on, her son, Augustine, was a challenging young man who had little use for Christianity. He was twenty-nine when he moved out independently to take up a life in Rome. She followed him, praying all the while. A bishop explained to her that it was pointless to attempt to argue religion with her intelligent son. He would discover the error of his thinking through his reading. The bishop encouraged her to continue praying. "It is not possible that the son of these tears should perish."

What joy and relief she experienced when her son was baptized in 387. A few weeks later, in her fifty-sixth year, Monica died far across the Mediterranean from her home in Thagaste, North Africa (now Algeria). She said, "Bury this body anywhere. Don't concern yourselves about it. Nothing is far from God."

Augustine confessed to God, "I wept for my mother for a small part of an hour, for she was dead who had wept for me that I should live in your sight."

AUGUST 28

Augustine (354–430)

☙ *Resisting conversion*

Augustine is one of the world's great minds. His writings have placed an indelible mark on Christian doctrine. He was as multi-dimensional as all of the rest of us, so it would not be fair to caricature him as "brainy" or cerebral, because he had an active and caring ministry during tough times for his people.

The story of the first three decades of his life records the tale of an intelligent pagan. He admitted that he was highly emotional and sensual. At one point in his life he was addicted to theater because he enjoyed the throat-constricting melodrama. Sex outside of marriage was also part of his experience for many years. His personal account of his conversion makes powerful and dramatic reading.

Aside from the unrelenting prayers of his mother, Monica, the influence of Bishop Ambrose (December 7) in Milan was important to his conversion. Augustine supported himself in Milan by teaching rhetoric. When he heard Ambrose comment that some troubling passages of Scripture can be interpreted allegorically rather than literally, Augustine's resistance began to weaken. He grew dissatisfied with his religious philosophy.

After Augustine wrestled with his own mind and spirit for years, a climactic and pivotal point came when he was sitting in a garden and heard the voice of a child repeating a chant, "Take up and read! Take up and read!" With a notion that God was prompting him to open the Bible, he picked it up and read from Paul's letter to the Romans. "Let us behave decently, as in the daytime, not in orgies and drunkenness, not in sexual immorality and debauchery, not in dissension and jealousy. Rather, clothe yourself with the Lord Jesus Christ, and do not think about how to gratify the desires of the sinful nature." Augustine recalled, "I had no desire, no need, to read further. In the instant that sentence ended, it was as if a peaceful light shone in my heart and all the darkness of doubt vanished."

Returning to North Africa after his mother's death, Augustine was ordained a priest. In 396, he became bishop of the city of Hippo. These were troubled years in church and political history. Constantinople and Rome were in a power struggle. Barbarians and Vandals were destroying Latin culture. The prosperity of North Africa was failing. Controversy and heresy were tearing apart the Christian Church in Africa. All the while, Augustine worked hard to maintain religious integrity.

When Rome fell in 410 to the army of Alaric the Visigoth, pagans suggested that Christianity had angered the Roman gods and brought about the catastrophe. In response, Augustine wrote *The City of God*, in which he contrasts Jerusalem and Babylon— those who are dedicated to God and those who are citizens of the pagan empire of this earth.

When Augustine died in August, 430, Vandals had the city of Hippo under siege. The intellectual properties of his fertile mind, however, were indestructible. His defining comments on the human condition and Christian theology remained the backbone of Christian thought for centuries. He continues to enter into conversation with our contemporary theologians, providing benchmarks for new ideas.

A sentence he wrote to God on the first page of his *Confessions* is often quoted by sensitive souls: "You have made us for yourself, and our hearts are restless until they rest in you."

AUGUST 29

John the Baptist (first century)

✒ *Forerunner*

The story of Jesus Christ begins with the ministry of John the Baptist. John, a cousin of Jesus, was born about six months before Jesus, but they grew up under radically different circumstances.

While Jesus was raised in the home of a carpenter in Nazareth, John was an ascetic with untrimmed hair—a dedicated Nazarite from birth who lived in the desert. Jesus grew up in a regular way with family responsibilities. He pronounced John the greatest of the prophets and more than a prophet. John was God's messenger, sent to prepare the way for the Christ.

With John, the voice of prophecy that had been silent for centuries again was heard. He went to the area beside the Jordan River and began to preach a message of repentance, offering baptism as a sacred rite.

As the last of a long line of prophets, John preached the nearness of the day of Christ. He knew a time of decision and judgment was coming soon. John reactivated the ancient Messianic expectancy of the Jews. He said that he was not worthy to untie the shoes of the one who was coming. John baptized with water, but the Christ would baptize with the Holy Spirit and with fire. When Jesus came to the Jordan to be baptized, John told his disciples to follow him, for Jesus was the "Lamb of God who would take away the sin of the world". John modestly hesitated to baptize Jesus, but Jesus insisted. This moment for Jesus was the turning point from a private to a public life. Afterward, John began to say, "He must increase and I must decrease."

John told people they could no longer trust their descent from Abraham as being sufficient for their acceptance with God. He told tax collectors they should not collect more money than appropriate. He was openly critical of King Herod for marrying his brother's wife, Herodias. Soon enough, Herodias pressed King Herod to have John arrested in order to stop his public objections to their relationship.

In prison, John began to have doubts. Perhaps they resulted from the dark confinement of one who was familiar with open air and sunshine. Maybe it was because Jesus wasn't doing the things John expected of a Messiah. He sent two of his disciples to Jesus to ask him directly, "Are you the one who was to come, or should we look for another?" Jesus sent an indirect answer to the uncertain John. "Blessed is he who is not offended in me." Like the rest of us, John had to respond in faith.

The account of John's execution by decapitation is strikingly told in Richard Strauss's opera *Salome,* which is based on a play by Oscar Wilde. The Scriptures tell us that Herodias encouraged her daughter, Salome, to ask for John's head as a reward for pleasing the King with a dance.

It is significant that the book of Acts records that twenty years after his death, in another part of the world, there were still people who proclaimed the baptism of John.

AUGUST 30

Margaret Ward (d. 1588)

❧*Steadfast support*

To appreciate the circumstances that led to the martyrdom of Margaret Ward, we must understand the religious tensions that accompanied the time of the Spanish Armada. Elizabeth I ruled England in 1588. Philip II of Spain was in economic rivalry with her. Gold was returning from the New World, and Spain was leading the building of an international empire. Philip attempted to gain influence in England by proposing marriage to Elizabeth. She refused, and began to work against him. Elizabeth supported the Anglican Church and opposed the Catholics. In response, Philip directed his shipyards to construct a large number of ships in order to invade England.

The thirty thousand Spanish sailors and soldiers faced severe challenges in the English Channel. Foggy weather, a shortage of drinking water, friction between Spanish and Portuguese crews, maneuverable English ships with long-range cannons, and inadequate planning doomed the Armada. Storms at sea added to their misery when they attempted to return home. Spain lost nearly ten thousand men and more than sixty-three ships. In failure, Philip turned his attention to France, but his influence in Europe began to wane.

Margaret Ward worked as a servant in London. Margaret came to the assistance of a priest named William Watson, an odd and notoriously controversial man. In and out of prison, caught up in political partisanship, Watson nearly starved to death while being questioned by his captors. To control his activities they moved him to an attic and required him to attend Anglican worship services.

Margaret began to visit him, bringing baskets of food. Gaining the confidence of those around Watson, she secretly brought him rope cut to the right length, and hired some Catholic sailors to have a boat in the river below his attic window in the wee hours of the morning. Watson thought he could keep the rope if he doubled it and pulled it down after him. Unfortunately, he fell, breaking an arm and a leg. The sailors recovered him and took him to a place of safety. The rope remained dangling and implicated Margaret. Along with Margaret, a young Irishman, John Roche, assisted in the priest's escape by exchanging clothes with him. Both Margaret and John were soon arrested.

As with many other prisoners, she faced mistreatment in that time and place. Margaret was placed in irons for more than a week, then suspended by her wrists and beaten before she made an appearance in court. The authorities charged Margaret and John with assisting a prisoner who was a traitor. They were offered freedom if they would apologize to the queen and attend the Anglican Church. Margaret replied that she had done nothing to offend the queen. They were condemned for disobeying an obligation, and were hanged in 1588.

AUGUST 31

Joseph of Arimathea and Nicodemus
(first century)

Attracted to Christ

No one is certain where Arimathea was located. The New Testament always attaches his community of origin to his name in order to distinguish him from the other Josephs. The Gospel narrative describes him as good and just. He was a respected member of the council, probably the Sanhedrin. Whatever his origin, Joseph lived in

Jerusalem long enough to become a respected citizen. Living among so many who were poor, Joseph was one of the wealthy. His property lay outside the city wall, and in his garden he had prepared a tomb for himself, hewn from solid rock.

Joseph shared the anticipation of the arrival of the Messiah. Reports of Jesus of Nazareth caught his attention. He concluded that it would not be possible for Jesus to accomplish the things he was doing if God were not with him. We don't know what contact Joseph had with Jesus, but he was convinced that he was the Christ.

Joseph remained a secret disciple. Keeping his ideas to himself, he never openly declared his faith. His friends would not have shared his belief in Jesus. He may have been cautious because his faith could have had negative social results.

It is possible that Joseph sat in the court that found Jesus guilty of blasphemy and sentenced him to death. Joseph's inner conflict must have been enormous, but he found it prudent to remain silent. Secret disciples may believe one way, but they are forced to act another.

The crucifixion took place very near Joseph's garden. At this point, he found his courage. The Gospels tell us that he walked boldly into the hall of Pilate and asked for the body of Jesus, openly identifying himself. Pilate was amazed that Jesus was dead and kept Joseph waiting until he had confirmation. With that, Pilate allowed Joseph to take the body and place it in his own personal tomb. Otherwise, Jesus' body would have been thrown into a garbage pit along with the bodies of the two thieves. As it turned out, the most significant event in human history occurred in the garden of Joseph of Arimathea: the resurrection of Jesus.

Nicodemus is another who attempted the impossible by being a secret follower of Jesus. He was a Pharisee, a member of a Jewish group practicing extreme patriotism and religious fervor. He held a responsible position of authority as a scholar and a teacher. Nicodemus recognized something authentic in Jesus.

The three mentions of Nicodemus in the Gospels always attach the explanation that he is the one who visited Jesus at night. Scripture implies that he came by night because he did not want to be seen. He was eager for conversation with our Lord, but he did not want his friends to know about it.

Jesus was sharp with Nicodemus, pointing to the necessity of his being reborn. Jesus seemed to demand an open confession of faith from him. While Nicodemus willingly speculated regarding religion, he did not intend to identify himself with Jesus. He wanted to stand personally aloof while engaged in an interesting discussion. Jesus assured him that from the detached point of view of a spectator, it would not be possible for him to understand the simplest things about God's kingdom. In fact, he was now faced with a life-or-death choice.

Nicodemus must have departed that nighttime meeting with his soul troubled. He had come to discuss and debate. Jesus had offered him an opportunity for decision and obedience.

When Jesus returned to Jerusalem a few months later, the opposition to him had grown stronger. It became difficult for Nicodemus to maintain a neutral position. Someone asked the gathered body, "Have any of the rulers of the Pharisees believed on him?" Nicodemus responded defensively, "Does our law judge anyone before it hears him and knows what he is doing?" They replied sharply, "Are you also a Galilean?"

We don't know what became of Nicodemus. In the last mention of him in the New Testament he is with his friend Joseph of Arimathea at the burial of Jesus. It is probable that both became committed followers.

SEPTEMBER 1
Giles (eighth century)
✒ *Christian influence*

St. Giles had great popularity in the Middle Ages. England dedicated more than a hundred and fifty churches to him, and even some Protestant churches use his name in our time. Hospitals also frequently use his name.

What we can say about Giles with any certainty is that he was an eighth-century hermit who founded a monastery where the town of Saint-Giles, France, is located today. His shrine became a popular pilgrimage site.

The remainder of his story is shrouded in legend, some of which is dramatic and gripping. One such tale regards a hunting accident. Hunters were pursuing a deer that ran for refuge to the hermit who shared its forest. As it stood near him, a hunter's arrow missed, and it struck and crippled Giles instead. A deer, an arrow, and a crutch often appear in artistic representations of Giles.

SEPTEMBER 2

John du Lau and Companions (d. 1792)
Courage

The French Revolution was a violent and bloody upheaval. On September 2 we remember the massacre of one hundred and ninety-one priests and bishops in 1792. The problem began when new laws stated that clergy were subject to secular authority. The law required church leaders to take an oath affirming government policy. In all of France, only four bishops and a handful of priests agreed to do so. The ones who refused were declared "enemies of the Revolution" and were told to leave France.

Believing rumors of an imminent invasion, an enraged mob broke into Paris jails, searching for counter-revolutionary Catholic priests. The large group honored today was being held in a Carmelite church on the Rue de Rennes until they could be deported. The mob burst into the church, and the archbishop of Arles, John du Lau, stepped forward to meet them. After confirming his identity, the wild crowd killed him with swords and pikes, beginning a killing frenzy that went on for hours. Each prisoner had one last opportunity to take the oath of allegiance. As they refused, the enraged men took them outside and murdered them, two at a time.

Most of the "companions" martyred in this grisly event remain anonymous in published histories. One of them, Francis de La Rochefoucauld Maumont, the bishop of Beauvais, stands out of the crowd because he was an invalid. After witnessing the steady stream of executions that continued until sundown, someone called his name. From his pallet, he answered, "Here I am, gentlemen. I'm ready to die, but I can't walk. Please carry me where you wish me to go." Declining to take the oath, he also was taken to the garden and hacked to pieces.

SEPTEMBER 3

Gregory the Great (ca. 540–604)

✠ *True greatness*

Illness and handicaps are not necessarily obstacles to spiritual greatness or holiness. Gregory was chronically ill during most of the time he was making history. The pain of gout and gastritis made life miserable, but it did not cloud his judgment. Even as he lay dying, Gregory busily dictated letters and took care of church business. In spite of the distractions of weak flesh, Gregory's achievements place him among the few honored with the title "Great" (*Magnus*). Gregory's own choice of a label was "servant of the servants of God."

By the time Gregory was born in the mid-sixth century, the fall of Rome was complete. The magnificent days of the Roman Empire were history, and the city was in ruins. Disorder and poverty followed the chaos of the Gothic War (536–53). Gregory became prefect of Rome at the age of thirty. His administrative skills brought expressions of praise and gratitude from the Roman citizenry.

Gregory was far more than an outstanding manager; he also had a sensitive spirit and lived devoutly. When his father died in 575, Gregory turned the fancy, family home into a monastery and became its first monk. By his own report, the next three years of prayer and fasting were the happiest of his life.

By 590, he was pope, and he turned out to be one of the most respected. Rome was no longer an economic dynamo or a political force in the world. Because no secular authority remained functional, Gregory essentially became, the mayor and city manager of Rome. The new pope dealt with floods, starvation among his people, and an epidemic of the plague. Aggressive Germanic Lombard armies that invaded northern Italy disturbed the peace. Vast multitudes of barbarians who knew nothing of Christ surrounded him.

The Venerable Bede (May 25) wrote that Gregory visited Rome's market and noticed some blond Anglo-Saxon slaves. He asked them where they were from and they explained that they were "Angles." Gregory commented, "They are well-named, because they have angelic faces and could be the companions of the angels in heaven." Though reports came from England that it was a savage and dangerous place, Gregory became eager to send Christian missionaries there.

Gregory's writing both influenced and reflected the mentality of the medieval period in Europe. He was neither a great theologian like Augustine (August 28) nor a brilliant writer like Jerome (September 30), but an author of popular religious works, including stories of the lives of saints. A huge collection of more than eight hundred of his letters reveals the human side of Gregory the Great, as well as the intimate qualities of church life in his times. In one letter, Gregory sent a friend who was having eye trouble, a pinch of iron filings from the iron chains that he believed had bound Peter and Paul (see June 29). He wrote, "Apply these to your eyes. Many miracles have been wrought by this same gift." Gregory's six-volume commentary on Job, *Magna moralia*, applies Augustinian theology to Scriptural interpretation. Interested in the development of church music, he will forever be associated with the Gregorian chant.

In the ruins of Rome, Gregory conceptualized a world filled with the supernatural presence of wizards, ghosts, and demons. Rational order had departed the universe, and people believed the end of the world was near. Only faith sustained life in the horror and terror of the seven centuries some now call the Dark Ages. Someone described Gregory as "the first completely medieval man." But his hand was so steady on the wheel, his integrity and insight so valuable to his times, that people would come to value his office as a stabilizing base for a society spinning out of control.

SEPTEMBER 4

Rose of Viterbo (1234–52)
✐*Mysticism*

Rose was born to a poor Italian family living at Viterbo. Religiously inclined from childhood, Rose had a mystical experience during an illness when she was eight, and she began to preach in the streets of her hometown. Her messages supported the pope, who was in considerable political difficulty. Crowds of the curious attempted to catch a glimpse of her at home. This distressed her father, who told her to stop speaking in public but relented at the parish priest's urging. Rose continued her street preaching for the next two years.

Opponents of the pope declared that Rose was not preaching, but meddling in politics. Emotions and pressures grew, until Viterbo's *podesta* banished Rose and her parents to Soriano.

Emperor Frederick II soon died, ending the contest with the pope that had been the subject of Rose's street messages, and the family safely returned home. She attempted to join the Poor Clare convent of St. Mary of the Roses at Viterbo, but the nuns repeatedly refused to admit her.

After her death as a young woman of eighteen, Rose was buried in the church of Santa Maria in Podio. Five years later, on September 4, 1252, her remains were exhumed and reburied at the convent of St. Mary of the Roses.

SEPTEMBER 5

Mother Teresa of Calcutta (1910–97)
✐*Selfless*

An exception to the normal five-year waiting period for beatification was made for this exceptional woman. Less than two years after Mother Teresa of Calcutta died, the shortest such interval in modern history, Pope John Paul II pronounced her "blessed."

There is little doubt that if Mother Teresa had lived in the early centuries of Christianity, the church would have declared her a saint before her grave was covered.

The defining moment in this Albanian woman's life came on September 10, 1946. For twenty years, Teresa had taught school in India. On this day, she was riding the train to Darjeeling when an overwhelming sense of divine calling came to her. She was convinced that God wanted her "to be poor with the poor." Responding to that divine impulse, she became the "Saint of the Gutters," and gave the world a new and defining example of applied Christianity.

Born in the Balkans at Skopje in 1910, she began life as Gonxha Agnes Bojaxhiu. After growing up under the care of her widowed mother, she left home in 1928 to join the Sisters of Loreto, in Ireland. Her religious name became Mary Teresa, after St. Thérèse of Lisieux (October 1), and soon the nineteen-year-old was on her way to Calcutta where she began to teach girls at St. Mary's School. In 1944 Mother Teresa became the school's principal, recognized for her organizational skill, hard work, loving care, and selflessness.

After the inspired moment of her train ride, her "call within a call," she established the Missionaries of Charity and waited two years for the Pope's official approval of the order. When the way was clear, she donned her now familiar white sari with a blue border, and entered the slums of Calcutta. She washed children's sores, cared for an old man lying on the road, and cared for a woman dying of tuberculosis and starvation. The following days began in the same manner. After communion she walked out, rosary in hand, looking for "the unwanted, the unloved, the uncared for." She did not have to search far. An overwhelming opportunity to minister in the name of Christ waited for her. As the months passed, her former students began to join in the work with her.

By the 1960s, Mother Teresa was sending sisters to other Indian cities. Thirty years later, her work had spread all over the world. "We are not social workers," she said. "We may be doing social work in the eyes of some people, but we must be contemplatives in the heart of the world. Do ordinary things with extraordinary love."

After Mother Teresa won the Nobel Peace Prize in 1979, she became the center of the media's attention, but her simple labor among the poor did not change. "Holiness is not the luxury of the few. It is a simple duty for you and for me." Others asked to join her in her work in Calcutta. She responded, "Find your own Calcutta. Don't search for God in far lands—he is not there. He is close to you, he is with you."

The government of India gave Mother Teresa a state funeral when she died on September 5, 1997. She was buried in the Mother House of the Missionaries of Charity. Her tomb soon became a shrine for people of many religions.

SEPTEMBER 6

Eleutherius of Spoleto (d. ca. 590)

❧ *Effective prayer*

When Gregory the Great (September 3) needed someone to pray for his health, he turned to Eleutherius. Being himself the beneficiary of a cure, Gregory included an article on the life of Eleutherius in his book of saints.

Known as a miracle worker, Eleutherius was abbot of St. Mark's near Spoleto, Italy. Moving to Rome, he became a monk at Gregory's monastery.

Eleutherius died in Rome.

SEPTEMBER 7

Clodoald (d. ca. 560)

❧ *Seeking solitude*

St. Cloud, Minnesota, and St. Cloud, Florida, carry the familiar name of Clodoald, the grandson of King Clovis, of France. His father died of a wound in Burgundy when the future saint was only three years old. Grandmother Clotilde reared Clodoald and his brothers with much loving attention. By the time Clodoald became a young man, he had seen murder, mayhem, assassinations, and political intrigue enough to make him weary of the world. He declined an opportunity to seize the French throne and decided instead to become a monk. Retreating to a hermit's cell, he attempted to master his life through austerity and prayer.

Uncomfortable with his proximity to Paris, where people knew and recognized him, Clodoald decided to move to Provence. But once he was there, many people then began to visit the hermit for healing and guidance. It became impossible for Clodoald to have enough personal time for solitude and prayer. He returned to Paris and was welcomed with celebrations of joy. In 551, Clodoald became an ordained priest. He founded the monastery of Nogent-sur-Seine near Versailles and became its abbot. Today, the church there is named St. Cloud.

Clodoald was only thirty-six when he died.

SEPTEMBER 8

Corbinian (670–730)

Proclamation of the Gospel

Corbinian originally took the name of his father, Waldegiso, but his mother renamed him after herself. Growing up near Fontainebleau, France, he became a hermit late in the seventh century. Retreating from society, Corbinian lived reclusively for fourteen years. The familiar trend of people in those days to seek divine guidance and miracles from Christian hermits disturbed his peace.

Searching for his proper place in the world, Corbinian arrived in Bavaria, Germany, and began to preach the gospel. Duke Grimoald of Bavaria was pleased to have him in his country and gave him both support and protection. Corbinian's preaching produced excellent results, with many conversions to Christ, but his relationship with Duke Grimoald soon turned sour.

The Duke married his brother's widow, Biltrudis. Corbinian interpreted church law as forbidding such a marriage. The duke agreed, but Biltrudis was outraged. She began to harass Corbinian, calling him a foreign interloper in Bavarian affairs. It became necessary for him to flee for safety. He remained in exile until both Grimoald and Biltrudis were deceased. Returning to Bavaria, Corbinian continued his missionary efforts.

SEPTEMBER 9

Peter Claver (1581–1654)

✥Kindly example

If we do not have the ability to stop a great social evil such as slavery, we can find a way to minister to its victims. Wanting to do something to help victims of slavery, Peter Claver, a Spanish Jesuit, went to Cartagena (Columbia), a busy port of entry to the Americas for African slaves. Each year about ten thousand slaves passed through Cartagena after a dangerous and inhumane voyage from West Africa. Slave traffickers packed their human cargo into the holds of ships with no concern for sanitation or freedom of movement. Given minimal food and water, and treated cruelly, about a third of each load died at sea. The desolate people who survived the voyage had one friend when they arrived—Peter Claver, who called himself the slave of slaves.

Peter met each ship as it pulled into port, went aboard, and tried to help its unwilling passengers. As the slaves were being sold at public auction, he gave them food, medicine, and other necessities. "We must speak to them with our hands," Peter said, "before we try to speak to them with our lips." Using pictures and a team of seven interpreters, he told them of Jesus Christ. He attempted the impossible task of giving the slaves a sense of the human dignity they had been denied, by telling them of God's love. Peter baptized an estimated three hundred thousand arrivals from Africa. He visited slaves as they worked on plantations and in the gold and silver mines, staying in the slaves' quarters rather than with the owners. Those who were making money in the slave trade suspected that Peter might be attempting to undermine their livelihood. If a slave misbehaved, they considered it Claver's fault. His presence was not always welcomed.

The plague destroyed Peter Claver's ability to function in 1650. He remained alone for four years, receiving barely enough attention to keep him alive, dying in 1654.

SEPTEMBER 10

Nicholas of Tolentino (1245–1305)
Making a difference

More than forty saints are named Nicholas. The saint we remember today, Nicholas of Tolentino, was an answer to a childless mother's prayer. An Augustinian friar, he wandered from place to place, never really settling down until he perceived a voice directing him, "To Tolentino, to Tolentino. Persevere there." He lived the remaining thirty years of his life in Tolentino.

This Italian town was in a state of disorder when Nicholas arrived. Immorality was rampant, and religion had become fragmented and diluted with paganism. Nicholas began three decades of preaching to the public on street corners and ministering to the needs of people outside the church. He died in 1305.

SEPTEMBER 11

Jean-Gabriel Perboyre (1802–40)
Religious persecution

Born in France, Jean-Gabriel Perboyre became a priest in 1826. His brother Louis died while on a voyage to mission work in China, and Jean-Gabriel volunteered to take his place. Arriving in China in 1835, Jean-Gabriel worked his way to Nanyang, Hunan, and devoted half a year to learning the language. He then began Christian ministry up the Yang Tze River at the lake region of Hupei.

Religious persecution began suddenly in 1839. Soldiers arrested Jean-Gabriel and treated him badly. There were many "trials" with repeated questioning. In an effort to get him to reveal the names of other Chinese Christians, the soldiers hung him by his thumbs and beat him with bamboo rods. Jean-Gabriel remained silent and suffered in the same manner exemplified by his Lord.

Sentenced to die by strangulation, Jean-Gabriel came to the end of his life on a hill named "Red Mountain." He was tied to a cross and strangled with a rope around his neck on September 11, 1840.

SEPTEMBER 12

Guy of Anderlecht (d. ca. 1012)

☙Service to Christ

"The poor man of Anderlecht" was a church janitor in Belgium during the eleventh century. He spent most of his time in a church near Brussels, sweeping the floors, polishing brass, and washing sacred vessels, but always found time to be friendly with others as poor as himself. A thick veneer of legendary material, composed long after his death in Anderlecht, hides from our eyes today the events in Guy's life.

SEPTEMBER 13

John Chrysostom (ca. 347–407)

☙Interpretation of Scripture

"Chrysostom" is a nickname. In English, it means "Golden-Mouthed." John Chrysostom was a powerful and eloquent preacher in the early years of Christianity, mingling scholarship with practical direction. The sermons he preached in Antioch, Syria, during the fourth century are easily found in print today, and comprise the best representations of biblical interpretation from his time. They remain surprisingly relevant.

Born an army officer's son in 347, John was nurtured by his widowed mother. At the age of twenty-four, he became a monk in a community in the hills not far from his home. His attempt at cave dwelling and fasting had a devastating effect on his health. He returned to Antioch and became a priest in 386, and by 398 was archbishop of Constantinople. His comments about politics, women's clothing, and everyday behavior brought him both fame and criticism.

In 404, John Chrysostom, one of the great teachers of the church, was banished to Armenia by a petulant empress. He died while being forced to travel on foot in hot weather and in a state of exhaustion.

SEPTEMBER 14
Notburga of Eben (d. 1313)
❧ *Generosity*

From the Tyrol Mountains of Austria, Notburga became a servant in a castle at Innsbruck. As cook for Count Henry of Rothenburg, she would pass food along to the poor. When Ottilia, the Count's wife, ordered Notburga to give any table scraps to the hogs, Notburga then began to save some of her own food to pass along to those who had little to eat.

Notburga has a reputation for being a hard worker who cared for others and regularly participated in public worship. As she was dying in 1313, she asked that her body be placed on an oxcart, and that she should be buried wherever it stopped. After a trip that sprinkled blessings along the way, the cart came to a stop at the door of the church of St. Rupert at Eben. She was buried there.

SEPTEMBER 15
Catherine of Genoa (1477–1510)
❧ *Activity and contemplation*

Mystical experiences are less common among saints than many realize. The mystic Catherine of Genoa was one of the less common. Her writings about the spiritual life are among the major classics. She reports that she felt God burning within her, like a flame. These experiences came to her with increasing frequency as the years passed, while she labored in the physical world, working at a variety of jobs.

We begin her story with an arranged marriage that may have been a good idea for two families at odds, but took no consideration of the personalities and affections of bride and groom. Sixteen-year-old Catherine suffered pure misery for ten years attempting to be the wife of Julian Adorno. He was careless with their money, inordinately sensual, ill-tempered, and frequently absent and unfaithful. When she turned twenty-five, she asked God to send her an illness that would make her bedridden.

On March 22, 1473, Catherine knelt for confession and had an intimate experience of the divine that made her conscious of her sins and confident of God's love. Someone heard her say, "No more world. No more sins." Bitterness and resentment evaporated from her spirit. From that early spring day, Catherine was a new person. She realized her life would be meaningful only if she lived it in service to others. Though she had grown up in a fastidious aristocratic family, Catherine sought out the most repulsive hospital patients and gave them personal care. Her happiness grew as she learned how to share the love of God.

Her husband was throwing their money away, seeking pleasure and distraction. Forced into bankruptcy, they sold their luxurious house and moved into an unpretentious cottage. Catherine told Julian the new place was much more to her liking. Touched by her spirit, and learning some tough lessons about life, Julian also experienced a change of heart and became a lay Franciscan. Eventually they moved into the hospital of Pemmatone, and Catherine became its director.

There is no doubt that Catherine was an able administrator and bookkeeper, but her main impact at the hospital continued to be her devotion to the care of the sick. In 1493, the plague killed four-fifths of the residents of Genoa. One day, Catherine kissed a dying woman and contracted the deadly illness herself. After lingering near death, she recovered, but before the year was over, Julian died.

In the years that followed, people responded to Catherine's spirituality and mission of charity. They came to help and they came to learn. Her wide-awake soul was an example of faith and works combined in a healthy way. The deeper her prayer life, the harder she labored. The more important her work, the more she prayed. Force applied at one end of the swing of the spiritual pendulum pushed it still higher at the other end of its arc. While having spiritual ecstasies, she also gave focused attention to caring for the needs of others.

Catherine of Genoa became seriously sick with an undiagnosed illness for the last three years of her life, dying in 1510.

SEPTEMBER 16

Cornelius and Cyprian (d. 258)

✍️ *Leadership*

Cornelius became pope in 251. Because of the Roman persecution of the Church, there had been no pope for more than a year. As Cornelius emerged as a leader, others vied for the position. One of the contestants, a priest named Novatian, had a strong opinion against forgiving the sins of church members who denied their faith when threatened with death. He found enough support to become an "anti-pope" to Cornelius, who held the opposite position, welcoming the return of apostate members to the Church. Though very much in the spirit of Christ, the gentle and forgiving view of Cornelius was unpopular with the rigorist faction.

Cornelius received written support from Cyprian [October 12}, a prominent lawyer in North Africa whose letter supporting Cornelius effectively defeated Novatian.

Under renewed persecution, Cornelius went into exile at Civita Vecchia. Though there is no evidence that he became a martyr, Cyprian described him as such. Visitors may still see his tomb in Rome.

SEPTEMBER 17

Hildegard of Bingen (1098–1179)

❦*Religious insight*

We may summarize the character and achievement of Hildegard of Bingen with three terms: Benedictine abbess, intellectual, and mystic. But this hardly does justice for one of the most remarkable German women of her times.

Hildegard was born in 1098. She grew up near a Benedictine abbey and became a nun while still in her teens. By 1136, she was its superior and relocated the growing community to Rupertsberg near Bingen about a decade later.

Mystical experiences were part of her life from childhood. "My visions were not like the dreams of sleep," she wrote. "I did not see them with my eyes or ears in hidden places. I saw them in full view when I was wide-awake and mentally alert. I perceived them with the eyes of the spirit and the inward ears." Hildegard's superiors instructed her to write down her experiences. With the help of a monk as a secretary, she devoted ten years of her life to preparing *Scivias* ("Know the Ways").

In the manner of other visionaries, Hildegard wrote letters to various leaders and rulers, criticizing their policies and offering better alternatives. Henry II of England heard from her, as did the emperor Frederick Barbarossa and Pope Eugenius III. She developed a concept of the "greenness" of God's life-giving force, and was an ecologist before anyone had coined the word.

One of her books was in the field of medicine. Hildegard dealt with the circulatory system, headaches, dizziness, insanity, and other maladies. She was knowledgeable regarding herbal therapy, and wrote about flora and fauna with a biologist's interest. She prepared commentaries on the Gospels, on the Athanasian Creed, and on the Rule of St. Benedict. Musicians are still performing her twelfth-century compositions and recording them on modern compact discs. Hildegard was an extraordinarily gifted woman with the widest imaginable range of interests built on a foundation of careful study.

Hildegard had almost reached her eightieth birthday when she died in 1179.

Joseph of Cupertino (1602–63)
❧*Patience and humility*

Cupertino is an Italian town where the dim-witted Joseph was born in a garden shed. Other children did not enjoy playing with him, nicknaming him "the Gaper" (*Boccaperta*) because he walked around with his mouth open. He failed as a kitchen helper with a Capuchin community, and then worked as a stable hand until it became clear to others that he was spiritually astute.

Although an exceptionally poor student, Joseph performed well on final examinations and became an ordained priest in 1628. He then began a unique ministry of healing and performed attention-getting miraculous stunts. Worshipers insisted they saw him fly over their heads from the church door to the altar. On one occasion, reliable witnesses reported seeing him levitate into an olive tree and kneel on one of its branches. The record of Joseph's life lists more than seventy instances of levitation. When ten workers failed to erect a cross thirty-six feet high, Joseph of Cupertino lifted it into place through the air "as if it were a straw." A new nickname, "The Flying Friar," replaced his unhappy childhood name. With all of that, Joseph remained humble, gentle, and cheerful. His demeanor was such that birds did not fly away when he approached.

We may smile at the credulity and pious exaggerations of seventeenth-century people, but historians do not doubt that his behavior embarrassed many religious people. Disturbing phenomena followed Joseph of Cupertino, disturbing enough for church authorities to put him out of sight in remote places during the final thirty-five years of his life. He died in strict seclusion in 1663. His canonization is not based on his startling displays, but on his extreme patience and humility.

SEPTEMBER 19

Januarius of Benevento (d. 304)

✒ *Martyred for faith*

Januarius, also known as Gennaro, did not make it very far into the pages of reliable history. We remember him chiefly because of a remarkable container of what is believed to be his blood.

Januarius was a fourth-century bishop of Benevento, Italy. He visited some imprisoned Christians during the Diocletian persecution and ended up in jail himself. The Romans martyred him along with the others about 304. Legend holds that they threw Januarius and his companions to the bears, but the animals refused to attack. Their captors then decapitated each of them. A woman named Eusebia collected some of the blood from the stone on which Januarius died and presented it to the bishop of Naples.

Today, an ornate reliquary contains hermetically sealed glass vials purported to contain the blood of Januarius. Thousands gather at the Naples Cathedral three times a year to witness the liquefaction of blood that is centuries old. The ritual itself began in the fourteenth century, a thousand years after Januarius was martyred. Skeptics point to the fact that the "blood" liquefied several times when jewelers repaired the reliquary. Chemists at the University of Pavia and colleagues in Milan have duplicated the phenomenon in their laboratories with chemicals that would have been readily available to medieval artists and alchemists. They created a gel that turns solid when undisturbed and liquefied when agitated. Regardless of such investigations, there is no proof that the substance in the reliquary is not blood, and Januarius remains the patron saint of Naples—a saint who died for his faith.

SEPTEMBER 20
Korean Martyrs (nineteenth century)
❦*Faith as risk*

Christianity is growing rapidly in South Korea today, and many churches are filled to overflowing. This was not the case in the nineteenth century. State-sponsored Confucianism officially banned Christianity. The first Korean Christian was actually baptized in China in 1784. Korean Christians returning home brought books with them. When a Chinese priest arrived in 1794, he discovered about four thousand Koreans who had been secretly attracted to Christ. Missionaries gradually arrived, and the number of "closet" Christians continued to increase.

It was impossible to keep such a large number of Christians hidden from official eyes indefinitely, even though they made heroic attempts to stay out of sight. Violent persecution broke out in the mid-nineteenth century, with many missionaries and their converts becoming martyrs. Of the thousands who were killed, one hundred and three were officially canonized in 1984, all but ten of them Korean.

SEPTEMBER 21
Matthew (first century)
❦*Beyond the apparent*

Matthew the tax collector worked for the Roman occupiers in a lucrative and unpopular occupation. Jesus made a point about God's love by being kind to Matthew, when the general population tended to snub him. Zaccheus, who climbed a sycamore tree in Jericho to see Jesus pass by, was also a tax collector. The fact that Christ wanted a tax collector as an apostle must have been shocking and scandalous in his cultural context. Religious people made the charge against Jesus that he ate with "tax collectors and sinners." Jesus made a sensible reply that reveals the depth of his spirituality. "Those who are well do not need a physician."

The inclusion of Matthew will forever remind Christians that though it may be easier to love the saint than the sinner, every sinner is a potential saint.

SEPTEMBER 22

Maurice and Companions (d. 287)

✒ *Allegiance to God*

It is necessary to distill the account of Maurice and his fellow soldiers to free it from enthusiastic exaggerations and thick layers of piety. But even after reducing the numbers involved, there is still a moving story of martyrdom.

In 287, the Roman army recruited a legion from Thebes in Upper Egypt. Every one of the new soldiers was a Christian. Rome sent them to help control rebellious Gauls near the lake of Geneva. The night before a decisive battle, all the combatants received instructions to sacrifice to the Roman gods. The Theban Legion declined pagan worship. The army considered this insubordination and used a standard technique to get compliance—decimation. Ten percent of the soldiers in the legion would be chosen by lot for execution. The remaining ninety percent should then be willing to sacrifice to the gods.

Because of the Theban Christians' strong religious convictions, the Roman plan failed to work. The officers used a second lottery and the soldiers continued to resist. "We are your soldiers, but we are also servants of the true God. We will obey your orders in every regard except in that which is against God's law. We took an oath to God before we took one to you."

Christians were causing problems for the Roman Empire in other parts of the world and could become military targets. The Theban legion knew this and did not want to fight against others who shared their faith in Christ. The Romans martyred the entire Theban legion. They offered no resistance as they were slain.

SEPTEMBER 23

Padre Pio (1887–1968)

✍*Inexplicable experience*

Padre Pio, as he is known today, was a poor boy who became a Capuchin friar in modern times. He lived at a Franciscan monastery, San Giovanni Rotundo, in the Apulian region of southern Italy. He would have preferred to blend anonymously into the community, but the very opposite happened when he became marked with the stigmata on his hands, feet, and side, similar to St. Francis of Assisi (October 4). These inexplicable open wounds appeared on his body in 1910 and remained there, bleeding, for fifty years.

Thousands came to see him and talk with him. Padre Pio of Pietrelcina was living proof of God's activity in the world, gifted with the complete range of supernatural gifts associated with a medieval saint. He performed miraculous healings, even giving sight to a man born without pupils in his eyes. He could "read" the hearts and minds of others so that they had no secrets with him. There are many reports that he could be in two places at once. These things were not happening in a gullible age of faith, but in our skeptical modern world that is suspicious of anything that defies scientific analysis.

Even religious experts responded negatively to Padre Pio. Church leaders did not want a monk who was a celebrity. They applied much effort to discredit and debunk the bizarre reports of his supernatural experiences. He was a troubling embarrassment, and they asked him to stay out of sight as much as possible.

Padre Pio, meanwhile, was truly suffering. The stigmata actually hurt and the notoriety caused him personal grief. The reaction of church officials brought him extraordinary stress. The wounds of the stigmata closed and healed shortly before his death on September 23, 1968. He became a canonized saint in 2002. Many books have been written about him.

SEPTEMBER 24
Gerard Sagredo (d. 1046)
✐*Evangelistic service*

"The Apostle of Hungary" began life in Venice, where he became a monk at San Giorgio Maggiore. While on a pilgrimage to Jerusalem, he passed through Hungary and met King Stephen, who wanted his country Christianized. Gerard agreed to tutor the king's son, Emeric. In 1035, Gerard became the first bishop of Csanad.

When King Stephen died in 1038, the forces of paganism broke out again. In 1046, soldiers killed Gerard in the area that in modern times has become Budapest. His murderers threw his body into the Danube River. Venetians venerate him as their first martyr.

SEPTEMBER 25
Sergius of Radonezh (1315–92)
✐*Simplicity*

There are two lists of official saints, Eastern and Western, reflecting the ancient division between Rome and Constantinople. Sergius is among the Russian Orthodox Church's most popular saints, and he is one of the very few who also appears on the Catholic calendar.

Sergius and his family settled down in Radonezh, near Moscow, early in his life. Civil war had stripped them of their position and wealth, forcing them to survive as peasants. When his parents died, Sergius and his brother Stephen became Christian hermits, living in the forest, struggling against the forces of the wild and their own human nature. Others gradually joined them to restore the dilapidated monastery of the Holy Trinity. Life at the monastery was simple and beautiful, if a little rough. Sergius was a mystic who also became involved in politics, but he steadfastly refused to depart from his life of prayer and devotion at the monastery.

SEPTEMBER 26

Cosmas and Damian (d. ? 303)

❦ *Christian service*

Here are two saints who exemplify the many who are "known only to God." All we know about them are their names. Some authorities are not even willing to place them in a particular century. Legend states that they were Arab brothers who were physicians. Famous for offering their services freely, they gained the nickname "Moneyless." Tradition holds that they were martyred near Antioch while Diocletian was Emperor of Rome. Fra Angelico and other artists left excellent paintings of their legendary experiences.

SEPTEMBER 27

Vincent de Paul (1581–1660)

❦ *Selfless giving*

Vincent's name will always be associated with charity for the poor. A French farm boy, Vincent de Paul became a priest when he was only nineteen or twenty. For the first decade of his seventeenth-century ministry, he enjoyed a comfortable life far from the dirt and heavy labor of his rural beginnings. The challenge of serving the poor waited for him in the future as he fulfilled a dream of rising above his early circumstances. He became a chaplain in the service of Queen Margaret of Valois, and gained the social skills to be at home among the affluent. He tutored in one of the wealthiest homes in Paris and grew familiar with eating well and dressing well.

At the same time, the connections Vincent were making opened doors that allowed him to perform valuable services for people in great need, such as working to improve prison conditions. He met Francis de Sales (January 24) and was profoundly influenced by him. Possibilities for a ministry focused on the world's forgotten poor began to take shape in his thinking. Like all people, those outside the circle of upper-class society had both physical and spiritual

225

needs. He decided to organize groups of lay people to become involved with the cause of the poor.

In 1625, Vincent founded the Congregation of the Mission (known also as Vincentians). Its members were secular priests who agreed to live in a community, train clergy, and serve in small towns and villages. He also began the Sisters of Charity, women who were committed to the poor and the sick. This was the first "unenclosed" congregation of women. "Their convent is the sickroom," he wrote, "their chapel the parish church, their cloister the streets of the city."

Vincent de Paul became a legendary figure while he remained at work. Wealthy people contributed funds and volunteered to help. The poor and victims of war benefited from his tireless service. He established hospitals, orphanages, and homes for the mentally ill, and raised funds to ransom Christian slaves in North Africa. Vincent told those who were sharing his ministry, "The poor are your masters and you are their servants." His work had spread across Europe by the time of his death in 1660.

SEPTEMBER 28

Lioba (d. ca. 781)

Christian example

A relative of Boniface (June 5), Lioba was an English nun in Wimborne abbey in Dorset. She stands tall as an early missionary of the Christian Church. After several years of correspondence with her distant cousin Boniface, she received an invitation to join him in a mission to evangelize Germany in 748. Her assignment was to establish convents. A group of about thirty nuns traveled with her to Tauberbischofsheim.

Rudolf of Fulda wrote Lioba's biography about fifty years after her death in 782. He had interviewed four nuns who knew her intimately. Lioba, they told him, was an attractive, intelligent, kind, and accessible woman. Her influence and example spread to other convents. People in responsible positions for both church and state came to her for advice.

SEPTEMBER 29
Richard Rolle (1300–49)
℘ *Life of prayer*

England's first great medieval mystic was born in Yorkshire in 1300, or possibly a few years earlier. Most of what we know about Richard Rolle is from the pages of his own books. He dropped out of Oxford to become a religious hermit, causing his family to worry about his sanity. With financial support from a few enthusiastic patrons, Richard Rolle sustained life as a religious hermit for thirty-one years.

Richard wrote about his religious experiences in books, two of which remain in general circulation: *Emendatio vitae (The Mending of Life)* and *Incendium amoris (The Fire of Love)*. "Once I was sitting in a chapel, singing the Psalms as well as I could in the evening before supper. It seemed as though I could hear stringed instruments playing above me. With my prayers, I reached out to these heavenly sounds. I experienced a blending of the internal melodies I was improvising with the heavenly harmonies. My meditation was transformed into music."

While Richard Rolle's writings include descriptions of such personal rapture, he also gives clear instruction to those who would live a Christian life. He did not hesitate to criticize misdirected interests of clergy or shallow religious behavior.

"Not everyone who leaves the things of this world behind comes to Christ. When Christ says 'sell everything,' he means change your point of view. If you are proud, now you must become humble. If you are angry, learn how to forgive. If you are greedy, be transformed into a generous person."

We would be mistaken to imagine Richard Rolle as one who lived a wild life in rags and avoided society. He enjoyed people and had a strong interest in seeing them grow spiritually.

The Black Death took Rolle's life on September 29, 1349.

SEPTEMBER 30

Jerome (ca. 341–420)
✐ *Christian dedication*

The word most frequently associated with Jerome is scholar. A consummate student and linguist, Jerome is one of the greatest scholars the Christian Church has ever produced. One of his contemporaries, St. Augustine (August 28), remarked, "If Jerome doesn't know it, no one knows it." Proficient in Hebrew, Aramaic, and Greek, the original languages of sacred Scripture, he produced a Latin Bible known as the *Vulgate*. The Latin he used was the language of the common people in his day, the "vulgar," everyday speech. Jerome's thorough and careful translation became the standard version of the Bible for more than a thousand years.

Jerome's mature years were lived in Bethlehem, where he founded a monastery in 386. He seemed to enjoy controversial debate on matters relating to Christianity, making enemies and gathering supporters. In 410, news of the destruction of Rome stunned Jerome, and the horrible reports from Roman refugees greatly moved him. He turned aside from his studies to organize and render assistance. "Today, we must translate words of the Scriptures into deeds."

Jerome is distinctive among the saints. While he lived a simple life and was devoted to the Church, his behavior and speech are not becoming. His temper, hatred, and anger were ferocious. His careful and invaluable scholarship makes him a saint, not his self-discipline.

Toward the end of his life, Jerome became distraught. Barbarians were overrunning Syria and Palestine. He wrote, "How many monasteries they captured! How many rivers run red with blood! The Roman world is falling." Growing old, he continued to work with his books day after day. He was writing a commentary on Jeremiah when he died in Jerusalem on September 30, 420.

OCTOBER 1

Thérèse of Lisieux (1873–1897)

✥ *Life of holiness*

The Story of a Soul, the autobiography of Thérèse of Lisieux, caught the attention of a worldwide readership. Millions of copies in thirty-eight languages have made it one of the best-sellers of all time. Thousands of statues of her stand on several continents. Her appeal and popularity are incredible. And yet, she lived barely twenty-four years, and only a handful of people ever knew her. She did nothing to attract any attention before tuberculosis ended her short life in 1897.

Born into an unremarkable French watchmaker's family in the little provincial town of Alençon, Thérèse grew up in obscurity, a shy and moody child. She essentially disappeared from the world when she joined some of her sisters in the cloister of the Carmelite convent of Lisieux. The little book she wrote behind its walls made her famous.

The Story of a Soul describes in simple terms a practical way to live a holy life in a commonplace world. Thérèse left us personal notes, observations, and insights jotted down on the way to sanctity. She calls it the "Little Way," by which she means doing everything and suffering everything with an awareness of God's presence. She could see nothing outstanding about herself, a "Little Flower," but understood she was precious in God's sight.

Therese said that she could not bring herself to search through stacks of books for prayers. The process gave her a headache. "For me, prayer is an upward leap of the heart, an untroubled glance towards heaven, a cry of gratitude and love which I utter from the depths of sorrow as well as from the heights of joy."

Therese thought about doing heroic and dramatic things for Christ, but accepted the fact that her "vocation is love." Her illness taught her that spiritual heroism can occur far from public battlefields. For the final eighteen months of her life she experienced an agonizingly slow and painful death, using it as another opportunity for acceptance and living in the spirit of love. She wrote most of the pages of her book under the duress of this period of her life.

"Don't think that I am overwhelmed with consolations. I'm not. My consolation is not to have any in this life. Jesus never appears or speaks to me. He teaches me in secret."

OCTOBER 2

Leodegar (ca. 616–78)

❦ Active faith

Born into a wealthy family and reared in the seventh-century court of King Clotaire II in what became France, Leodegar (sometimes Leodegarius or Leger) occupied himself with both sacred and secular matters. He became a monk at Maxentius Abbey in 650 and its abbot the next year, bringing it under the Benedictine Rule.

Leodegar tutored the children of Queen Bathild (January 30), who often sought his advice. Later, he supported an unsuccessful candidate for the throne and briefly experienced exile. He died violently after two years of imprisonment and torture in Normandy.

OCTOBER 3

Gerard of Brogne (d. 959)

❦ Spiritually alert

This Belgian soldier became a courtier of the count of Namur during the tenth century. While stationed at the embassy in Paris, Gerard became a monk at the Benedictine abbey of St. Denis. His reputation was that of a genuinely nice person who was sensitive to God's presence. Upon his return home in 914 he founded a monastery which, under his leadership, was at the center of monastic reform in northwestern Europe.

OCTOBER 4
Francis of Assisi (1181–1226)
❧ *Total commitment*

Francis of Assisi defies brief characterization. Francis comes down to us across seven centuries trailing clouds of glory.

Assisi, Umbria, in the Appenine Mountains of Italy, is the location of the birth of Francis. A wealthy cloth merchant's son, Francis lived a frivolous and protected life of romance and adventure. Fastidious, he had always avoided the poor and the sick. One day when he was riding on horseback he saw a hideous leper, and something overcame him. Dismounting, he put his cloak around the leper's shoulders and impulsively kissed the loathsome man's cheek. From that moment his outlook on life began to change.

An experience while praying in a small, rundown chapel sharpened the focus of his new life. An inner voice said to him, "Francis, repair my church." He took the order literally and began working to repair the structure. Eventually, he understood that "my church" involved a much larger, more spiritual meaning. It was his assignment to bring the Christian Church back to the simple gospel expressed through poverty.

To finance the church's repair, Francis sold cloth from his father's warehouse. His father took him to court for his rash action. He acknowledged his guilt and returned to his father the money he had gained. Before the spectators in the market place where the trial was conducted, Francis then stripped off his fine clothes, saying, "I have called you Father. From here on I say, 'Our Father who is in heaven.'"

Completely rejecting his wealthy status, Francis began to live outdoors, doing manual labor and ministering to the sick. For a while the head-wagging citizens of Assisi made fun of him, but gradually others began to join him, forming the Friars Minor. A monk might dine on simple food, but he knew supper was always there for him. A friar had no idea where he might find his next meal. Sometimes women joined their number. Even Clare of Assisi (August 11) would sneak out in the darkness of night to join with him.

Legends about Francis abound. Ugolino gathered this largely oral tradition in a volume he entitled *The Acts of St. Francis and His Companions*. The book soon appeared in a slightly shorter Italian edition known as *The Little Flowers of St. Francis (I Fioretti di San Francesco)*. It contains wonderful stories and became a popular book. This is where we can read such pieces as "The Wolf of Gubbio," "How to Find Perfect Joy," "A Sermon for the Birds," and "Two Saints Dine Together."

Francis saw his kinship with all of God's creation, speaking of "Brother Sun and Sister Moon." Everything from living creatures to inanimate rocks was a respected part of a community he shared. His identification with Christ reached its apex when the wounds of crucifixion appeared on his hands and feet while he prayed alone in 1224. Two years later, he died, welcoming "Sister Death."

OCTOBER 5

Mary Faustina Kowalska (1905–38)

God's mercy

Baptized as Helena, Mary Kowalska was born into a large family of Polish peasants in Glogowiec. She left home at sixteen to work as a housekeeper. At twenty, she became a Sister of Our Lady of Mercy and took the name Mary Faustina. Doing menial chores, she remained with that congregation for thirteen years. No one noticed what was going on inside Mary as she went about routine chores, but she had a close, living relationship with God. The spiritual world was as vivid for her as the physical world.

In her personal diary she wrote, "Neither graces, nor revelations, nor raptures, nor gifts granted to a soul make it perfect, but rather the intimate union of the soul with God." The result of her spiritual awareness became an emphasis in her mission of teaching the mercy of God for the world.

She died of tuberculosis on October 5, 1938, less than two months past her thirty-third birthday. She is buried, appropriately, at the Shrine of Divine Mercy in Kraków-Lagiewniki, Poland.

OCTOBER 6

Bruno (ca. 1035–1101)

✒ *Changing vocations*

The Carthusian Order owes its existence to Bruno. After distinguished service at the cathedral in Cologne, Germany, Bruno became a grammar and theology lecturer at Reims, his alma mater. Some of the students he taught during his eighteen-year tenure there became outstanding leaders of the Church.

Bruno's life and ministry took a radical change when he returned to Cologne, became a monk, and began living as a hermit. Soon he moved on to Grenoble and came under the influence of Bishop Hugh (April 1). Hugh encouraged Bruno and six others who were with him to live in solitude. In 1084 Hugh led them to the beautiful Chartreuse area, where they constructed private cells around a chapel for prayer. The name "Carthusian" is a derivative of "Chartreuse." Bruno and his friends lived in austere solitude, taking their pattern from the practices of Egyptian monks. They devoted much of their time to copying the Bible by hand. Three copies of their Bibles still exist, the only ones saved after an avalanche destroyed their buildings. Bruno continued his monastic life at a safer site farther down the mountain slope.

Pope Urban II, one of his former students, summoned Bruno to Rome, where he participated in decision-making, but Bruno continually declined to become involved in continuing administrative duties. His interest remained with his Carthusian monks, helping them to define and refine their pattern of life. Bruno's death in 1101 left the monastery with an influential organization that prospered in the following centuries. Seventy-two years after his death, Carthusian monks, under Hugh of Lincoln (November 17), arrived in England and became a vital part of the working out of church history.

OCTOBER 7

Osyth (d. ca. 700)

☙ Commitment

England's village of St. Osyth, Essex, commemorates a saint who is almost without historical record. Bede (May 25) makes no mention of her in his *Ecclesiastical History*. Reared in a convent by her more strongly documented aunts, Osyth desired to become an abbess, but instead became a political pawn. Her parents were supposedly Frewald, a chieftain of the seventh-century Mercians, and Wilburga, the daughter of king Penda of Mercia. Her parents married their Saxon princess daughter to Sighere of Essex, "king" of the East Angles, by whom she had a son, Offa. Her son eventually took his father's position.

Osyth won her husband's permission to enter a convent. She established a monastery on land donated by Sighere, and there she served as abbess. She died a violent death, apparently at the hands of Danish Viking robbers.

John Aubrey, author of *Brief Lives*, noted, "In those days, when they went to bed they did rake up the fire, make an X on the ashes, and pray to God and St. Osyth to deliver them from fire, and from water, and from all misadventure."

OCTOBER 8

Pelagia the Penitent (d. ? 457)

☙ Repentance

Pelagia's inspiring story originates in what is probably a fifth-century biography that uses fictional glamour as an antidote to the dull monotony of everyday life in a monastery. Before her conversion, Pelagia considered herself a dancer, but others described her "dancing" as stripping in front of ogling men. Many editions of her tale are in existence. They span several centuries, and the writers often embellished the basic story with new details. Painters relished her as a subject for their canvasses and illustrations.

While some scholars do not take the legends surrounding Pelagia seriously, there is a basic story that may contain historic facts. John Chrysostom (November 13) wrote a sermon based on the Gospel of Matthew that includes an illustrative reference to an performer who lived in Antioch, who was suddenly converted and lived her remaining years in a convent, refusing to receive her former friends and associates.

The way the writers ordinarily tell the story, the attractive Pelagia was an immoral actress who had many lovers, expensive jewels, and a large entourage. She happened to pass by one day when some bishops were listening to an outdoor sermon at a saint's tomb. She was "provocatively dressed" and surrounded by a cluster of admirers. The stunned bishops averted their gaze, but the preacher pointed her out as a stripper who made an effort to improve her appearance, but did nothing for God.

The next day the same preacher was at work in the church at Antioch when Pelagia wandered in. She converted immediately and requested baptism. Giving away the luxurious things her work had brought her, she became a hermit, dressing in men's clothing to avoid attention, and living on Jerusalem's Mount of Olives. Others spoke of her as the "Beardless Hermit." Those who knew her at this final stage of her life did not know her true identity and sex until after her death.

OCTOBER 9

Louis Bertrand (1526–81)

✍*Christian mission*

When Louis Bertrand (Luis Bertrán) began his life in Valencia, Spain, in 1526, the excitement of the discovery of a "new world" was reaching fever pitch. Reports of "savages" living in South America led Louis, at the age of thirty-six, to go there with a desire and a commission to preach the gospel to Native Americans.

Speaking only Spanish, he preached through an interpreter, although there are reports that God granted him a gift of tongues that occasionally made him immediately understandable. Six years of ministry in Panama, Colombia, and the Indies resulted in thousands being converted to Christianity.

The behavior of Spanish adventurers in the New World shocked Louis. Their avarice and cruelty went beyond what he could accept as normal commerce.

Louis returned to Spain in 1569 and began to teach another generation how to present the gospel. He insisted that fervent prayer had to be the background for effective preaching, and that one's behavior gave power to what one said.

While Louis was preaching in the cathedral at Valencia, a lingering illness caught up with him, and friends carried him from the church to his bed. He remained in bed for eighteen months, dying on October 9, 1581, at the age of fifty-five.

OCTOBER 10
Daniel Comboni (1831–81)
Missionary insight

Africa beckoned to a young man attending a school for poor children in Verona, Italy. The director of that school loved Africa and often talked about it with his students. They nicknamed him "Father Congo." With this inspiration, Daniel Comboni dedicated his life to the evangelization of Africa. In 1849 he began serious studies in language, medicine, and theology.

Ordained a priest, Daniel departed for Africa with five other missionaries in 1857. Their voyage to Khartoum, capital of Sudan, lasted four months. He recognized immediately that his task would be difficult. The Africans in that region had learned to distrust Europeans because of the slave trade. The hot, humid climate was unbearable, and the labor was exhausting. Some of his fellow missionaries died. In a letter to his parents he wrote, "We are called to labor, to sweat, even to die, but the thought that we labor and die for love of Jesus Christ and for the salvation of the most abandoned souls, is too sweet for us to falter in this great commitment."

Poor health forced him to return to Italy after two years. Only he and two others survived the trip to Khartoum. The missionary effort failed, but Daniel Comboni did not lose sight of his dream. He began to travel all across Europe, raising funds for a new kind of mission in Africa. He wanted to convert Africa through Africans. Working to rescue Africans from slavery, he made a Herculean effort to bring an end to slave trading. Eight trips to Africa gave him an opportunity to turn much mission work over to the Africans themselves. He compiled a dictionary of the Nubian language.

He died in Khartoum, among the people he served and loved.

OCTOBER 11

Mary Soledad (1826–87)

❦Serving the sick

Mary was born a shopkeeper's daughter in Madrid, Spain, and given the name Bibiana Antonia Emanuela. She had a stable and sturdy home life. The Daughters of Charity led her education, and during these early years she demonstrated more interest in sharing her food with poor playmates, and teaching them prayers, than in games.

A committed religious life appealed to Emanuela from childhood. When she became old enough to strike out on her own, she applied to become a Dominican, but was rejected because of her poor health. In 1848, Don Michael Martinez y Sanz, a lay member of the Servites, asked her to be one of seven women devoted to Christian service as nurses for the poor. She took the name Mary Soledad. Soledad translates as "solitude," or "desolate," a name implying "alone and grief-stricken." An English equivalent term refers to the Virgin Mary as "Our Lady of Sorrows." The group called themselves "Handmaids of Mary Serving the Sick."

It was not an easy life. A cholera epidemic struck Madrid almost as soon as the nurses were organized. Getting more help proved a difficult challenge. When Don Martinez sent half of the group to West Africa in 1856, Mary Soledad tried to keep the work going with only six others assisting. When they were subjected to slander and bureaucratic bickering, it took the involvement of the queen of Spain to put the ministry on solid footing. In 1865 cholera broke out again, this time with ferocity. Mary and her sisters did a remarkable job of caring for the many victims, winning the community's praise for their selfless devotion.

Strife returned when some of her helpers left to work with another religious order about 1870. Detractors criticized her program. One friend commented, "Mother Mary is like an anvil. She constantly takes a beating." Again, things eventually improved, and she opened her first foreign house in Santiago, Cuba, about 1875. Forty-six other houses followed worldwide.

Mary devoted thirty-five years of her life to leading the order. Serenity reached her toward the end of her life. From her deathbed, she said to her well-organized and skillful nuns, "Children, live together in peace and harmony." A modern saint, she was officially canonized in 1970.

OCTOBER 12

Cyprian of Carthage (ca. 200–58)

Conversion

Christ changed a pagan Roman lawyer, Thascius Cecilianus Cyprianus, into an effective Christian preacher. The dramatic redirection of his life was declared miraculous. Discarding his library of pagan books, he used his skills as a lawyer to become an interpreter of Scripture. He devoured works by Christian writers, calling Tertullian his most important teacher. In his own writing, he never once quoted a pagan author.

In 248, Christians in Carthage asked Cyprian to be their bishop. He accepted, but Roman persecution of the Church under the emperor Decius soon forced him into hiding. He guided his people by writing letters in which he explained basic Christianity. Here are some of his comments on prayer:

Pray with all of your attention. Eliminate distractions. Concentrate on God. When your priest prepares you for prayer by saying, "Lift up your hearts," you may respond, "We lift them up to the Lord." This is a reminder to think of nothing but the Lord.

Do not pray naked prayers. Let there be some leaves and fruit on the branches of your prayers. Petition that merely begs for something from God is barren. Action needs to accompany your words. Any tree that does not bear good fruit is cut down and cast into the fire. Let fasting and almsgiving accompany your prayers.

When the Roman persecution ended, Cyprian led the Church into gentle acceptance of Christians who had been frightened away. Unfortunately, persecution of the Church returned under Valerian, and Cyprian was beheaded in 258.

OCTOBER 13

Edward the Confessor (1003–66)

✒ *Christian leadership*

King Edward of England was a popular saint in the Middle Ages. The basis for his reputation as a holy person was his openness to his subjects, his generosity to the poor, his simplicity, his gentleness, and the reports of his suppression of sexual desire. Charming, though possibly legendary, anecdotes recall his personality and character. Three times he caught a servant stealing and let him get away with it, commenting, "The poor fellow needs the gold more than I." He would greet beggars and lepers at the gate to his palace, conversing with them and sometimes healing them with a touch. He enjoyed hunting and falconry for days at a time, but never failed to be present at Mass each morning. King Edward also strengthened the English Church's relationship with Rome.

Edward ascended to the throne in 1042 at the age of forty. He had lived in exile in Normandy for the previous twenty-seven years, because Scandinavians had seized power in England. His performance as king gets mixed reviews. Some historians believe his vacillation set up the nation for the Norman Conquest. On the other hand, he inherited a political quagmire that years of wars had not improved, and his twenty-four year reign was a time of relative peace. Under Edward, England became prosperous, people lived in security, and the nation's churches were repaired.

Edward played a major role in the founding of Westminster Abbey. He gave ten percent of his income, a tithe, for the project, endowing it with grants of land. The gigantic Romanesque church, the size of a football field, became the place for the coronation and burial of the kings and queens of England. Royal weddings are resplendent in such a setting. Edward was too ill to attend the consecration of Westminster Abbey. He was buried there in 1066. Nearly forty years later, workmen discovered that his body had not decayed—an indicator of saintliness in those times.

Edward's remains were solemnly buried again on October 13, 1163, a day of national celebration. Ailred of Rievaulx delivered the sermon and wrote a biography of the king. Henry III employed Italian craftsmen to build an elaborately decorated shrine for Edward at Westminster Abbey in 1269. This became a target for vandalism during the Reformation, but Edward's body remained undisturbed.

OCTOBER 14

Callistus I (d. ca. 222)
✎ Following Christ

Callistus was born a Roman slave. Courts convicted him twice for possible embezzlement and careless money handling, and for brawling with Jews in a synagogue. Callistus worked for a while as a cemetery superintendent, but ended his life as pope. Always supporting leniency and forgiveness, he became a third-century martyr. His enemies, who disapproved of his less than strict dealing with sinners, record most of what we know about Callistus. Other narratives about him are spurious legends.

Hippolytus of Rome, an important Christian writer of his time, published a scathing attack against the laxity of Callistus called *Philosophumena*. This book confirms that the five years Callistus was pope were unusually controversial. Callistus took an unpopular stand recognizing marriage between slave and free, which was forbidden by Roman civil law. He allowed priests to marry and ordained some who had been divorced. Callistus never struck back at Hippolytus, not even when the latter opened shop as a rival pope. The death of Callistus in 222 occurred during a public riot and was not the result of political persecution.

OCTOBER 15

Teresa of Avila (1515–82)

Action and Contemplation

Teresa of Avila destroys every notion that there are two kinds of religious personalities: active and contemplative. The story of Mary and Martha recorded in the Gospels, so beloved by every author of spiritual literature, makes us think that the two patterns of behavior are clear opposites, mutually exclusive. The Christian is either an active Martha, busy with the dishes; or a contemplative Mary, sitting at the feet of Jesus in quiet conversation. Such a simple distinction is inaccurate. Teresa is an outstanding example of a thorough blending of both.

At the age of twenty-one, Teresa responded to a lifelong urge and became a Carmelite nun in her hometown, Avila, Spain. As an active Christian, she reformed her order and founded fourteen monasteries. Her spirit of reform affected the male Carmelites through the cooperation of St. John of the Cross (December 14). They used the terms "calced" and "discalced" (with or without shoes) to denote the difference they had brought about. Plagued with poor health, Teresa somehow managed to attend to a multitude of administrative details. She directed the work of laborers the way a modern contractor hires and oversees employees. She dealt with royalty and "city hall" like a diplomat. She put in an exhausting day that began with worship at five in the morning and often kept her at her desk until well past midnight. A favorite quotation from her autobiography is "Rest? I don't need rest. What I need is crosses!"

This same busy, creative, determined administrator is also one of the greatest contemplative spirits in history. While signing contracts or confuting her critics, she had an awareness of living in the presence of God. She had a personal experience of mystical union with God through a remarkable prayer life that dominated her existence. Her prayer life was the source of her energetic activity.

Interior Castle is her most distinctive book. In this volume she ignores the interesting details of her life and work, and concentrates exclusively on her spiritual discoveries. While she was, by nature, a rambling writer who followed her stream of consciousness before the pedagogues ever coined the term, *Interior Castle* possesses form and comeliness. She describes a seven-tiered spiritual awareness in a style that is unsophisticated and direct. "Our soul is like a castle created out of a single diamond or some other similarly clear crystal."

To read Teresa is to sit down for a chat with her. She did not read what she had written with a critical eye, scratching out this line and that, amending and shaping, correcting and refining. She simply sat down and wrote what was on her mind, often reminding the reader that she was not very good at it. But in fact, she was a wizard at wringing profound meaning from the Spanish language, delicately playing one word against another in puns so subtle that modern translators often miss them. "They figure it must be a rapture (*arrobamiento*). I call it foolishness (*abobamiento*)."

OCTOBER 16

Gall (ca. 550– ca. 645)

❧ *Solitude*

A monk who lived in Bangor, Ireland, in the sixth century, Gall traveled with Columban (November 23) to England and France, assisting in the founding of several monasteries, including the abbey at Luxeuil in Burgundy. When Columban departed for Italy, Gall began life as a hermit in Switzerland and became an early leader in the propagation of Christianity among the Swiss. The area where he camped is now the location of a fine Benedictine abbey named after him. In fact, St. Gall is the name of the town that grew up around the monastery.

OCTOBER 17

Ignatius of Antioch (d. ca. 107)
Expressing faith

The nicknames applied to saints can be revealing. Ignatius of Antioch carried the name *Theophorus*, which translates *Bearer of God*. He also had a moniker for himself: *God's Wheat*.

We have very little reliable evidence of his early life and later career as bishop of Antioch, but tradition holds that a disciple of John (December 27) converted Ignatius of Antioch to Christ. We can certainly place him in the second half of the first century, and we know that he was arrested during Trajan's reign, carried to Rome, and thrown to the lions during a public entertainment. While he was on the way to Rome, he wrote some letters of great doctrinal interest that survive to our day.

An important feature of this early Christian correspondence is that it demonstrates first-century faith in the divinity and resurrection of Christ. "If what our Lord did is a sham, so is my being in chains." The letters refer to the Lord's Supper as an instrument of unity. "We are not only to be *called* Christians, but to *be* Christians." Ignatius is also confident that Peter and Paul (June 29) founded the church in Rome. He called the squad of Roman soldiers who were escorting him "ten leopards," observing that their behavior "gets worse the better they are treated."

Of himself, he wrote, "Let me be fodder for wild beasts—that is how I can get to God. I am God's wheat and I am being ground by the teeth of wild beasts to make a pure loaf for Christ."

The Romans turned two fierce lions loose on Ignatius of Antioch. His death was mercifully quick.

OCTOBER 18

Luke (first century)
ꙮForming the gospel

The man the apostle Paul (June 29) called *the beloved physician* is the only non-Jewish writer in the Bible. Luke is the probable author of the Gospel that bears his name as well as the Acts of the Apostles. His background and education were Greek. Evidence points to Luke as Paul's personal physician who traveled with him on much of his missionary work. Paul's letters assure us that Luke stuck with him to the bitter end.

Luke was devout, loyal, urbane, self-effacing, and happy. He wrote classical Greek, and did so in the introductory sentences of his Gospel, but preferred to communicate in the more common Greek spoken among the Jews of his day.

Without Luke's Gospel we would not have the beautiful narrative of the birth of Christ at Bethlehem. We would never have heard Christ's parables of the prodigal son and the good Samaritan. Only Luke reports the moving account of the distraught woman who wept on Jesus' feet and wiped them with her hair. Only Luke tells us about the contrasting prayers of the Pharisee and the publican at the temple. The New Testament would be much the poorer without the work of Luke, who disappears from history after the death of Paul.

OCTOBER 19

Peter of Alcantara (1499–1562)
ꙮSelf–denial

When he was sixteen, Peter departed his hometown of Alcantara, Spain, and became a Franciscan Observant in 1515. Life among the Franciscans was strictly regulated, and Peter followed the rules carefully. A well-respected preacher and Christian mystic, he wrote a book on prayer that became popular.

In his fortieth year, Peter founded the first friary of the "Strict Observance," going beyond the austerities and asceticism he had already practiced as a Franciscan. He designed his own cell in a confined way that prevented him from ever stretching out when lying down. He ate sparingly and wore rough and basic clothing without shoes.

Among the people he influenced were Teresa of Avila (October 15). He recognized her spirituality and encouraged her to continue her own reforms among the Carmelites. She described his austerities as "incomprehensible to the human mind," noting that he looked "as though he were made from the roots and dried bark of trees rather than flesh." Their meeting in 1560 made a deep impression on her. "He told me that he only sleeps about an hour and a half a day, and that he never put up his hood, regardless of sun or rain. One of his companions told me he sometimes ate nothing at all when he prayed for days at a time. I saw one of his great raptures."

Teresa also reported that he was a man of few words, but that he was worthy of attention because what he did say had great insight and understanding. She gave him credit for the success of her own religious work.

Peter of Alcantara died while kneeling in prayer.

OCTOBER 20

Acca (ca. 660–740)

✎ Resourceful

Acca was a Northumbrian who kept good company. He traveled with Wilfrid (October 12) for thirteen years, and some of the writings of the Venerable Bede (May 25) are dedicated to him. Bede's *Ecclesiastical History* contains material Acca found in his personal theological library. He also suggested that Bede write a concise commentary on the Gospel of Luke because the one Ambrose (December 7) wrote was too long and complicated.

Acca became bishop of Hexham, which is on the Tyne River in England. He had a wonderful singing voice and brought about a renewed British interest in religious vocal music. Acca died a natural death.

OCTOBER 21

Malchus of Khalkis (d. ca. 390)
❦*Religious adventure*

Jerome (September 30) wrote the life of the Syrian monk Malchus after meeting him at Khalkis near Antioch. Malchus reported his adventures as he traveled in a caravan that Bedouin raiders attacked. They carried him off beyond the Euphrates River, and he lived a nomadic life with them, tending sheep and goats while consuming dates, cheese, and milk. His captors wanted him to take one of their women for a bride. She was already married, but seemed willing to cooperate with the group's plan. Malchus, faithful to his monastic vows, declined. He did agree to allow her to live with him, appearing to be her husband, while not sleeping with her. Later Malchus said he loved this woman as a sister, but "never quite trusted her as a sister."

After seven years the two of them determined to escape. She would return to her original husband and Malchus to his monastery. They packed food in goatskins that also served as inflatable life rafts to take them across the Euphrates. Traveling on foot for three days, they left a trail in the sand for their Bedouin master and a cohort to follow on camels. Upon their discovery, the lethal action of a lioness saved their lives. Seizing the camels, they raced away to a place of safety.

The woman lived her remaining years near Malchus because she never found her husband. Malchus first went to his monastery at Khalkis and then moved on to Maronia, where he met Jerome.

OCTOBER 22

Salome (first century)
❦*Devotion to Christ*

There are two Salomes in the Gospels. One is the unsaintly daughter of Herodias who danced for King Herod and requested the head of John the Baptist as her reward. The other is a Galilean

follower of Jesus who may have been Zebedee's wife and mother of
the apostles, James (July 25) and John (December 27). She was
among the faithful women present at the Crucifixion and a witness
to Christ's resurrection when she went early on Easter morning to
anoint the body of Jesus. It is possible to conjecture on the basis of
scriptural evidence that she was Mary's cousin.

OCTOBER 23

Rafqa Petronilla al-Rayès (1832–1914)

Suffering

Rafqa was Lebanese, like the bride in the Song of Songs. Her
middle name is a feminization of Peter because she was born on his
feast day, June 29, 1832. Known as the "Little Flower of Lebanon,"
this blind woman had profound spiritual vision.

Her early years were difficult. She lost her mother when she was
only six and had to work as a housemaid to support herself. As a
nun, later in life, she suffered poor health. Even so, she continually
practiced self-denial, eating only leftovers and working steadily at
manual labor. The final seventeen years of her life, Rafqa was blind
and paralytic, in constant pain. She demonstrated how one can unite
personal suffering with Christ's. No one ever heard her complain
about her situation. She actually thanked God for her suffering. "I
know that the sickness I have is for the good of my soul and his
glory. Sickness accepted with patience and thanksgiving purifies the
soul as fire purifies gold."

OCTOBER 24

Antony Claret (1807–70)

Communicating

Antony, like his father, was a Spanish weaver. With a natural
intellectual curiosity, he learned Latin and printing. He went on to
attend seminary and become an ordained priest in 1835. Traveling

to Rome, Antony joined the Jesuits, intending to become a foreign missionary. Poor health intervened, and he returned to Spain, realizing that much evangelizing waited for him at home. Antony devoted the next ten years of his life to presenting the gospel in the Catalonia region, founding a group that now uses his name: the Claretians.

His sudden appointment as archbishop of Cuba brought with it enormous difficulties, challenges, and risks. Assassination attempts left him seriously wounded. An upset young man whose girlfriend had returned to a moral life under Antony's direction inflicted the wound. In 1857 he resigned his post in Cuba and returned to Spain in order to become the confessor of Queen Isabella II. In this position, he engaged in speaking and writing. Understanding the value of the printed word, he published many religious books and pamphlets.

When Queen Isabella went into exile during the Spanish Revolution of 1868, Antony went with her. He never returned home. Antony died at a Cistercian monastery in France.

OCTOBER 25

Gaudentius of Brescia (ca. 360– ca. 410)
✒ Dedicated life

Gaudentius called Philastrius, the bishop of Brescia, Italy, his "adopted father." Philastrius provided an education for Gaudentius, leading him toward a religious vocation. Gaudentius gained the respect and admiration of the people of Brescia, but left Italy to become a monk at Caesarea in Cappodocia, Asia Minor. The Brescians did not forget about him, and when Philastrius died, they sent for him. Gaudentius became bishop of Brescia, consecrated by Ambrose (December 7) around 387.

Gaudentius gained the love of all who knew him. He is particularly remembered for Easter sermons he wrote out for a man who was too sick to attend church.

Pope Innocent I and the emperor Honorius sent Gaudentius to Constantinople to defend John Chrysostom (September 13). This trip, in 405, turned out to be an unhappy experience. Gaudentius was not welcomed in Constantinople, and few had any interest in what he had to say. Chrysostom sent him a letter of thanks, but it all came to no good. Gaudentius and those who traveled with him experienced imprisonment and rough treatment. Gaudentius died five years after his voyage to Constantinople.

OCTOBER 26

Cedd (d. 644)
⫻ *Faithful living*

The Venerable Bede (May 25) wrote nearly everything we know about Cedd, a seventh-century Northumbrian monk. Cedd and his three brothers all became priests after receiving an education from Finan of Lindisfarne (February 17). Cedd became the bishop of the East Saxons. We have few details of his experience until Florence of Worcester reports that Cedd died of pestilence on October 26, 664.

He founded several monasteries, none of which survived the Viking incursions.

OCTOBER 27

Frumentius and Aedisius (fourth century)
⫻ *Bane and blessing*

It is likely that these two were brothers. Both were influential in establishing the Ethiopian church. Their uncle, Meropius of Tyre, took them there when they were children. Frumentius and Aedisius were the only survivors of a disastrous voyage to Arabia. After an argument, Ethiopians attacked and killed all the crew and the other passengers on the ill-fated ship. The "king" of what is now Tigre, Ethiopia, enjoyed the wit and charm of the boys and gave special attention to their education. Aedisius became his cupbearer and Frumentius his treasurer and secretary of state. Later, Frumentius became the bishop of Ethiopia.

OCTOBER 28
Simon the Zealot / Jude (first century)
❦*Following Christ*

The only mention of Simon the Zealot in Scripture is in the lists of names of the apostles. Luke's list refers to him as Simon the Zealot, but the lists in Matthew and Mark call him Simon the Canaanean, which does not mean "from Canaan," but "enthusiast." The tag was probably applied to Simon because he had joined others who were outspoken against the Roman occupation of Palestine. These "Zealots" were radical patriots who wanted to restore divine rule in their country.

Rome ruled more of the known world for a longer time than any other empire in human history. The Romans built excellent roads and public water supplies. Travel was safe, and trade prospered under Roman rule. Rome used a firm hand in the maintenance of public order and was promptly ruthless in suppressing revolt, but liberal toward religion and local customs. The Romans highly valued peace because it avoided costly wars.

In the time of Jesus, a huge undercurrent of resistance to Rome sometimes became violent. There were many Zealots, but no army could defeat mighty Rome. As a child, Jesus probably saw the horror of such confrontations in his neighborhood. Thoughtful Jews attempted to sway public opinion regarding such things as taxes and tariffs rather than engage in futile military conflict. The aggressive Zealots, though, were feared by both the Romans and by other Jews who cooperated with Rome. No one was really sure which neighbor might be a Zealot. When Jesus chose both a tax collector and a Zealot to be apostles he reached out broadly.

The fact that Simon the Zealot is listed among the apostles who were waiting for the coming of the Holy Spirit affirms his lasting loyalty to Jesus. What his fellow disciples thought about Matthew, the tax collector who had collaborated with Rome, we can only imagine. Regardless, their love of Jesus Christ united their spirits.

Another apostle, Jude, shares this day. Matthew and Mark refer to him as Lebbaeus or Thaddaeus, Aramaic words meaning "courageous" and "lively." Luke designates him as Judas, son of James. In every case the Gospel writers make an effort to distinguish him from Judas Iscariot. John tells us he was "Judas (not Iscariot)."

The Bible records only one thing this apostle ever said. It was during the Last Supper that he spoke. Jesus had said, "In a little while the world will not see me any more, but you will see me." The apostle, still unaware of what was coming, asked, "Lord, how is it that we will see you, but others will not?" In reply, Jesus told him it would be a matter of spiritual perception. The one who loves will be the one who sees.

OCTOBER 29

Narcissus of Jerusalem (d. ca. 222)

Dedicated service

St. Narcissus is not to be confused with the character in Greek mythology who enjoyed his own reflection to an inordinate degree and turned into a flower. This Narcissus was a Greek living in Jerusalem. He was in his eighties when he became one of Jerusalem's first bishops about 180, but he watched over the church with youthful energy. Narcissus received broad admiration and respect.

Narcissus made an unpopular decision when a council met in 195 to consider the proper date for the celebration of Easter, which is associated with the Jewish Passover. The important thing, as Narcissus saw it, was that the Church should observe Easter on Sunday, the Lord's Day, rather than the actual day of Passover. The rule became, for those of us west of Constantinople, that Easter falls on the first Sunday following the first full moon after the first day of spring. The support Narcissus gave this radical idea distressed church members in Jerusalem, and they began to make false accusations against their bishop, subjecting him to vicious, open slander.

The heated unrest prompted Narcissus to resign in order to keep peace in the church, and to retreat into the desert as a hermit, but eventually emotions cooled and he returned to be bishop of Jerusalem until a very old age, some think 110.

One story remains from his time as bishop of Jerusalem. The night of a vigil before Easter, the church had run out of lamp oil. Narcissus asked for water from a nearby well, blessed it, and asked that it be put in the lamps. For years, the church at Jerusalem kept that little vial of miraculous oil.

OCTOBER 30

Marcellus the Centurion (d. 298)

❦ *Conscientious objection*

About the year 298, a birthday party for the Roman emperor Maximian Herculeus on the Strait of Gibraltar in Tangier, Spain, presented a problem for a centurion named Marcellus. This Roman soldier declined an opportunity to take part in the pagan offering ceremony. Throwing down his shield and sword, he announced that he was a Christian and refused to participate. "I am a soldier of Christ, the eternal King."

Marcellus spent the remainder of the festival locked in jail. At his trial, he continued to affirm his faith. Aurelian Agricolanus pronounced a sentence of death upon him, but the court notary, Cassian, refused to write down the sentence, declaring it unjust. Cassian immediately received the same sentence.

Marcellus became a Christian martyr by being beheaded on October 30. Cassian met the same fate a few weeks later.

OCTOBER 31

Wolfgang of Regensburg (924–94)

❦ *Service to Christ*

A native of Swabia, Germany, Wolfgang traveled as a boy to the abbey of Reichenau, located on an island in Lake Constance. A proficient student, he made a close friend in the brother of the Bishop of Würzburg. This connection resulted in his becoming dean of the cathedral school at Trier.

In 964, Wolfgang became a Benedictine monk in Switzerland. He accepted responsibility for administration of the school at the monastery in Einsiedeln and became an ordained priest. In 972, he became bishop of Regensburg in Bavaria. In this position, Wolfgang worked to improve standards of education, as well as to organize church administration, and devoted himself to serving the poor. Behind all of his accomplishments was a dedicated life of prayer.

Wolfgang became seriously ill while traveling down the Danube River into Austria. He died near Linz.

NOVEMBER 1

All Saints

☜ *Cloud of witnesses*

Since there are many more Christian saints than the three hundred and sixty-five days of the year, this day is set aside to honor all of them. The official list of canonized saints, as large as it is, does not claim to include every saint. Many have never had their names mentioned beyond a very small circle of friends.

Not all saints are alike. Spiritual gifts are as varied as the many interests and abilities that exist in the broad spectrum of people. Some saints have mystical experiences; others do not. Some saints stay busily at work in the world; other saints have neither the energy nor the social skills for that. Many saints have no idea that they are saints. One saint will rediscover the value of tradition, while another saint will open new doors of innovation. Each life has a purpose and fits into God's grand scheme the way plants—an oak or a trillium— grow in a forest.

NOVEMBER 2
Victorinus of Pettau (d. ca. 304)
❧*Interpreting Scripture*

Our earliest known commentator on Scripture is Victorinus. He served as bishop of Pettau in what is now Slovenia. He was a competent writer, and his exegetical commentary on the book of Revelation still exists. The esoteric nature of the Apocalypse fascinated him, and he attempted to make it understandable. Victorinus died a martyr during the Diocletian persecution about the year 304.

NOVEMBER 3
Martin de Porres (1569–1639)
❧*Spiritual sensitivity*

For many years, barbershops have called attention to themselves with red and white striped poles. The red represents human blood, and the white symbolizes a bandage. The barber pole goes back to a time when barbers were also surgeons who treated wounds, pulled teeth, and engaged in bloodletting. Martin de Porres was a young South American barber/surgeon who became a Dominican lay brother.

Martin was the illegitimate child of a Spanish father and a darkskinned Peruvian woman. His father would eventually become governor of Panama, but he showed little interest in Martin. At the age of fifteen, Martin asked to be admitted to a Dominican monastery as a janitorial helper. The skills he had learned in his previous trade soon attracted notice, and the monks placed him in charge of the infirmary. His use of herbal medicine and his special touch as a healer were remarkable. Stories began to circulate about his ability to diagnose an illness and cure patients by simply being present in the room with them.

Martin did not confine his medical ministry to the monastery. He went out into the slums of Lima to help neglected street people. Sometimes he would take a sick person back to his own bed. His superior ordered him to stop doing this, and when another indigent person was found in his bed, he severely chastised Martin. "Please forgive my mistake," Martin said. "I did not know that obedience took precedence over charity."

Martin also became something of a veterinarian, treating animals as lovingly as he cared for humans. Apparently he could communicate directly with them. A monk was amazed to see a dog, a cat, and a mouse eating together from a bowl that Martin had filled for them.

As people became familiar with Martin's humble love and piety, his superiors urged him to become a full lay brother. Many reliable witnesses reported supernatural activity similar to the phenomena observed in Padre Pio (September 23) almost three hundred years later. Levitation, bilocation (people met him in China while he remained in Lima), clairvoyance, healing, and even invisibility are attributed to this simple man.

As Martin lay on his deathbed at the age of sixty, the Spanish viceroy knelt beside him and sought his blessing. He died on November 3, 1639, but was not canonized a saint until 1962.

NOVEMBER 4

Charles Borromeo (1538–94)

☜Steadying influence

The Catholic Church desperately needed someone like Charles Borromeo in the sixteenth century. The Protestant Reformation spurred the need for Counter-Reformation during these seriously troubled times. A capable, steady hand at the helm was essential. Charles Borromeo became the most accomplished Italian bishop of his century.

Charles grew up familiar with the rich and the powerful. His mother was a Medici, and his uncle became Pope Pius IV. While he was not a handsome boy, and he was handicapped with a speech impediment, he had a strong spirit and an indomitable will. As a young man in his early twenties, he accepted an appointment as a cardinal. His attention to detail and organizational skills confirmed the trust others placed in him.

Soon enough, Charles Borromeo became archbishop of Milan and helped his uncle, the pope, to implement the reforms of the 1562-63 Council of Trent. He set up soup kitchens and hospitals when the plague of 1567 devastated Milan. His work was not universally appreciated. An unhappy friar even attempted to assassinate him in 1569.

Wearing himself out with his ministerial activities, Charles died at the age of forty-six.

NOVEMBER 5
Elizabeth (first century)
❦ Chosen

Elizabeth was the wife of the Jewish priest Zechariah. She had no children and, like Sarah and Hannah in the Old Testament, was beyond the normal age for child bearing. While Zechariah was performing his duties at the temple in Jerusalem, the angel Gabriel announced to him that a child would be born to them in their maturity. Six months later, the same angel would be present when her relative Mary conceived a child.

The Gospel of Luke tells us that Mary went to visit Elizabeth. When Elizabeth greeted Mary, she said, "Blessed are you among women, and blessed is the fruit of your womb." Elizabeth told Mary that her baby leapt for joy when Mary spoke to her. Her baby would grow up to be John the Baptist (August 29).

NOVEMBER 6
Illtyd (d. ca. 505)
❦ Early leadership

Illtyd is one of the most familiar Welsh saints, but most of the biographical material about him is full of implausible legends assembled hundreds of years after his life.

As a monk, he founded the large monastery of Llanilltyd Fawr near Cardiff. Other saints of Wales emerged from his monastery. Illtyd died near Dol in Brittany. A number of churches in Wales are dedicated to him. The presence of churches and communities bearing his name in Brittany affirms the likely fact that Illtyd sailed to Brittany on a ship loaded with wheat for famine relief.

NOVEMBER 7

Willibrord (ca. 658–739)

❦ *Missionary effort*

A Northumbrian, Willibrord received an education under Wilfrid of York (October 12) at Ripon, England. He continued his studies for twelve years with Egbert of Iona in Ireland.

In 690, Willibrord joined eleven other Anglo-Saxon monks on a voyage to Friesland, Netherlands. Together they conducted a missionary effort among the pagans there and in Denmark. Ultimately, Willibrord founded the monastery of Echternach in Luxembourg. He died at the age of eighty-one.

NOVEMBER 8

Elizabeth of the Trinity (1880–1906)

❦ *Exemplary prayer*

As a young girl growing up in Bourges, France, Elizabeth Catez was popular and effusive, with skills as a pianist, but she was also stubborn and self-centered. At the age of fourteen, her personality matured and she decided to become a Carmelite nun. Her mother disapproved and attempted to distract Elizabeth by involving her in the party circuit, encouraging young men to seek her hand.

In her twenty-first year, Elizabeth joined the Carmelites at Dijon, and immediately felt perfectly at home. In a letter, she wrote, "In the morning, let us wake in love. All day long let us surrender ourselves to love, by doing the will of God, under his gaze, with him, in him, for him. When evening comes, let us go to sleep still in love."

With an exemplary personal prayer life, Elizabeth developed the idea of the Trinity living in the person at prayer. Now the formerly strong-willed personality could say, "In order to have peace, one must forget about oneself."

Addison's disease prematurely claimed her life in 1906.

NOVEMBER 9

Benignus of Armagh (d. ca. 466)

✒*Faithful service*

Even the most rational mind will acknowledge that things happen in human experience that defy analysis and explanation. Miracles do happen. Prayer produces results. God is active in our world and is not restricted by the "laws" of his own creation. Damage results when pious imaginations conceive false tales. The skeptic concludes that if *some* stories about saints are phony, then *all* of them are. If there are twenty-three skulls of the twelve apostles venerated in ancient shrines, can any one of them be authentic? If there are enough pieces of the "true cross" in reliquaries to fill a lumberyard, and several pounds of iron nails used to crucify Jesus, can we accept a few as genuine?

Clearly, some kind of screening needed to be done for the stories of the lives of the saints. Addressing this issue, Jean Bolland organized a group of Jesuits in the sixteenth century to research the historical record of saints and their relics. The Bollandists labored for two centuries, producing many volumes of the *Acta Sanctorum*. In it, they attempted to separate historical fact from fiction. They demythologized the stories of the saints. Religious scholars today do not hesitate to announce the absence of credibility on any aspect of the lives of the saints, without diminishing a particular saint's value to the faithful. No one is injured, and most are helped, when researchers declare, "The story of Benignus is uncertain. The legend that he died after joining Patrick at Glastonbury is falsified and worthless history. The bodies buried there belong to other worthy persons."

We may be certain that Benignus of Armagh was St. Patrick's (March 17) close disciple who traveled with him on various missions. A gifted musician who effectively arranged choral music, Benignus acquired the title, "Patrick's Psalm Singer." As the abbot of Drumlease for twenty years, he helped to compile the *Irish Code of Laws*. Benignus succeeded St. Patrick as bishop of Armagh, Ireland, dying around the year 466.

NOVEMBER 10

Leo the Great (d. 461)

ℳ*Steadying hand*

Leo was born to a Tuscan family in Rome near the beginning of the fifth century. When he was elected pope in 440, the Roman Empire had collapsed. Vandals and barbarians were approaching with destruction and pillage on their minds. Heresies perforated Christianity. The Church was in trouble, and it needed Leo's firm control and common sense.

Leo came up with the terminology that helped to resolve the lengthy debate regarding the nature of Christ. His *Tomos*, or treatise, to the Council of Chalcedon in 451 spoke of *one Person* with *two natures*. In Christ, he said, the human and the divine are united without confusion. Leo's concept became orthodox doctrine.

A heart-stopping moment of history dramatically demonstrates Leo's flair for negotiation. Attila the Hun's army was poised to invade Rome in 452. Leo, in the company of two Roman senators but without any arms or protection, went out to meet the ruthless warrior and convinced him to withdraw. The massive army that had sacked and burned thriving cities throughout the civilized world marched back over the Alps to Hungary.

Leo's death in 461 left a church that had survived when civil government collapsed. In fact, the Church became the most influential and steadying international institution of medieval times.

Martin of Tours (ca. 316–97)

❧*Pioneering service*

Martin was born in Hungary, the son of a pagan Roman officer, early in the fourth century. At fifteen, Martin himself was conscripted into the Roman cavalry. With an inclination to become Christian, Martin grew dissatisfied with his military role. When he spoke out as a conscientious objector, officers imprisoned him. After he was ultimately discharged in 357, Martin had a moving experience when he helped a beggar at Amiens. He cut his cloak in half and put it on the nearly naked man. Later, Christ appeared to Martin in a dream, wearing the cloak he had given the beggar. Martin was soon baptized and became a devout Christian.

St. Hilary (January 13) returned to Poitiers from exile in 360. Becoming a disciple of Hilary, Martin and others built the first monastery in Gaul at Ligugé. Martin remained a solitary monk here until he became bishop of Tours in 372. Continuing to live in his cell, the new bishop worked at his difficult responsibilities with dedicated fervor. He played a central part in the handling of the unending doctrinal disputes.

One of the possibilities for pioneering ministry that occurred to Martin was the evangelization of rural areas. Most Christians were in the cities. The very word *pagan* is a derivative of *pagani*, referring to people living in the country. Martin tore down pagan altars and sacred trees as he moved among his people, converting them to Christ.

Martin died in 397 at Candes, France, and was buried at Tours.

Agostina Livia Pietrantoni (1864–94)

❧*Devoted service*

Agostina began life as Livia, and the story of her experiences reads like a classical Italian opera libretto. It is a tragic tale that is filled with faith, struggle, conflict, beauty, and emotion.

Livia was the second of eleven children born to an Italian farming couple. She learned honesty, industry, thrift, and religion as she grew up. Because there was always work to do on the farm, she was not able to attend school on a regular basis. At the age of seven she worked as a child laborer hauling bags of sand and stone for highway construction. When she was twelve she joined other seasonal workers picking olives in Tivoli.

Traveling to Rome in 1886, she proved herself worthy of becoming a Sister of Charity, a servant of the poor. Taking the religious name Agostina, she went to an ancient hospital, Santo Spirito. The secularization of the hospital was total. There were no religious icons of any kind. Sisters were grudgingly permitted to work among the patients, but were forbidden to mention God. Though she was able to do good for the needy, her personal life at Santo Spirito was miserable. She worked first in a children's ward and then moved on to work with tuberculosis patients. Agostina's exposure to the contagious disease brought tuberculosis to her own lungs, but she was miraculously healed.

One of the tuberculosis patients had a difficult personality. Giuseppe Romanelli was vulgar, disrespectful, and violent, especially toward Agostina, who kept him in her prayers and tried to give the disagreeable man special attention. Because of his behavior toward the women working in the hospital's laundry, the director discharged him.

Romanelli became extraordinarily hostile and selected Agostina as his target. He began to send her notes with threatening messages. "You only have a month to live." "I will kill you with my own hands." The insanely violent former patient caught her by surprise on November 13, 1894, stabbing her to death. Her final words to him were words of forgiveness.

NOVEMBER 13

Abbo of Fleury (ca. 945–1004)

❦ *Teaching ministry*

Born near Orléans, France, Abbo became a Benedictine monk at Fleury. A consummate student, he became one of the greatest scholars of his time. The subjects of his writing included astronomy and mathematics, as well as religious subjects.

In 985, Oswald of Worcester invited Abbo to Ramsey Abbey, England, to serve as headmaster of his school. Abbo encouraged his students in serious study, and at least one of them, Byrthferth of Ramsey, produced important writings. Abbo himself wrote a biography of Edmund, King of East Anglia (November 20), using interviews with Edmund's standard-bearer as his chief source. Abbo dedicated this book to Dunstan (May 19).

When Abbo returned to Fleury in 988 as abbot, his monks copied and studied Aristotle's *Categories* and *Analytics*. Abbo served as a mediator between the pope and the French king. On a visit to the monastery of La Réole in Gascony to lead the the monks there in reform, Abbo tried to calm a fight between monks and refectory servers, and was killed in the melee.

NOVEMBER 14

Dubricius (d. ca. 545)

❦ *Faithful service*

Dubricius, also known as Dyfrig, was one of the founders of monasticism in Wales. Among the earliest saints of South Wales, he played a leading role in securing a foothold for Christianity there. The historical record regarding his personal life is garbled.

Dubricius appointed a monk named Samson (July 28) abbot of Caldey and then ordained him bishop. When a biography of Samson appeared in the seventh century, the far-ranging influence of Dubricius became a matter of record. Alfred Lord Tennyson praises Dubricius (Dyfrig) in his *Coming of Arthur*. There is even an unsubstantiated claim that Dubricius actually crowned King Arthur.

Dubricius retired as an old man to Bardsey Island. He died there about 545.

NOVEMBER 15

Albert the Great (ca. 1200–80)

✒Dedicated life

If we evaluated teachers by the achievements of their students, Albert would get high scores. He taught Thomas Aquinas (January 28) at Cologne, introducing him to Aristotle's thought.

From Swabia, Germany, Albert joined the new Dominican Order as a student at the University of Padua. He became a bishop in 1260, but did not enjoy administrative detail. He resigned the post less than two years later and devoted his attention to teaching and writing. Albert's broad expertise earned him the nickname "Universal Doctor." He wrote treatises on the widest spectrum of studies: theology, Scripture, logic, rhetoric, ethics, philosophy, mathematics, physics, astronomy, mineralogy, chemistry, biology, geography, geology, and botany. Albert also pioneered studies in human and animal physiology. His writings fill thirty-eight volumes and provide the foundation for blending faith and reason. He had a mind in harmony with the Dominican idea of "general studies."

Albert was still actively teaching when he died at Cologne in 1280.

NOVEMBER 16

Agnes of Assisi (1197–1253)

✒Dedicated

Agnes was the younger sister of Clare (August 11). About two weeks after Clare left home to join the Benedictine convent of St. Angelo in Panso near Assisi, Italy, Agnes followed at the age of sixteen.

This greatly distressed her father, who sent members of his family to persuade, and perhaps force, Agnes to return home. Her great struggle against these "rescuers" impressed Francis of Assisi (October 4). When he saw her dedication, he cut her hair short, as he had cut her sister's, and welcomed her to the life of poverty.

In 1219, Agnes became the first Poor Clare abbess of Monticelli at Florence. She was actively involved in the establishment of other convents in Italy.

In 1253, three months after her sister's death, Agnes died at San Damiano. Her remains rest near those of her mother and sisters in the church of St. Clare at Assisi.

NOVEMBER 17

Hugh of Lincoln (1140–1200)
✒ *Christian leadership*

Hugh originated in the Grenoble region of France. In 1160, he joined the Carthusian monks at Chartreuse. King Henry II of England asked Hugh to establish the first English Carthusian foundation at a dilapidated charterhouse at Witham in Somerset. Under Hugh's guidance it was soon flourishing and attracted some outstanding fellow monks.

Hugh began the construction of the cathedral of Lincoln where he had become bishop. After an earthquake damaged the structure, Hugh went to the site to be present with the laborers, working on the cathedral with his own hands. Only a few stones of the walls remain today.

Hugh's high interest in education brought new life to the schools in Lincoln. He also had excellent relations with the Jewish community in that city, and on one occasion, took great risks in a riot in order to save the lives of targeted Jews.

Hugh was both a friend and a critic of several kings. His sense of humor turned away the wrath of both Henry II and Richard I. When Hugh died in London, the kings of England and Scotland accompanied his body on its return to Lincoln.

Odo of Cluny (ca. 879–942)

ℨ *Extended influence*

In spite of being an obscure saint, Odo of Cluny achieved important and significant work in the early years of the tenth century. It amuses some who have a musical ear that Odo was the son of Abbo. While not many parents are naming their sons Odo today, it was a common name then, and there are five or six other saints from his era with similar names.

Odo studied music and theology for four years in Paris. When, in 909, he read the Rule of Benedict (July 11), he decided to become a Benedictine monk at Baume. He brought everything he owned with him—about one hundred books. He became abbot of Baume in 924. Three years later, he became abbot of Cluny, another Benedictine monastery in France. Odo was able to free Cluny from secular control, and the monastery prospered for several hundred years, becoming one of the most important abbeys in Europe. Odo insisted upon silence, abstinence, and a strict interpretation of the Benedictine Rule. Other monasteries were slack by comparison.

In Rome, Odo reformed St. Paul's-Outside-the-Walls, and his influence extended to other monasteries in Italy. In his mature years, Odo gained respect as a mediator in political issues. He died at the monastery of St. Julian at Tours.

Mechtild of Hackeborn (d. 1298)

ℨ *Visionary*

The Benedictine convent of Helfta in Saxony was home to several extraordinary Christian mystics in the thirteenth century. Gertrude of Helfta's *The Herald of Divine Love* remains in print today. Mechthild of Magdeburg wrote a classic spiritual journal now called *The Flowing Light of the Godhead*.

Mechtild of Hackeborn entered the convent when she was only seven years old, and Gertrude became something of a mother to her. Mechtild's mystical experiences began early. The first was a vision of Christ during communion. Many others followed over the years. Mechtild gained respect among those who lived and prayed with her. Gertrude wrote down the reports and interpretations Mechtild made of her visions that became known as *The Book of Special Grace.*

Mechtild died November 19, 1298.

NOVEMBER 20
Edmund (849–70)
✒️*Loyalty to Christ*

King Edmund, of East Anglia, England, was born a Saxon and grew up in a Christian home. During his reign, the Danes invaded Edmund's territory. He led an army against them, but was defeated and taken captive. The historical record lacks details, but apparently, Edmund declined the two options given him by Ingwar, the leader of the invading hoard: He declined to deny his faith in Christ, and he refused to become a vassal ruling as a figurehead for Ingwar.

Suffering the same fate as the young Sebastian (January 20), Edmund was used for target practice by archers. They then beheaded him in a field called Hellesden in Suffolk. They buried him in 869, and when his remains were exhumed in 915, they were incorrupt. They were relocated to Bedricsworth, which took on the new name of Bury St. Edmunds. A community founded at his shrine in 925 grew to be one of the most important English Benedictine abbeys. His relics were moved several times across the centuries, and are now lost.

NOVEMBER 21
Columbanus (ca. 543–615)
✒ *Christian missions*

Irish monasteries played a huge role in keeping education and civilization alive during the Dark Ages. We owe a tremendous debt to the enthusiastic people who flocked to these religious safe havens and spread Christianity across the islands and onto the European continent.

Columbanus was an outstanding Irish missionary who took a dozen fellow monks to Gaul and established a monastery in Burgundy. His work flourished and he soon needed to build additional facilities. French Christians did not like his radical organizational structure and thought his Celtic spirituality, with its harsh corporal punishment, severe. They asked the Irish monks, who considered themselves in "voluntary exile for Christ," to leave.

Moving on to Milan, Italy, by way of Switzerland and Austria, Columbanus established a string of monasteries. The Benedictines eventually displaced his strict Rule, but Columbanus helped to generate a popular European trend toward monastic life.

NOVEMBER 22
Cecilia (second or third century)
✒ *Famous in obscurity*

Musicians have sung about St. Cecilia since the sixteenth century. The Academy of Music in Rome named her as its patron saint when it opened in 1584. There is no historical record that associates Cecilia with music.

In fact, there is little reliable historical record of any kind relating to this honored second or third century saint. All of the colorful material is legendary. Her death is one of the strong moments in Geoffrey Chaucer's *Canterbury Tales*. A pagan judge, Almachius, sentenced Cecilia to death, telling the guards to take her home:

". . . and burn her in her house," said he,
"Within a bath of fire all flaming red."
And this was carried out as he had said;
For in a bath they shut her, and they light
A fire beneath, and feed it day and night.

All the long night and all next day again,
In spite of all the bath's heat and the fire,
She sat quite cold, and felt no kind of pain,
Nor did the flames make her a drop perspire.
Yet in that bath at last she must expire,
For Almachius in his wicked wrath
Ordered that they should slay her in the bath.

Three strikes the executioner delivered
Upon her neck, but by no kind of chance
Could strike so that her neck was wholly severed;
And since in that day, by an ordinance,
None was allowed a man's pain to enhance
By a fourth stroke, however light or sore,
This executioner dared do no more.

Chaucer's grisly verse goes on to relate how Cecilia lingered near death for three days, continuing to instruct all who came to her in the ways of Christ. Following her passing, Pope Urban I turned her house into a church.

Cecilia's remains are buried in the cemetery of St. Callistus (October 14).

NOVEMBER 23

Amphilochius (ca. 340– ca. 95)
ℐ Champion of orthodoxy

Known as one of the Cappodocian Fathers, Amphilochius studied with Basil (January 2) in Constantinople, and became a lawyer there. Basil made Amphilochius bishop of Iconium in 373. Rampant heresies greatly troubled Asia Minor during his twenty-year tenure as bishop, and he became deeply involved in defining and supporting Christian orthodoxy. Though references to important writings by Amphilochius exist, most of his original writings have not survived the centuries.

NOVEMBER 24

Martyrs of Vietnam (1745–1862)

Persecution

More than one hundred thousand Christians became martyrs in the Vietnam area during the first two hundred years of missionary activity. The earliest missionaries arrived about 1530, but results did not begin to look promising until the Jesuits arrived in Hanoi in 1615.

Today memorializes one hundred and seventeen European and Asian martyrs who died in the period between 1745 and 1862. They represent the largest mass canonization in history. Ninety-six were Vietnamese, eleven were Dominican missionaries from Spain, and ten were French missionaries from the Paris Foreign Mission Society. Largely, they were victims of violent reaction to colonialism. *Ta dao*, which means "false religion," was written on the foreheads of Christians in Vietnamese characters. Families were cruelly separated and their homes destroyed.

NOVEMBER 25

Maria Corsini (1884–1965)

Sheltering others

Maria was the daughter of Angiolo Corsini, a military officer. Because of his occupation, the family moved frequently. Maria was born in Florence, Italy, and by the time she was nine she had lived in four cities. Her education began in one of Rome's parochial schools, but her father took her out and placed her in a public school when he heard a report that one of the nuns had been critical of the king.

Maria married Luigi Quattrocchi and became the mother of four children. They opened their home as a refugee shelter during the Second World War. She became a college professor and wrote about education. Italian women's gatherings often responded enthusiastically to her talks on religious subjects.

Maria died of natural causes in 1965, and Pope John Paul II officially beatified her in 2001.

NOVEMBER 26

Umile da Bisignano (1582–1637)
Infused knowledge

Luca Antonio Pirozzo was born in Bisignano, Italy. His religious name was Umile (humble), an entirely fitting name for this Franciscan who prayed fervently and possessed remarkable mystical gifts. Other Franciscans called him the "ecstatic friar."

His ecstatic religious experiences began to be noticed by the public, and this brought him difficult times. He was accused of fraud, and of responding to the devil. Umile quietly bowed his head during this period of misunderstanding and distrust.

Never a good student and unable to read, Umile demonstrated the gift of "infused knowledge." His understanding of Scripture and doctrine amazed noted scholars. The archbishop of Reggio Calabria and a team of theology professors examined Umile with regard for his supernatural wisdom. Without hedging, he gave clear, precise answers to their questions.

Umile died as he had lived—in prayer.

NOVEMBER 27
James Intercisus (d. 421)
✼*Confession of faith*

James was a fifth-century Persian Christian military officer and courtier of high rank. In order to maintain political privilege, he renounced his faith. When the king he served died, members of the family reprimanded James for his apostasy. "Where is this king you made such a sacrifice for? He is dead like any other man. He is dust. Can he save you from eternal torture?" Responding to a nagging conscience, James told the new king that he was a Christian.

King Bahram showed little mercy and condemned him for his faith. He died a martyr by being slowly cut into twenty-eight pieces. His name, Intercisus, means "cut to pieces." A final blow of the sword to his neck ended his life in 421.

NOVEMBER 28
Joseph Pignatelli (1737–1811)
✼*Devoted service*

The trouble began on April 2, 1767. Spanish soldiers surrounded Jesuit houses all over the country, awakened the residents, and read them an edict from King Charles III of Spain, expelling every member of the Society of Jesus. He considered Jesuits to be standing in the way of his control and power, both in Spain and in Spanish colonies in the New World. King Charles and his advisors determined to eradicate the Jesuits and seize their property.

That the Jesuits survived is largely credited to Joseph Pignatelli, the "second founder" of the Society of Jesus. He joined five thousand other Jesuits from Spain at the Catalan border. They sailed in overcrowded ships for three weeks, looking for a port that would accept them. For a while, they set up shop in Corsica, but soon were adrift at sea again. Italy, France, and Portugal did not want them. Under political pressure, Pope Clement XIV formally disbanded the Jesuits in every part of the world. In essence, he fired twenty-three thousand

Jesuit priests. Unemployed, Pignatelli went to Bologna and became a student-in-residence for about twenty years.

One stubborn woman kept the Society alive. Empress Catherine the Great of Russia refused to permit the reading or implementation of the pope's brief of suppression. In her territory of the world, Jesuits continued to function. Pignatelli received news of this turn of events and asked the Russians to receive him as an affiliate. They agreed, and in 1797, Pignatelli became the only Jesuit in Italy. By 1804, conditions had improved.

Joseph Pignatelli died three years before the Jesuits were fully restored.

NOVEMBER 29

Cuthbert Mayne (1544–77)

Religious persecution

Cuthbert grew up in one of England's Protestant families and became an Anglican minister. While studying for a degree in arts at Oxford he came under the influence of Edmund Campion, and through that influence converted to Roman Catholicism. Ordained a priest in 1575, he received a bachelor of theology degree in 1576.

Cuthbert went to Cornwall and worked incognito as a servant at Golden Manor, the household of Francis Tregian, all the while ministering secretly to Catholics who refused to participate in the public worship of the Church of England. On June 8, 1577, one hundred armed men arrested Cuthbert Mayne and most of Tregian's household. He became a prisoner at Launceston Castle.

Cuthbert Mayne became the first English seminary priest to be tried. The authorities decided to make an example of him, "as a terror to the papists." When he refused to agree that the queen was the head of the Church, he was executed. His skull is preserved at the Carmelite monastery of Lanherne in Cornwall.

NOVEMBER 30

Andrew (first century)

The importance of second place

"Simon Peter's brother" is the phrase most often used to identify Andrew. It is never spoken in reverse. Peter (June 29) was a powerful personality and a natural leader whose activity and comments take a prominent position in the New Testament. Andrew receives mention in only a few places.

But it was Andrew who brought Peter to Jesus. The Fourth Gospel tells us that Andrew and another person were followers of John the Baptist (August 29) before meeting Jesus. When they heard John pronounce Jesus "the Lamb of God," they followed Jesus home. Time with Jesus convinced Andrew that Jesus was the Messiah, and he eagerly sought Simon Peter. His enthusiastic behavior makes it reasonable to call Andrew the first Christian evangelist.

Matthew, Mark, and Luke tell the second part of the story. Simon, Andrew, and others were fishing on the Sea of Galilee when Jesus called them. Their immediate response suggests that they were spiritually prepared for this moment by an earlier conversation with Christ.

At the miracle of the feeding of the five thousand, Andrew called attention to the boy with five barley loaves and two fish. Andrew was also among the disciples consulted when some Greeks wanted to meet Jesus.

Church tradition continues Andrew's story by holding that he became a missionary to Russia, Greece, and Turkey. Tradition states that Andrew died a martyr's death on November 30 in the year 69.

Although his brother's reputation may have overshadowed Andrew's, there is no trace of jealousy or antagonism in Andrew's behavior. His only concern seems to have been serving Jesus Christ.

DECEMBER 1
Eligius of Noyon (588–660)
✐*Holy crafts*

Exceptional talent does not depend upon social status. Eligius is an example of an extraordinarily gifted craftsman born in poor circumstances in Limoges, France. King Clotaire commissioned him to construct a throne inlaid with gold and jewels, giving him a supply of precious metal and stones. Eligius determined that the generous supply of raw material exceeded what he needed to make the throne. With the extra gold and jewels, he produced a second throne for the king.

Impressed by such honesty, the king made Eligius his royal goldsmith. Eligius's hands created the coinage of the realm and dazzling objects of art for the French court as well as for dozens of churches and religious houses.

Eligius resigned from his position with the government in 640 and became a priest. As bishop of Noyon, he worked to evangelize Flanders until his death in 660.

There were still examples of his golden art scattered around the country when the French Revolution began, but thoughtless revolutionaries destroyed it all. One fragment of his work possibly survived.

DECEMBER 2
Chromatius of Aquileia (d. ca. 407)
✐*Friendship*

The enviable thing about Chromatius is the outstanding company he kept. Remarkable people were his friends. It was Ambrose (December 7) who consecrated him bishop. Jerome (September 30) and Rufinus headed the religious community in Aquileia mentioned above. When John Chrysostom (September 13) needed a defender, Chromatius stood up for him.

Of Chromatius, the scholars always state that he was a great theologian and interpreter of the Bible, but little of his writing remains today. Aside from the fact that he was bishop of Aquileia, Italy, from 387 until his death, and had something to do with a community of ascetics there, we have no record of his activity.

Francis Xavier (1506–52)

❦ *Missionary journey*

Cultural shock would be an understatement if used to describe the experience of a young European arriving in the Orient in the sixteenth century. Francis Xavier engaged in one of the greatest missionary journeys since Paul (June 29) evangelized the northeast Mediterranean area in the first century.

Francis was among the first half-dozen men to join Ignatius of Loyola's Society of Jesus (July 31). These Basque Spaniards had been friends and fellow students at the University of Paris during the early 1530s. In 1534 they were ordained priests in Venice.

Foreign missions were a prime objective of the Society of Jesus. In 1541, Francis began his personal effort by sailing from Portugal to Goa in order to evangelize the East Indies. The voyage took thirteen months, and Francis had a distressing susceptibility to seasickness.

The remaining ten years of his life produced outstanding and lasting results. The Portuguese had already established a Christian foothold at Goa, but the church and Christian living were hardly recognizable. Many Portuguese Christians were more interested in profit and pleasure than in religious devotion. They were cruel to their slaves, neglected the poor, and took advantage of females.

The first task facing the newly arrived missionary and his companion, Simon Rodriguez, was correcting the poor example of these "nominal" Christians. By making every effort to make Christ visible in his behavior, by carefully learning the languages and dialects, by delivering appealing sermons, and by setting Bible verses to popular tunes, Francis Xavier began the slow process of winning good will and respect. He lived among the poor as a poor man himself. Conversions to Christianity among lower-caste Paravas resulted from his next seven years of labor in southern India, Ceylon, Malacca, the Molucca islands, and the Malay Peninsula.

Reports began to reach Francis about Japan, an island beyond the awareness of most of the Western world. Japan had no central government at that time. Several hundred local leaders ran the country, making immigration a simple task. In 1549 he disembarked on the shores of Japan and began the next stage of his missionary journey.

Francis translated a short statement of Christian doctrine into the Japanese language and within a year had converted a hundred citizens of Kagoshima, helped them form a congregation, and began to travel to other cities. Gaining respect for Japanese culture, he saw the necessity of changing his style of mission. Francis discovered he could not meet with the Mikado at Miyako (Kyoto today) unless he presented gifts that were more expensive than he could afford. Instead of continuing his life of obvious poverty, he began to clothe himself with fine robes and obtained unique items from Portugal to use as gifts. He associated with the indigenous culture, and as a result he received protection and the use of an abandoned Buddhist monastery.

Within a little over two years of personal ministry, Francis Xavier gathered a flock of about 2,000 dedicated new Christians who clung to their faith even in the face of life-threatening persecution in subsequent years (February 6). He prepared the spiritual soil of Japan for other missionaries who would follow to plant and harvest.

China beckoned as Francis looked for ways to extend his missionary journeys. Even though that great nation discouraged foreign travelers, he felt an overwhelming urge to take the gospel to China. In 1552, on a difficult and clandestine voyage to Canton, Francis became seriously ill with a fever. Because his seasickness made the illness unbearable, he asked to be put ashore on an island in sight of the Chinese coastline. Exhausted and increasingly weak, Francis Xavier died in this lonely spot at the age of forty-six. Four people attended his funeral.

DECEMBER 4

Giovanni Calabria (1873–1954)

❧Demonstrating love

From Verona, Italy, Giovanni Calabria was the seventh child of a shoemaker and a housemaid. The couple never seemed to have enough income to support their family. When Giovanni was in the fourth grade, his father died. As with many poor children, working became more important than getting an education. A local priest recognized the latent abilities of the boy and began to tutor him, with a plan to send him to seminary. Giovanni became a theological student and performed well. He was ordained in 1901 and began a ministry of charity to the poor and underprivileged. One of his best references came to Pope Paul VI in a letter from a Jewish woman physician he helped hide from Nazi-Fascist persecution. After his death she wrote: "Every instant of his life was a personification of St. Paul's marvelous hymn on love," a reference to the famous passage in 1 Corinthians 13.

A gifted organizer, Giovanni founded and led a variety of groups that rendered service to the poor and neglected. He guided laity into productive religious service, and continued his forward-thinking ministry until his death on this day in 1954.

DECEMBER 5

Sabas of Jerusalem (439–532)

❧Called apart

Sometimes called Sabas the Great, this Cappadocian devoted his long life of more than ninety years to the service of Christ. After having lived in a monastery for a decade, at the age of eighteen Sabas went to Jerusalem, where he became noteworthy for his hard manual labor in service to the Christian community. When he turned thirty, he began to live a solitary life in a cave, weaving baskets from palm fronds.

His parents urged him to give up the monastic life, but he refused, moving down the Cedron brook to live for four years alone in the desert. In time, as many as a hundred and fifty others joined with him. With widespread encouragement, Sabas accepted ordination as a priest in 491, and his widowed mother arrived to run a guesthouse and hospitals.

On a visit by Sabas to Constantinople, the doorkeeper at the house of the emperor Anastasias turned Sabas away, thinking he was a beggar. But because he had a letter of recommendation, he finally gained admission and spent a winter there preaching and teaching. Sabas returned to Constantinople at the age of ninety, and the emperor Justinian received him warmly. He soon departed, having obtained the emperor's promise to build a hostel for religious pilgrims to Jerusalem, a fort for the protection of monks against raiders, and to lower taxes in Palestine.

Sabas died soon after returning to Jerusalem. His monastery there, Mar Saba, is still in operation, inhabited by Eastern Orthodox monks. In 1965, a church in Venice made an ecumenical gesture by returning his remains to this location

DECEMBER 6

Nicholas (d. 350)

ᨠ*Beyond the record*6

Few details exist regarding the life and experience of St. Nicholas. We know he was bishop of Myra, the capital city of Lycia, in Asia Minor. A history professor lecturing on the significant Council of Nicea, commented, "Santa Claus was there." Legend reports the remainder of what we remember about him. Stories of Nicholas and children abound. There is a famous tale of how he secretly tossed gold coins at night through the open window of a poor father who was thinking of selling his daughters. The coins fell into the children's stockings, which they had hung by their beds. It was enough to pay their dowry.

Hundreds of churches use the name of Nicholas, as many as four hundred in England alone. People in many parts of the world celebrate his feast day, December 6, enthusiastically exchanging gifts. Stained glass, sculptures, frescoes, and mosaics in widely scattered locations tell the adventures of his life. Many variations of his name continue to be popular: Colin, Nicholson, Nixon, Nicola, Nicolette and others. The composer Benjamin Britten wrote a musical drama about him. The remains of Nicholas are found in Bari, Italy, where raiders took them in 1087 after the Saracens conquered Myra.

The metamorphosis of the saint into the commercial Christmas icon in a red suit is not difficult to trace. It began in New York when that city was still called New Amsterdam. The Dutch are very fond of St. Nicholas, who according to their tradition brings gifts to their children on this day each year. Dutch Protestants in America receive the most credit for mixing with "Father Christmas" the Scandinavian legends of a magical elf who punished naughty children and gave gifts as rewards to good children.

American advertising also played a part in the transformation. In the Victorian era, an artist named Thomas Nast drew pictures of Santa Claus that gradually became the accepted icon. In an attempt to secularize the person to fit a marketplace that wanted to attract all kinds of customers, the actual saint disappeared, and the rosy-cheeked plump fellow with a long white beard wearing a fur-trimmed red suit took over.

Like St. Valentine (February 14), St. Nicholas would be astonished by what has evolved.

DECEMBER 7

Ambrose (ca. 339–97)

✒*Inspired leadership*

Anyone who reads Augustine's *Confessions* (August 28) will gain a profound respect for Ambrose. The meeting of these two men was one of the great moments in the history of the Christian Church. Here is a modern paraphrase of Augustine's report of that event.

It was in Milan that I met Bishop Ambrose. He was widely known as one of the world's best men, a devout and eloquent preacher. God led me to him in order that he might lead me to God. He welcomed me like a father. When I began to love him it was not because I expected to find any truth in him, but simply because he was kind to me.

I paid no particular attention to what Ambrose said. I only cared about how he said it. I began to see that Christianity could be rational. I was especially impressed with his figurative explanation of certain Old Testament passages which had killed my interest when I had taken them literally. His sermons convinced me that all those deceptive knots that others had tied around the Scripture could be untied. As I listened to him, I was ashamed that I had been barking all those years, not against Christianity, but against imaginary doctrines. The Church never taught the things I accused her of teaching. Ambrose drew aside the veil of mystery and made clear the spiritual meaning of things which could not be accepted literally.

Anyone could approach him without an announcement, but when we did we would often see him reading silently and we would not want to interrupt his study. We would sit quietly and watch him at work for a while, and then go away.

Ambrose taught Augustine the elements of Christianity and baptized him in 386. The rest is history.

Born into the home of a high-ranking official of the Roman government, Ambrose learned politics firsthand and became a provincial governor himself in northern Italy, with offices in Milan. When the bishop of Milan died, the church there was in doctrinal turmoil. Christians split into factions and were unable to agree on who should become their next bishop. Because emotions ran high and violence was likely to occur, Ambrose stepped forward as the community's civil servant, urging the people to reach a decision in a rational and peaceful manner. A young person in the basilica where he was speaking was impressed enough by his diplomatic approach to cry out, "Ambrose for bishop!" Many others soon joined in, chanting in unison.

Ambrose was disturbed by this turn of events. He was a secular person who had never been baptized and had no desire for the position. While the Christians continued to call his name, Ambrose quietly slipped out of the building and went into hiding. A week later, on December 7, 374, he received the sacrament of baptism and was consecrated bishop of Milan.

Desiring to become a competent bishop, Ambrose engaged in a crash course of religious education. He gave away his possessions, began daily prayer and in-depth study of Scripture and Christian theology. He began to preach every Sunday at the basilica in Milan and took a personal interest in teaching new converts and those preparing for ministry. He served as an outstanding bishop, carefully leading the church through a critical period of its history. It is not an exaggeration to say that Ambrose was the most influential Christian in Italy. Pivotal moments in church history turned in healthy ways under his leadership.

Not only did Ambrose help define orthodox Christian doctrine, he also stood firmly against the abuse of secular power. The emperor Valentinian attempted to bring a peaceful resolution to theological squabbles among his subjects by directing Ambrose to let a heretical group control one of his churches. Ambrose resolutely refused, and the emperor sent troops to enforce his order. They laid siege to the church with Ambrose and his congregation inside. He sent a statement of his position to the palace: "The emperor is in the church, he is not above it." Valentinian blinked and backed down.

Another direct confrontation with political authority occurred when another emperor, Theodosius, called for a massacre in Thessalonica in retaliation for the murder of its governor. Imperial troops killed thousands of innocent Thessalonican citizens. Horrified, Ambrose sent a letter to the emperor barring him from communion and urging him to do penance: "What has happened at Thessalonica is unparalleled in human memory. You are human, and temptation has overtaken you. I implore you to penance. The devil took away your crown of piety. Drive him from you while you can." Theodosius did as his bishop had directed. Later, Ambrose conducted the funeral for Theodosius, commenting, "He stripped himself of every sign of royalty and bewailed his sin openly in the church. The emperor was not ashamed to do the public penance which lesser individuals try to avoid. To the end of his life he never ceased to grieve for his error."

A famous mosaic image of Ambrose depicts him as a young man impressively dressed as a bishop, but with his head slightly tilted in humility. He died at the age of fifty-seven on Good Friday, 397. It is significant that his feast day is set on the day of his consecration as bishop.

DECEMBER 8
Romaric (d. 653)
From moneyed to monk

After his conversion, Romaric, a nobleman in the court of France's Clotaire II, became a monk. Because of his selfless example, some of the serfs he freed joined him. We know little about him beyond the fact that he helped to found a monastery on his estate in the Vosges Mountains near Alsace-Lorraine. Many tourists seek this gently beautiful landscape today, enjoying hikes through the woods, skiing on the hills, and kayaking down its streams. He died peacefully in 653.

DECEMBER 9
Peter Fourier (1565–1640)
Teaching others

In 1597, Peter Fourier accepted an appointment to one of France's most neglected parishes. Mattaincourt in Lorraine presented enormous difficulties for the thirty-two-year-old priest and theology professor. He selected the parish from a list because it seemed to be the neediest.

Peter undergirded his new ministry and all of his activity with intense prayer. His manner of living exemplified simple faith in action. He considered the free education of children the thing the neighborhood needed most, and began by attempting to teach boys, but he failed. With four female volunteers, he opened a free school for girls.

Peter himself had a prodigious memory and a reputation for knowing by heart all of *Summa Theologica* by Thomas Aquinas (January 28). He instructed the four women on a daily basis. He wanted them to teach older girls how to prepare invoices and receipts. Speaking and writing proper French was also important, but above all, he wanted the girls to be taught about the love of God and morality. He wrote some dialogues about virtues and vices that the children would recite for adults in church on Sunday afternoons. He aimed these directly at the weaknesses he observed in his parish.

Peter Fourier spent the final four years of his life in political exile, teaching in one of the schools opened under his guidance. After his death, his influence spread across the Atlantic to Canada and the United States.

DECEMBER 10

Brian Lacey (d. 1591)

Martyred for faith

Brian Lacy was a sixteenth-century country gentleman in Yorkshire, England, and cousin to a Catholic priest during a notorious time of persecution. Authorities arrested Brian in 1586, accusing him of assisting and hiding priests. He survived that ordeal only to be turned in by his betraying brother Richard in 1591. At the prison in Bridewell, Brian was tortured until he revealed the identities of others who were also providing cover for priests. Ultimately Brian Lacey was sentenced to death for supporting the Catholic Church. He died by hanging on December 10, 1591, in London.

DECEMBER 11

Maria Maravillas de Jesús Pidal y Chico de Guzmán (1891–1974)

☙ *Saintly influence*

Maria, the daughter of a Spanish ambassador, reminds us that saints are also a part of modern times. She was born in Madrid in 1891 and was profoundly influenced by the writings of John of the Cross (December 14) and Teresa of Avila (see October 15), sixteenth-century Christian mystics who wrote in the Spanish language. Just as many people today are attracted to Trappist monasteries by reading the writings of Thomas Merton, through her reading Maria determined to become a shoeless Carmelite nun. When her father died in 1913, her mother discouraged her from taking such a radical step. On October 12, 1919, Maria fulfilled her desire by joining the Discalced Carmelites of El Escorial in Madrid.

Sensitive to the guidance of God, Maria worked with three other Carmelites to establish *Cerro de los Ángeles,* the first of several Teresan Carmelite Monasteries she would found around the world. Her goal was to provide living according to the spirit and ideals of Teresa of Avila and John of the Cross. When someone criticized the flimsy structures and bare walls of her convents, she replied, "It is not our concern to plant a seed. The Discalced Carmelites have already been founded. Even if our convents collapse, nothing will happen."

Mother Maravillas, as she was called, gained the respect and admiration of those in her communities, but her spiritual life was a private affair, known only to her spiritual directors. In fact, she experienced discouraging times of spiritual dryness and stress. Her solution was total abandonment to God's will as she understood it.

Maria founded the Association of Saint Teresa two years before her death. Her last words were uttered repeatedly: "What happiness to die a Carmelite!"

DECEMBER 12

Jane de Chantal (1572–1641)

✍ *Gentle in spirit*

Many fine young women today are known as "Viz girls." They cheer with enthusiasm at athletic events, perform music with competence, demonstrate academic excellence, and sometimes see a sign on their way to the school parking lot that says, "Remember, Drive Gently." These are the students of Visitation Schools, scattered worldwide.

Jane-Frances Frémiot de Chantal worked with Francis de Sales (January 24) to found the Order of the Visitation of the Blessed Virgin Mary. This new order began with the intention of providing for frail women an alternative to the austerity of traditional convents. By the time she died in 1641, Jane had founded more than eighty popular houses for women fully committed to the religious life.

Jane was born to a wealthy church-supporting family in Dijon, France, in 1572. When she was twenty she married Christopher de Rabutin, Baron de Chantal, and lived an ordinary, happy life as the mother of four children (three others had died in infancy). Widowed after nine years by a hunting accident, Jane decided she would not marry again. Her father-in-law treated her harshly, and she struggled with depression. Faith in God sustained her during this difficult period of her life.

Jane de Chantal stands out as a shining example of how God uses men and women in profoundly spiritual relationships. Three great pairings that come to mind are Teresa of Avila and John of the Cross, Clare and Francis of Assisi, and Jane de Chantal and Francis de Sales.

Life took a dramatic turn for Jane in 1604 when she met the bishop of Geneva, Francis de Sales (January 24). There was a harmony of spirit between these two that resulted in much good for the Church and the world, and Jane asked Francis to be her spiritual director. The correspondence between them is one of the most revealing records we have of the depth and genuineness of the spirituality of both and is a spiritual treasure for readers today.

Life was not easy for Jane. In poor health, she dealt with criticism, opposition, lack of funds, and the death of her children and close friends. Maintaining a cheerful countenance, she survived for sixty-nine years, founding eighty-seven international houses of the Visitation. A sentence in her surviving writings may be taken as something of her motto: "Regardless of what happens, be gentle with yourself."

DECEMBER 13
Lucy of Syracuse (d. 304)
Christian dedication

Lucy is one of the most famous virgin/martyrs of the early fourth century. Christians suffered persecution under the Emperor Diocletian of Rome. Unfortunately, her colorful biographical sketches are highly unreliable. The stories told about her have to do with miraculous healings, rescues, and the avoidance of male advances.

The only historically accurate things we can say about Lucy is that she became a Christian martyr at Syracuse, Sicily, and that she had a significant following for centuries throughout Europe. Churches bore her name in Rome, Naples, Venice, and England. Venice claims to have her remains in a shrine. In Sweden, many people celebrate her feast on this day of brief sunlight with a festival of light in which the youngest daughter of a household dresses in white and wakes the family with coffee, rolls, and the widely known song, *Santa Lucia*.

DECEMBER 14
John of the Cross (1542–91)
Mystical experience

Few who knew this intellectual genius and intense spirit had any idea of his spiritual depth. Anyone wanting to become acquainted with him today should begin with his poetry.

On a dark night,
Burning with yearning love (oh, happy chance!)
I went out secretly,
While everyone else was asleep. . . .
The only light I had was the light that flamed in my heart,
But that light guided me better than the noonday sun
To the place where the one I knew was waiting for me.

Then move on to some of his masterful books: *Ascent of Mount Carmel, Dark Night of the Soul, Spiritual Canticle, Living Flame of Love.* No one else has articulated Christian spirituality as eloquently and meaningfully as John of the Cross. The unchallenged master of all mystical theologians, he found a way to express the inexpressible.

Juan de Yepes began life near Avila, Spain. His father's parents had wealth, but they disinherited their son because he married a girl beneath their social level. Juan never knew his father, who died when he was an infant, leaving his family in poverty. In spite of these difficulties, Juan sought an education. He studied philosophy and scholastic theology at the Carmelite College in Salamanca, one of the most respected universities in Europe. He became a Carmelite friar at the age of twenty-one, taking the name *Juan de la Cruz*, John of the Cross.

Spanish Carmelites attracted notice for their deep interest in personal spirituality. They encouraged quiet, internal prayer, though many had become careless and self-righteous by the time John joined them.

Another of the great meetings of male and female saints occurred when John was twenty-five and Teresa of Avila (October 15) was fifty-two. It was 1567, the year of John's ordination. Each recognized a familiar spirituality in the other. Teresa was already hard at work reforming Carmelite nuns, and she had been looking for a man to lead a similar task with the friars. A spiritual bond rapidly grew between them.

The publication of new religious insights in those times brought risks. The Spanish Inquisition hunted for heresy and independent thinking. Church leaders were keenly conscious of this threat. Even more distressing were internal conflicts and power struggles. In 1577 rivals carted John off to a Carmelite monastery in Toledo where they imprisoned and tortured him. "I have a great love of suffering. God gave me a high idea of its value when I was in prison at Toledo." The poem, a paraphrased fragment of which is printed above, was composed during this imprisonment. After eight or nine months of solitary confinement and beatings that left him marred for life, marginally sustained with bread and water, John escaped in the dark of the night, taking his poems with him.

Returning to his own community, he faced petty bickering among friars, while others were jealous of his abilities and worked in nasty ways to prevent his leadership. It was during this turmoil that John wrote his most renowned books, none of them given any attention while he was alive. Plagued by lingering illness, John died alone on December 14, 1591.

Contemplating this spiritual giant's life and accomplishments can leave a sensitive person a little numb. Silence seems more appropriate than discussion. One of his most respected translators, Allison Peers, in his introduction to *Ascent of Mount Carmel,* points out that John had read everything he could find regarding Christian spirituality, had absorbed it and made it his own. Rather than quoting the classics, he expresses thoroughly digested ideas in his own way. The writing of medieval mystics is "often vague and undisciplined; they need someone to select from them and unify them, to give them clarity and order, so that their treatment of mystical theology may have the solidity and substance of scholastic theology. To have done this is one of the achievements of St. John of the Cross."

DECEMBER 15

Mary-Crucifixa di Rosa (1813–55)

❧ *A caring life*

Mary-Crucifixa di Rosa's Italian parents named her Paula at birth. She quit school at seventeen and began to take care of things at home. Clement di Rosa, her father, began trying to find her a husband. It surprised her when he brought a young man to her, and she took no interest in him. She poured out her dismay to the wise priest who had counseled her for years. The priest went to her father and gently told him not to pressure his daughter into marriage. She remained at home for the next ten years, doing increasing amounts of social work among poor girls. A deadly outbreak of cholera in 1836 provided Paula with an opportunity to work in a hospital. This led the intelligent young woman into several other ventures of service to young women in difficulty.

When she founded The Handmaids of Charity, local physicians and hospitals welcomed the work she and her companions rendered the sick on a full-time basis. The Handmaids considered both the physical and the spiritual needs of their patients.

Political upheaval in northern Italy brought open warfare, with both military and civilian casualties. The military took care of their own wounded, but the Handmaids of Charity ministered to wounded civilians and prisoners of war. Mary-Crucifixa di Rosa died in her early forties.

DECEMBER 16
Adelaide (ca. 930–99)
❧ *Faithful courage*

It was common in medieval times for Christians to practice holiness by withdrawing from the world, and Adelaide's enemies encouraged her to do that. But Adelaide's story is a different one. She preferred to stay active in worldly affairs. Daughter of the king of Burgundy and widow of King Lothair of Italy, Adelaide became regent of the Holy Roman Empire. She was familiar with politics, diplomacy, and the ways of the world, so her life story does not read like that of most saints.

There was justifiable suspicion that King Lothair had been poisoned by his successor, Berengarius. Berengarius pressed Adelaide to marry his son, and when she refused, he had her brutally punished and locked away in a castle on Lake Garda. Eventually, Otto the Great of Germany invaded northern Italy, defeated Berengarius, and became a friend of Adelaide. Though Otto was twenty years older, they were married on Christmas Day, 951, at Pavia. The political consequence of this wedding was the consolidation of Otto's Italian power.

Otto and Adelaide had five children, but problems arose when a son by his first wife became jealous of his stepmother. This young man attempted to start a rebellion, but he could not induce the German population to think ill of Adelaide. In 962, Otto was declared emperor at Rome. Ten years later, he died, and Adelaide's oldest son took his place as Otto II. In a sad moment of political intrigue, the newly powerful son turned against his mother. Such turmoil and struggles for power within the family continued until 991 when the elderly Adelaide became regent. Though feeble, she was able to restore monasteries and convents in her realm. She died on December 16, 999, at a monastery she had founded near Strasbourg.

DECEMBER 17

José Manyanet y Vives (1833–1901)

Family nurture

José's father died when he was less than two years old. He grew up under the close supervision of a Spanish priest who became his spiritual director. This, in conjunction with his mother's devotion, led him into a life of ministry. Ordained in 1859, he became a seminary librarian with additional duties of pastoral visitation. Spiritually nurturing families became his lifelong passion. The magazine he started, *La Sagrada Familia (The Holy Family)*, remains in publication today. His concept was that the home life of Jesus in Nazareth could be a workable pattern for modern families.

Frail, and coping with many obstacles, José Manyanet found the inner strength to lead a vital ministry to families that spread around the world. For sixteen years he carried wounds in his side that refused to be healed. He called them "God's mercies."

José died in Barcelona in 1901. The last words he spoke were a prayer he had used many times throughout his life: "Jesus, Joseph, and Mary, may my soul pass away in peace with you."

DECEMBER 18

Flannan (seventh century)
❧ *Wandering preacher*

An Irish monk, Flannan received his ordination in Rome (a charming fable contends he got there on a floating stone) and returned to become the first bishop of Killaloe. Irish monks like Flannan were often wandering preachers. A group of small islands west of Scotland carries his name because he spent some time in religious activity on them. A few stones remaining on one of them may mark Flannan's chapel.

DECEMBER 19

Nemesius of Alexandria (d. 250)
❧ *Faithful courage*

During the persecution of Christians in Egypt by the emperor Trajanus Decius, the police arrested Nemesius and two other men for being thieves. When he was proven innocent of that charge, they then accused Nemesius of being a Christian, a charge he did not deny. The result was a Roman scourging of the cruelest sort and a sentence of death. The authorities burned him alive in Alexandria, executing him between two criminals, in the year 250.

DECEMBER 20

Dominic of Silos (ca. 1000–73)
❧ *Restoration of property and freedom*

Many Dominics populate the history of the Christian Church. The one we remember today was a self-educated farm boy who became a priest. A mother who prayed for a child at the shrine of Dominic of Silos gratefully applied Dominic's name to her son. *That* baby grew up to become the founder of the Dominicans (August 8).

Dominic of Silos fell into disfavor with Garcia III of Navarre, who exiled him to Castile. Ferdinand I of Castile extended a welcome and in 1041 sent Dominic to restore the monastery of Silos. It had fallen into ruin, though still occupied and functioning with six resident monks. Mass was being celebrated when Dominic arrived. The monk who was officiating was at one point supposed to say, *Dominus vobiscum.* Instead, he impulsively called out, "Behold, the restorer is here!" The story goes that the choir responded, "It is the Lord who sent him."

Dominic of Silos achieved remarkable success. He rebuilt the chapel and designed new cloisters. With his guidance, the abbey turned into a proficient producer of manuscripts, some of which still exist.

Dominic did not confine his work to this monastery that ultimately took his name. While there, his reputation attracted many in need of healing. By the end of his life in 1073, the monastery had more than forty monks who worked as craftsmen in gold and silver, earning enough to do significant charitable work in the surrounding area. Dominic would often visit prisoners and pay their ransom. Visitors to the chapel's vault today may see balls-and-chains, handcuffs, and other hardware used by the Spanish Moors to hold the captives Dominic helped free.

DECEMBER 21

Thomas (first century)

First–hand knowledge

This apostle of Christ is stuck forever with a nickname. "Doubting Thomas" has come into the English language as a term for any habitually doubtful person. But there is another side to doubt. Tennyson wrote: "There lives more faith in honest doubt, believe me, than in half the creeds." Thomas is not a one-dimensional character. "Doubting Thomas" is a partial truth.

Actually, Thomas was one of the most loyal and dedicated of the twelve apostles. His nickname according to the Gospel of John is "Thomas, called the Twin." He turns up at several interesting places in John's narrative.

Thomas spoke up when Jesus prepared to visit some special friends in a small town near Jerusalem. Mary, Martha, and Lazarus lived in Bethany, and their home was one of his favorite stops. News reached Jesus that Lazarus had died. As Jesus decided to go see Mary and Martha, his disciples were horrified. They knew he would be walking into a beehive of hostility in that neighborhood. Twice, in the past four months, religious leaders in Jerusalem had tried to kill Jesus. They hesitated to accompany him into such a deadly environment. It was Thomas who encouraged the others to go along with Jesus: "Let us also go, that we may die with him."

That was not the melancholy comment of a pessimist. Thomas was facing a reality that Calvary confirmed. As a realist, he saw the dangers, but he was still able to think clearly and act effectively. "Let's go" are the words of a hero, a true leader who will not be deterred by any threat.

The next time we hear of Thomas is at the Last Supper in the Upper Room. Jesus has been pouring his heart out, saying, "I go and prepare a place for you." A bewildered Thomas jumped in with a sharp question. "Lord, we do not know where you are going! How can we know the way?"

Jesus was talking about the way to heaven, and Thomas wanted a road map. Thomas is an example of a practical mind dealing with mysticism. His common sense bumped into divine knowledge. Once again, Thomas faced the tension between the real and the ideal, between emotion and reason.

The famous doubting scene occurred when the resurrected Jesus appeared to some women and his disciples. For an unexplained reason, Thomas was not present for Christ's early appearances. When the women and the disciples told him about it, his response was that he could not believe them unless he could see and touch Christ's wounds. Eight days later, Jesus returned and invited Thomas to make his reality checks. Interestingly, the Gospel does not tell us that Thomas actually touched Jesus' wounds. He simply said, "My Lord and my God!

DECEMBER 22

Peter Canisius (1521–97)

✥*Positive response*

A positive response to the Reformation that was sweeping across Europe with the force of an avalanche in the sixteenth century began with a few individual leaders. Their names do not immediately come to mind as certainly as Luther and Calvin, but they emerged from the turmoil and despair with a desire to make a difference. They confidently turned to God, willing to learn new lessons.

Peter Canisius, born in Nijmegen, Holland, was one of the great, steadying influences in the history of the church in Central Europe. He understood it was time for Roman Catholics to make important changes. Some Protestants called him "the dog," making a play on the literal translation of his last name.

Peter was an early Jesuit, the eighth person to join the Society of Jesus. His ministry took him to Sicily, Rome, Bavaria, Vienna, Germany, Poland, and Switzerland, traveling thousands of miles on horseback and on his own two feet. He led the action of the Counter-Reformation in two significant directions.

Most important, Peter was confident that the gospel message was positive and healing. Jesus Christ was above human controversy. In the manner of Francis de Sales (January 24), Peter Canisius was an outstanding Christian diplomat. He treated his Protestant adversaries with courtesy and respect. His *Catechism*, published in the doctrinal heat of 1555, makes no reference to the positions taken by Protestant leaders. It is simply a clear, concise, and systematic statement of faith in question and answer form. Welcomed like a desert oasis, his work was translated into many languages and was respected on both sides of the theological debate. His condensed versions became enormously popular. Peter Canisius expressed the wholesome, universal appeal of the gospel of Jesus Christ.

The sixteenth century offered an opportunity to find ways to use the press for communication and evangelism. Martin Luther comprehended the new potency of the printed word, but church leaders were often slow to catch on. Canisius put his pen to work, writing for the public as well as for students. Publishing became one of his major interests.

Peter Canisius died at Fribourg, Switzerland, after a crippling illness that forced him to write through an amanuensis.

DECEMBER 23

Servulus (d. ca. 590)

☙ *Faithful exmple*

It is not unusual in large cities today to see homeless people camped out on church porticos. In the sixth century, Servulus was a tetraplegic beggar whose mother and brother carried him every day to a place near the door of St. Clement's in ancient Rome. Since birth, it was impossible for him to stand, sit upright, turn from one side to the other, or to lift a hand to his mouth. Living on the handouts of passersby, he shared the small gifts he received with other homeless beggars. He enjoyed having the Bible read to him and memorized many passages. Gregory the Great (September 3) delivered a moving sermon, based on his personal experiences with Servulus, that remains in print today.

DECEMBER 24

Paola Elisabetta (1816–65)

☙ *Commitment*

Beginning her life as Costanza Cerioli, this frail Italian child was the youngest in a family of sixteen children. After a difficult life marked with illness, grief, and many stresses, she placed herself into the hands of God, praying constantly for faith.

At thirty-eight, she determined to become a nurturer of others. Expressing the love of God in Christ became her single interest. Orphans, struggling to survive life in the streets, moved her to extreme generosity. Others expressed astonishment by the degree of her commitment to such children, but some were impressed enough to join her in her work.

In 1857 this "mother of many orphans" founded the Institute of the Sisters of the Holy Family, taking the name Paola Elisabetta. She directed those who shared her ministry to exhibit "the same spirit of humble labor that Jesus, Mary, and Joseph lived."

Her death came without warning at the age of forty-nine, on December 24, 1865.

DECEMBER 25

The Nativity of Christ

✒ *Incarnation*

The Gospel record of the birth of Jesus reminds us of two vitally important things: He was God's only begotten Son, and he was fully human, complete with umbilical cord and an infant's dependent vulnerability.

The earliest Christian preaching and teaching emphasized Jesus' death and resurrection. In this, we have evidence of God at work in our world. Eventually, the first evangelists began to recount the things Jesus said, and they reported his activity among people. Details regarding the conception, birth, and childhood of Jesus appear to have come later in the process of telling others about him.

Behind various episodes in the familiar Christmas story there are firm points of agreement. Mary and Joseph were engaged, but had not had sexual relations. Joseph was a descendent of King David. Angels announced the birth and stated the name of Jesus. God's Holy Spirit was involved in Mary's pregnancy. Bethlehem during the reign of King Herod was the place and time of his birth. Jesus grew up in Nazareth.

All of this, though satisfying to a scholar, fails to recognize the "music" of this day. It is a mixture of celebration and quietness, of joy and sorrow, of flesh and spirit, of heaven and earth.

DECEMBER 26

Stephen (first century)
❧ *Courage of conviction*

The first person to die for believing in Christ was a young man with a good reputation. Stephen became one of the first seven deacons chosen by the Apostles to serve tables. Everything we know about him is contained in the book of Acts.

After making a stirring speech to a hostile audience with "a face like the face of an angel," Stephen was stoned to death. With his final breath, he reported a mystical vision of Jesus sitting at the right hand of God. He prayed, "Lord Jesus, receive my spirit. Do not hold this against them."

A "young man named Saul" (June 29) stood there holding the cloaks of the murderers, "consenting to his death."

DECEMBER 27

John (first century)
❧ *Centrality of love*

One of two "sons of Thunder" among the disciples of Jesus, John needed a lot of spiritual guidance. For instance, John criticized an independent healer who was using the name of Jesus. Jesus rebuked John by saying, "He that is not against us is for us." And it was John with his brother James (July 25) who presumptuously asked "to sit one on your right hand and one on your left in your glory," only to have Jesus tell them, "You don't know what you are asking." As much as he needed to develop spiritually, Scripture makes it clear that John was "the disciple Jesus loved." He sat next to Jesus at the Last Supper.

It was to John that Jesus, from the cross, entrusted the care of his mother. It was John who recognized and identified his risen Savior when the disciples were fishing on the Sea of Galilee: "It is the Lord!" It was John who joined Peter and James to be with Jesus at the highest spiritual moments of his ministry—the resuscitation of the daughter of Jairus, the transfiguration on the mountain, and the agony of prayer in the Garden of Gethsemane the night of his betrayal.

Jerome (September 30) put in writing an old tale that was in circulation about John. As the last surviving apostle, he accepted an invitation to speak at the Ephesian church. This was a highly publicized event, and the church overflowed with eager listeners. When John arrived he was so feeble he had to be carried into the church. Following a lengthy worship service and an eloquent introduction, attendants lifted John to his feet before a hushed and expectant congregation. The old man said, "Little children, love one another, love one another, love one another," and then sat down, having presented the heart of the gospel.

DECEMBER 28
Anthony of Lérins (d. ca. 520)
Solitude

Anthony grew up in the ancient Roman province of Pannonia, which was in today's Balkan Mountain area. Anthony was only eight years old when his father died. Passed around from guardian to guardian, he was about twenty in the year 488 when he sought solitude near Lake Como in Italy. Living in a cave, Anthony engaged in prayer, study, and gardening. Against his wishes, he attracted many visitors who interrupted his time alone.

Because he thought the notoriety and fame he was acquiring were harmful, he crossed the Alps into southern France and became a monk at Lérins. He lived there as quietly as possible until his death nearly two years later.

DECEMBER 29

Thomas Becket (1118–70)

Faithful service

Despite being good friends, King Henry II and Thomas Becket engaged in a perilous struggle to determine the line of authority between church and state. King Henry II appointed Thomas his royal chancellor, a position of responsibility and power second only to that of the king himself. The chancellor held the purse strings and performed important administrative duties. Thomas proved to be an extraordinarily supportive and capable assistant.

King Henry wanted to consolidate his power by making Thomas archbishop of Canterbury. He proposed the idea to Thomas upon the death of archbishop Theobold in 1162. Thomas hesitated, but allowed the king to carry out his plan. He was ordained a priest and soon enough was consecrated archbishop of Canterbury in a spectacular event.

As in most such schemes, there was a transparency in the king's motives. The leaders already in place at the cathedral did not welcome their new archbishop from beside the throne. But a curious thing happened. Thomas Becket took his new position seriously and began to claim independence from Henry by resigning his office of chancellor. He began to fast and pray with earnest devotion.

Systematically, and in bold and dramatic ways, Thomas began to untangle the church in England from civil authority. In 1164 King Henry secured the enactment of the Constitutions of Clarendon that limited the right of appeal to Rome in ecclesiastical cases, restricted the power of excommunication, subjected clergy to civil courts, and put the election of bishops under the control of the king. At this point, Thomas Becket openly broke with Henry II. For his own safety, Thomas fled to France until the situation cooled.

In July, 1170, Henry met Thomas on the beach at Normandy, where they made amends. After what was essentially a six-year exile, Thomas returned to Canterbury. The issues of church and state, however, remained unsettled. Emotions raged and tempers flared. Four Norman knights determined to execute Thomas Becket after they heard King Henry II say, "What a set of idle cowards I keep in my kingdom who allow me to be mocked so shamefully by a low-born clerk." They took these words as an order rather than as an expression of exasperation. When they arrived at Canterbury on December 29, they cornered Becket. He offered no resistance as they murdered him with their swords. As he lay dying, Becket quoted Jesus, saying, "Into thy hands, Lord, I commend my spirit." A thunderstorm began to rage as the murderers ran out of the cloister.

Though the common people may not have fully understood every facet of the contest, they knew that Thomas Becket was a man of principle who was killed for standing in the way of an autocratic king. The tomb of Thomas Becket became one of the most popularly visited shrines in Western Europe. The site, and what it represented, was an irritation to King Henry VIII, who ordered it destroyed.

DECEMBER 30

Egwin (d. 717)

Leadership

Egwin was bishop of Worcester in England from 693 to 711, and the probable founder of Evesham Abbey, one of the great Benedictine houses of medieval England. As with many other saints from his time, the stories about him were written years after his death. Popular taste demanded fabulous tales full of magic and mystery. We do him no service to repeat such material here.

Egwin died in 717 and was buried at Evesham Abbey.

DECEMBER 31

Melania and Pinian (ca. 383–438)

Faith at work

Melania was born in Rome to an extraordinarily wealthy family, about the year 383. She and her husband, Pinian, opened their home to others and gave their money away to the poor. They traveled to

Roman northern Africa and became friends with Augustine (August 28). Their journeys eventually took them to Jerusalem in 417. In 431, a year after Pinian died, Melania founded a nunnery on the Mount of Olives, where her own life came to an end six years later.

❦Acknowledgments

My gratitude for the labor of Lil Copan at Paraclete Press is profound. This book is the offspring of her mind and spirit. Lil conceived the volume and offered invaluable guidance during the many months of its production. I would also like to thank my wife, Anna, for consulting with me regarding the complex history surrounding many of the saints, and for reading and correcting the original draft.

Patron Saints
Condensed list of saints included in this volume

Abandoned people: Germaine Cousin
Abuse victims: Adelaide,
    Rita of Cascia
Accountants: Matthew
Advertisers: Bernardino of Sienna
Agricultural workers: Isidore the
    Farmer
Air passengers and aviators:
    Joseph of Cupertino,
    Thérèse of Lisieux
Amputees: Anthony of Padua
Animals and birds: Francis of Assisi,
    Antony of Egypt
Apothecaries: Nicholas
Apple Orchards: Charles Borromeo
Apprentices: John Bosco
Archaeologists: Jerome
Archers: George, Sebastian
Architects: Thomas
Artists: Luke
Astronomers: Dominic
Athletes: Sebastian
Authors: Francis de Sales
Bankers: Matthew
Basket makers: Antony of Egypt
Beekeepers: Ambrose, Bernard,
    Modomnoc O'Neil
Beggars: Martin of Tours, Benedict
    Joseph Labre
Bishops: Ambrose, Charles Borromeo
Blacksmiths: Brigid of Ireland,
    Dunstan
Blind: Dunstan, Thomas
Blood banks: Januarius
Bookkeepers: Matthew
Bowel disorders: Bonaventure
Boys: Nicholas
Bricklayers: Stephen
Bridgebuilders: Benezet of Avignon
Burns: John
Bursars: Joseph
Canonists: Raymund of Peñafort
Carpenters: Joseph
Castle-chapels: George

Catechists: Charles Borromeo,
Childless people: Catherine of Genoa
Children: Nicholas
Chimney sweeps: Florian
Coachmen: Richard of Chichester
Conservationists: Francis of Assisi
Convulsions: John the Baptist,
    Willibrord
Cripples: Giles
Deacons: Stephen
Death of Children:
    Elizabeth Ann Seton
Desperate cases: Jude, Rita of Cascia
Disasters: Genevieve
Doctors: Luke, Cosmas and Damian
Ecologists: Francis of Assisi
Editors: Antony Claret, John Bosco
Elderly people: Anthony of Padua
Evangelists: Paul
Fear of snakes: Patrick
Firefighters: Catherine of Siena,
    Florian, John of God
Fishermen, anglers: Andrew, Peter,
    Nicholas
Florists: Rose of Lima
Foot problems: Peter
Fugitives: Brigid of Ireland
Funeral directors: Joseph of Arimathea
Gardeners: Rose of Lima
Girls: Agnes, Nicholas
Goldsmiths: Dunstan
Hairdressers (women):
    Mary Magdalene
Hairdressers (men): Martin de Porres,
    Cosmas and Damian
Headache sufferers: Stephen
Heart patients: John of God
Hermits: Antony, Giles
Homeless: Benedict Joseph Labre
Hopeless cases: Jude
Horses: Giles
Hospitals: Camillus de Lellis,
    John of God
Husbandmen: George

Infantrymen: Maurice
In-law problems: Elizabeth Ann Seton
Insect bites: Mark, Narcissus
Internet: Isidore of Seville
Jealousy, victims of:
   Elizabeth of Portugal
Journalists: Francis de Sales
Kings: Henry II
Knights: George
Lawyers: Hilary, Thomas More
Lepers: Giles
Librarians: Jerome
Longevity: Peter
Loss of parents: Elizabeth Ann Seton
Lost articles: Antony of Padua
Lovers: Valentine
Mail: Anthony of Padua
Married women: Monica
Merchants: Nicholas
Midwives: Panteleon
Missionaries: Francis Xavier,
   Thérèsa of Lisieux
Missionary bishops: Paul
Monks: John the Baptist, Benedict
Musicians: Cecilia
Mystics and mystical theologians:
   John of the Cross
Nail makers: Clodoald
Naturalists: Albert the Great
Navigators: Brendan the Navigator,
   Nicholas
Net makers: Peter
Nuns: Scholastica
Nurses: Camillus of Lellis, John of God
Opposition of Church authorities:
   Elizabeth Ann Seton
Orphans: Anthony of Padua
Painters: Luke
Parish priests: John-Baptiste Vianney
Pawnbrokers: Nicholas
Penitents: Mary Magdalene
People ridiculed for piety:
   Elizabeth Ann Seton
Perfumers: Nicholas

Pilgrims: James
Poets: John of the Cross
Politicians: Thomas More
Poor: Antony of Padua,
   Martin de Porres, Nicholas,
   Vincent de Paul
Popes: Peter, Gregory the Great
Preachers: John Chrysostom,
   Bernardino of Siena
Printers: Augustine, John of God
Publishers: John
Race relations: Martin de Porres,
   Peter Claver
Retreatants: Ignatius of Loyola
Rheumatism sufferers: Philip Neri
Salesmen: Lucy of Syracuse
Sailors: Nicholas, Francis of Paola
Scholars: Venerable Bede, Jerome
Scientists: Albert the Great
Scouts: George
Secretaries: Mark
Sick People: Camillus de Lellis
Singers: Cecilia
Slavery: Peter Claver
Soldiers: George
Spiritual help: Vincent de Paul
Starving: Antony of Padua
Students: Thomas Aquinas
Surgeons: Cosmas and Damian, Luke
Tax collectors: Matthew
Teachers: John Baptist de la Salle
Telephones: Claire of Assisi
Theologians: John, Augustine,
   Thomas Aquinas, Alphonsus Liguori
Throat sufferers: Blaise of Sebaste
Tourists: Francis Xavier
Unhappily married women:
   Rita of Cascia
Widows: Elizabeth Ann Seton,
   Frances of Rome, Monica, Paula
Writers: John, Francis de Sales
Youth: John Bosco
Zoos: Francis of Assisi

For a listing of 4,930 patron saints under 1,790 topics, visit
www.catholic-forum.com/saints/patronnf.htm

✎ Index

David of Scotland 5/24
David of Wales 3/1
Deogratias 3/22
Dominic 8/8
Dominic of Silos 12/20
Dubricius 11/14
Dunstan 5/19
Edigio Maria of St. Joseph 2/7
Edith Stein 8/9
Edmund 11/20
Edward the Confessor 10/13
Egwin 12/30
Eleutherius of Spoleto 9/6
Eligius of Noyon 12/1
Elizabeth 11/5
Elizabeth Ann Seton 1/5
Elizabeth of Portugal 7/4
Elizabeth of the Trinity 11/8
Enrique De Osso Y Cervello 1/27
Eucherius of Orléans 2/20
Euphrasia 3/13
Euplus 8/12
Eusebius of Vercelli 8/2
Eustathius of Antioch 7/16
Fidelis of Sigmaringen 4/24
Fillan of Glendochart 8/26
Finan of Lindisfarne 2/17
First Roman Martyrs 6/30
Flannan 12/18
Florian 5/4
Frances of Rome 3/9
Francis (Gabriel) Possenti 2/27
Francis Caracciolo 6/4
Francis de Sales 1/24
Francis di Girolamo 5/11
Francis of Assisi 10/4
Francis of Paola 4/2
Francis Xavier 12/3
Frumentius and Aedisius 10/27
Gall 10/16
Gaudentius of Brescia 10/25
Genevieve 1/3
Genoveva Torres Morales 1/5
George 4/23
Gerard of Brogne 10/3

Gerard Sagredo 9/24
Germaine Cousin 6/15
Germanus of Paris 5/28
Gildas the Wise 1/29
Giles 9/1
Giovanni Calabria 12/4
Gregory the Great 9/3
Guy of Anderlecht 9/12
Guy of Pomposa 3/31
Hannibal Di Francia 6/1
Henry II 7/13
Hilary of Aries 5/5
Hilary of Poitiers 1/13
Hildegard of Bingen 9/17
Hildegund 4/20
Honoratus of Arles 1/16
Hormisdas 8/6
Hugh of Grenoble 4/1
Hugh of Lincoln 11/17
Hypatius of Chalcedon 6/17
Ignatius of Antioch 10/17
Ignatius of Loyola 7/31
Illtyd 11/6
Irenaeus 6/28
Irenaeus of Sirmium 3/24
Isidore of Seville 4/4
Isidore the Farmer 5/15
James 7/25
James Intercisus 11/27
James Salomone 5/31
James the Less 5/3
Jane de Chantal 12/12
Januarius of Benevento 9/19
Jean-Gabriel Perboyre 9/11
Jerome 9/30
Joan of Arc 5/30
Joan of the Cross 8/17
John 12/27
John Baptist de La Salle 4/7
John Bosco 1/31
John Chrysostom 9/13
John de Britto 2/4
John de Ribera 1/6
John du Lau and Companions 9/2
John Eudes 8/19

Index

About Paraclete Press

Who We Are

Paraclete Press is an ecumenical publisher of books and recordings on Christian spirituality. Our publishing represents a full expression of Christian belief and practice—from Catholic to Evangelical, from Protestant to Orthodox.

Paraclete Press is the publishing arm of the Community of Jesus, an ecumenical monastic community in the Benedictine tradition. As such, we are uniquely positioned in the marketplace without connection to a large corporation and with informal relationships to many branches and denominations of faith.

We like it best when people buy our books from booksellers, our partners in successfully reaching as wide an audience as possible.

What We Are Doing

Books

Paraclete Press publishes books that show the richness and depth of what it means to be Christian. Although Benedictine spirituality is at the heart of all that we do, we publish books that reflect the Christian experience across many cultures, time periods, and houses of worship.

We publish books that nourish the vibrant life of the church and its people—books about spiritual practice, formation, history, ideas, and customs.

We have several different series of books within Paraclete Press, including the bestselling Living Library series of modernized classic texts; A Voice from the Monastery—giving voice to men and women monastics about what it means to live a spiritual life today; award-winning literary faith fiction; and books that explore Judaism and Islam and discover how these faiths inform Christian thought and practice.

Recordings

From Gregorian chant to contemporary American choral works, our music recordings celebrate the richness of sacred choral music through the centuries. Paraclete is proud to distribute the recordings of the internationally acclaimed choir Gloriæ Dei Cantores, who have been praised for their "rapt and fathomless spiritual intensity" by American Record Guide, and the Gloriæ Dei Cantores Schola, which specializes in the study and performance of Gregorian chant. Paraclete is also the exclusive North American distributor of the recordings of the Monastic Choir of St. Peter's Abbey in Solesmes, France, long considered to be a leading authority on Gregorian chant performance.

Learn more about us at our Web site:
www.paracletepress.com,
or call us toll-free at
1-800-451-5006.

Also Available

INCANDESCENCE
365 Readings with Women Mystics
Carmen Acevedo Butcher

296 pages
ISBN: 978-1-55725-418-4
$16.95, Trade Paper

Turn to any page in this beautiful collection and you will discover the women mystics of Christian tradition. These fascinating women offer a way to peace, laughter, love, and connection with each other, and they show us a picture of a tender, nurturing, forgiving God who is as intimate as our own breath.

Incandescence offers fresh translations from the writings of famous and not-so-famous mystics—Julian of Norwich, Mechthild of Magdeburg, Catherine of Siena, Hildegard of Bingen, Gertrude of Helfta, Margery Kempe, and others.

"In these pages, the images of the spiritual life are the erotic ones of the feminine experience. They are the stuff of very physically present women who loved their Lord with a ferocity and passion that could be reported only in those experiences of the flesh . . . there is peace here in the company of these good women."
—from the foreword by Phyllis Tickle

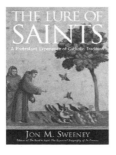

THE LURE OF SAINTS
A Protestant Experience of Catholic Tradition
Jon M. Sweeney

240 pages
ISBN: 978-1-55725-506-8
$15.95, Hardcover

This compelling guide includes profiles of ancient, medieval, and modern figures, East and West, the sublime and the unusual, with special chapters exploring:

*Differences between Catholic and Protestant imaginations.
*How saints were made in the past and how they are made today.
*Devotions and spiritual practices.
*The radical triumph of the Protestant idea.
*Miracles, doubt, and belief.
*Tears, pain, foolishness, apparitions, stigmata, and stranger saintly behavior.

"A satisfying blend of the concrete
(prayers, a list of feast days, ten steps to living like a saint) with Sweeney's personal observations and historical information."
—*Publishers Weekly*

Available from most booksellers or through Paraclete Press:
www.paracletepress.com; 1-800-451-5006.
Try your local bookstore first.